W9-AXC-160

ASIMOV ON SCIENCE FICTION

Isaac Asimov

No one knows science fiction as well as Isaac Asimov, and no one has made a greater contribution to its popularity. ASIMOV ON SCIENCE FICTION collects the thoughts of a lifetime on the subject; there is no other book like it, nor is there likely to be one. Every fan ought to have a copy; if you're a would-be Asimov, it's absolutely indispensable.

Asimov was already writing when John Campbell took over *Astounding Stories* and ushered in the modern era of science fiction. He has been a participant in and an observer of every significant development; he knows all the present practitioners of the art and knew most of the greats of earlier days; and his familiarity with the history and literature of sf is unsurpassed, from the fantastic traveling tales of classical antiquity through More's *Utopia*, Mary

(continued on back flap)

Science Fiction by Isaac Asimov

PEBBLE IN THE SKY

I, ROBOT

THE STARS, LIKE DUST—

FOUNDATION

FOUNDATION AND EMPIRE

THE CURRENTS OF SPACE

SECOND FOUNDATION

THE CAVES OF STEEL

THE MARTIAN WAY AND OTHER STORIES

THE END OF ETERNITY

THE NAKED SUN

EARTH IS ROOM ENOUGH

NINE TOMORROWS

FANTASTIC VOYAGE

ASIMOV'S MYSTERIES

NIGHTFALL AND OTHER STORIES

THE GODS THEMSELVES

THE EARLY ASIMOV

THE BEST OF ISAAC ASIMOV

BUY JUPITER AND OTHER STORIES

THE BICENTENNIAL MAN AND OTHER STORIES

ASIMOV
on Science Fiction

ISAAC ASIMOV

1981
Doubleday & Company, Inc.
Garden City, New York

ISBN: 0-385-17443-8
Library of Congress Catalog Card Number 80-2246

The following essays are reprinted from *Isaac Asimov's Science Fiction Magazine*, where they appeared as editorials in the indicated issues:

"Anniversaries," January 1980; "The Articles of Science Fiction," April 1979; "The Brotherhood of Science Fiction," January–February 1978; "By No Means Vulgar," September–October 1978; "The Dean of Science Fiction," November 1979; "Extraordinary Voyages," March–April 1978; "Golden Age Ahead," June 1979; "Hints," March 1979; "Hollywood and I," May 1979; "The Hugo," January 1979; "Isaac Asimov's Science Fiction Magazine," Spring 1977; "It's a Funny Thing," July–August 1978; "Learning Device," August 1979; "The Letter Column," May 1980; "The Mosaic and the Plate Glass," August 1980; "The Name of Our Field," May–June 1978; "Our Conventions," Winter 1977; "Rejection Slips," December 1979; "The Reluctant Critic," November–December 1978; "The Scientist as Villain," October 1979; "Try to Write!," Summer 1977; "The Vocabulary of Science Fiction," September 1979.
Copyright © 1977, 1978, 1979, 1980 by Davis Publications, Inc.

"Adventure!" is reprinted from *Asimov's Science Fiction Adventure Magazine*, Fall 1978, copyright © 1978 by Davis Publications, Inc.
"The Answer to *Star Wars?*," originally titled "*Battlestar Galactica*: Creativity (?) in Full Force," is reprinted from *Newsday*, September 17, 1978, copyright © 1978 by *Newsday*.
"Arthur C. Clarke" is reprinted from material accompanying the recording "*Childhood's End* by Arthur C. Clarke," copyright © 1979 by Caedmon Records, Inc.
"Beyond Our Brain" is reprinted from *Mind and Supermind*, edited by Albert Rosenfeld, copyright © 1977 by Saturday Review, Inc.
"The Boom in Science Fiction" is reprinted from *Asimov's Science Fiction Adventure Magazine*, Fall 1979, copyright © 1979 by Davis Publications, Inc.
"The Campbell Touch" is reprinted from *New Voices II: The Campbell Award Nominees*, ed. George R. R. Martin, Macmillan, Inc., copyright © 1980 by Isaac Asimov.
"The First Science Fiction Novel" is reprinted from material accompanying the recording "*Frankenstein* by Mary Shelley," copyright © 1977 by Caedmon Records, Inc.
"The First Science Fiction Writer" is reprinted from material accompanying

Dedicated to:
Martin H. Greenberg ("Marty the Other")
who, among other things, suggested
this book.

CONTENTS

INTRODUCTION

In my autobiographical volumes—In Memory Yet Green *and* In Joy Still Felt—*I carefully listed my more-than-two-hundred books in an appendix and, for the convenience of the reader, divided the list into separate categories.*

There may be those enthusiasts who have the ambition to collect every word I have written in whatever category, but most people, I imagine, feel themselves to be more restricted than that. Some are more interested in my science fiction than in my mysteries; in my histories than in my astronomy; in my humor than in my biblical studies (or vice versa in each case).

In an attempt to make sure I would be as helpful as possible, I ended by dividing my books into no less than nineteen different categories.

Anyone glancing over these categories would see that I have written books on every branch of science, on mathematics, on history, on literature, on humor—but the odd thing is that I've never written a book on science fiction.

I have written science fiction itself, to be sure, in all lengths and for all age levels. Just the same, I've never written a book about science fiction.

I know a reasonable amount about all the subjects I've written on, but what I am an acknowledged expert on is science fiction, yet I've never written a book about—but I'm repeating myself.

This doesn't mean I haven't thought about science fiction. In fact, I have written essays on almost every phase of science fiction and published them here, there, and everywhere. It just never occurred to me to get some of those articles into one place for those who are interested and can't very well go chasing over the face of the earth to get the individual essays.

Who knows when I would have thought of it, if ever, if Martin H. Greenberg (with whom I have been doing some anthologies recently) hadn't said, "Why don't you put together a group of essays that would make up a book you could call Asimov on Science Fiction."

It's funny how a small remark like that can set off a chain of free associations and end up with something remarkable. I considered Marty's suggestion, let it ferment in my head and develop for a while, and then the thought came to me out of left field.

"Hey," I said to myself, "why don't I put together a group of essays that would make up a book I could call Asimov on Science Fiction?"

It was the work of a moment (well, of a great many moments, actually) to go through my card catalog, search through my files, select and gather the essays, put them into a logical order and, in short, here is Asimov on Science Fiction.

I must warn you that some of the articles are slightly modified to eliminate unwanted repetition, or references that make sense only in the place of original appearance. You'll forgive me that, I know.

And now—let's go.

I
SCIENCE FICTION
IN GENERAL

(My Own View)

>   *One of the favorite games played by science fiction enthusiasts is that of trying to define just what science fiction is; and how, for instance, it is to be differentiated from fantasy.*
>   *I've tried my hand at the game, and done so more than once. I did so once when I was asked to write an introduction for* The Encyclopedia of Science Fiction, *edited by Robert Holdstock, and here it is.*

1. MY OWN VIEW*

I suppose it is a measure of the richness of the field of science fiction that no two of its practitioners are liable to agree on even something as fundamental as its definition—or on the boundaries that encompass it and on where one draws the dividing line between itself and realistic fiction, or between itself and fantasy.

Realistic fiction, as I see it, deals with events played against social backgrounds not significantly different from those that are thought to exist now or to have existed at some time in the past. There is no reason to suppose that the events in realistic fiction could not, conceivably, have taken place exactly as described.

Science fiction and fantasy (which we may lump together as "surrealistic fiction" if we wish) deal, on the other hand, with events played against social backgrounds that do not exist today and have not existed in the past. Examples would include the social satire of *Gulliver's Travels*, the talking animals of *The Jungle Book* or *The Voyages of Dr. Dolittle*, the supernatural influences of *Paradise Lost* or *The Lord of the Rings*, and the scientific extrapolation of *War of the Worlds* or *Rendezvous with Rama*.

To distinguish between the two major varieties of surrealistic fiction, I would say that the surreal background of the story in science fiction could, conceivably, be derived from our own by appropriate changes in the level of science and technology. The change could represent an advance, as in the development of colonies on Mars, or in the successful interpretations of signals from extraterrestrial life-forms. It could represent a retreat, as in a study of the destruction of our technological civilization by nuclear or ecological disaster. By a liberal interpretation of what scientific advances we can make, we could include such not-likely items as time travel, faster-than-light velocities, and so on.

Fantasy, on the other hand, portrays surreal backgrounds that cannot reasonably be supposed to be derived from our own by any change in the level of science and technology. (Or if they can be so derived, given enough ingenuity, the author does not bother to do so—as Tolkien scorns to try to fit Middle-Earth anywhere into human history.)

Given this definition of science fiction, we can see that the field can scarcely have existed in its true sense until the time came when the concept of social change through alterations in the level of science and technology had been evolved in the first place.

Through all of history, science and technology did advance and did, in so doing, alter society. (Consider the use of fire, for instance, or the invention of printing with movable type.) Through most of history, however, those changes progressed so slowly in time and spread so slowly in space that, within an individual's own lifetime, no change was visible. Hence, human history—barring trivial changes through war and dynastic succession, or fantasy changes through supernatural intervention—was viewed as essentially static.

The advance of science and technology, however, is cumulative, and each advance tends to encourage a more rapid further advance. Eventually, the rate of change, and the extent of the effect of that change on society, becomes great enough to be detected in the space of an individual lifetime. The future is then, for the first time, discovered.

This took place, clearly, with the development of the Industrial Revolution. It makes sense, then, to suppose that science fiction had to be born some time after 1800 and most likely in Great

Britain, and that its birth came about as the literary response to this discovery.

Brian Aldiss considers *Frankenstein*, published in Great Britain in 1818, to be the first true science fiction story, and I tend to agree with him.

In supplying a society that is technologically changed from that of the present, there is no need to produce one that will, in actual fact, some day come to exist. One which is not at all likely to come into being in any way can still be just as entertaining and have all the necessary dramatic values to be successful.

In the search, however, for a society which, although different, will carry conviction, and which will be consistent with the science and society of today, a writer does sometimes deal with matters which, to one degree or another, eventually come to pass. Atomic bombs and trips to the Moon are classic examples.

To suppose that this predictive aspect of science fiction, this foreseeing of details, is the truly impressive thing about science fiction, serves, however, only to trivialize the field.

What is important about science fiction, even crucial, is the very thing that gave it birth—the perception of change through technology. It is not that science fiction predicts this particular change or that that makes it important, it is that it predicts *change*.

Since the Industrial Revolution first made the perception of change through technology clear, the rate has continued to increase, until now the wind of change has risen from a zephyr to a hurricane.

It is change, continuing change, inevitable change, that is the dominant factor in society today. No sensible decision can be made any longer without taking into account not only the world as it is, but the world as it will be—and naturally this means that there must be an accurate perception of the world as it will be. This, in turn, means that our statesmen, our businessmen, our everyman† must take on a science fictional way of thinking,

† I use "man" in its most general sense, as including all human beings of either sex.

whether he likes it or not, or even whether he knows it or not.
Only so can the deadly problems of today be solved.

Individual science fiction stories may seem as trivial as ever to
the blinder critics and philosophers of today—but the core of science fiction, its essence, the concept about which it revolves, has
become crucial to our salvation if we are to be saved at all.

Foreword 2

(Extraordinary Voyages)

Just to show you that there is sufficient complexity in even the simple matter of a definition of science fiction, here is a second essay on the subject, one that is also by me but approaches that definition in quite a different manner.

This second essay appeared first as an editorial in the March–April 1978 issue of Isaac Asimov's Science Fiction Magazine, a periodical I will henceforth refer to as "my magazine" to avoid wearisome repetition of my name.

My magazine began* with the Spring 1977 issue as a quarterly, went to bimonthly publication in 1978, to monthly publication in 1979 and to tetraweekly publication in 1981. It has proved to be a gratifying success.

The actual editor of the magazine is George Scithers, and Shawna McCarthy is managing editor. I may call it "my" magazine, but it is they who do the real day-to-day work. Still, I have my chores, and one of them is to write an editorial in each issue.

I have a free hand in the subject matter of these editorials but I almost always deal with some phase of science fiction. In consequence, about two dozen of these editorials are included in this collection—so modified as to remove those occasional sentences that only make sense if you are holding an issue of the magazine in your hand.

* In chapter 51, I describe, briefly, how it came to be.

2. EXTRAORDINARY VOYAGES†

There are probably as many definitions of science fiction as there are definers, and the definitions range from those of the extreme exclusionists, who want their science fiction pure and hard, to those of the extreme inclusionists, who want their science fiction to embrace everything in sight.

Here is an extreme exclusionist definition of my own: "Science fiction deals with scientists working at science in the future."

Here is an extreme inclusionist definition of John Campbell's: "Science fiction stories are whatever science fiction editors buy."

A moderate definition (again mine) is: "Science fiction is that branch of literature that deals with human responses to changes in the level of science and technology." This leaves it open as to whether the changes are advances or retrogressions, and whether, with the accent on "human response," one need do more than refer glancingly and without detail to those changes.

To some writers, in fact, the necessity for discussing science seems so minimal that they object to the use of the word in the name of the genre. They prefer to call whatever it is they write "speculative fiction," thus keeping the abbreviation "s.f."‡

Occasionally, I feel the need to think it all out afresh and so why not approach the definition historically? For instance—

What is the first product of Western literature, which we have intact and which could be considered by inclusionists to be science fiction?

How about Homer's *Odyssey*? It doesn't deal with science, in a world which had not yet invented it, but it does deal with the equivalent of extraterrestrial monsters, like Polyphemus, and with

† Copyright © 1978 by Davis Publications, Inc.
‡ I don't favor the term "speculative fiction" except insofar as it might abolish that abominable abbreviation "sci-fi." But then it might substitute "spec-fic" which is even worse (see chapters 3 and 47).

people disposing of the equivalent of an advanced science, like Circe.

Yet most people would think of the *Odyssey* as a "travel tale." But that's all right. The two views are not necessarily mutually exclusive. The "travel tale," after all, was the original fantasy, the natural fantasy. Why not? Until contemporary times, travel was the arduous luxury of the very few, who alone could see what the vast hordes of humanity could not.

Most people, till lately, lived and died in the same town, the same valley, the same patch of earth, in which they were born. To them, whatever lay beyond the horizon was fantasy. It could be anything—and anything told of that distant wonderland fifty miles away could be believed. Pliny was not too sophisticated to believe the fantasies he was told of distant lands, and a thousand years of readers believed Pliny. Sir John Mandeville had no trouble passing off his fictional travel tales as the real thing.

And for twenty-five centuries after Homer, when anyone wanted to write a fantasy, he wrote a travel tale.

Imagine someone who goes to sea, lands upon an unknown island, and finds wonders. Isn't that Sinbad the Sailor and his tales of the Rukh and of the Old Man of the Sea? Isn't that Lemuel Gulliver and his encounters with Lilliputians and Brobdingnabians? As a matter of fact, isn't that King Kong?

The Lord of the Rings, together with what promises to be a vast horde of slavish imitations, are travel tales, too.

Yet are not these travel tales fantasies rather than science fiction? Where does "real" science fiction come in?

Consider the first professional science fiction writer, the first writer who made his living out of undoubted science fiction—Jules Verne (see chapters 27 and 28). He didn't think of himself as writing science fiction, for the term had not yet been invented, and for a dozen years he wrote for the French stage with indifferent success.

But he was a frustrated traveler and explorer and, in 1863, he suddenly hit pay dirt with his book *Five Weeks in a Balloon*. He thought of the book as a travel tale, but an unusual one since it made use of a device made possible by scientific advance.

Verne followed up his success by using other scientific devices, of the present and possible future, to carry his heroes farther and farther afield in other *"voyages extraordinaire"*—to the polar regions, to the sea bottom, to the Earth's center, to the Moon.

The Moon had been a staple of the tellers of travel tales ever since Lucian of Samosata in the first century AD. It was thought of as just another distant land, but what made it different in Verne's case was that he made the effort to get his heroes there by scientific principles that had not yet been applied in real life (though his method was unworkable as described).

After him, other writers took men on longer voyages to Mars and to other planets and finally, in 1928, E. E. Smith, in his *The Skylark of Space*, broke all bonds with his "inertialess drive" and carried humanity out to the distant stars.

So science fiction began as an outgrowth of the travel tale, differing chiefly in that the conveyances used do not yet exist but might exist if the level of science and technology is extrapolated to greater heights in the future.

But surely not all science fiction can be viewed as travel tales. What of stories that remain right here on Earth but deal with robots, or with nuclear or ecological disaster, or with new interpretations of the distant past, for that matter?

None of that, however, is "right here" on Earth. Following Verne's lead, whatever happens on Earth is made possible by continuing changes (usually advances) in the level of science and technology so that the story must take place "right there" on future Earth.

What, then, do you think of this definition: "Science fiction stories are extraordinary voyages into any of the infinite supply of conceivable futures"?

Almost everything about science fiction is a matter of controversy. This, perhaps, is not really strange. It may be because the writers, the fans, and even the casual readers happen one and all to be afflicted with eloquence, articulateness, and firm opinions. They will argue endlessly on any aspect of their beloved field and, in all probability, like each other all the better for the chance they had of expressing themselves vigorously.

Even the phrase "science fiction" itself manages to evoke dreadful nose-to-nose confrontations and I am not in the least backward about my opinion, either, as witness the following essay.

3. THE NAME OF OUR FIELD*

In the preceding essay, I talked of Jules Verne's "extraordinary voyages" and that brings up the point of how difficult it was to find a name for the kind of items that are published in the magazines of our field.

Such magazines contain "stories," and "story" is simply a shortened form of "history," a recounting of events in orderly detail. The recounting could, in either case, be of real incidents or of made-up ones, but we have become used to thinking of a "history" as real and of a "story" as made-up.

A "tale" is something that is "told" (from the Anglo-Saxon) and a "narrative" is something that is "narrated" (from the Latin). Either "tale" or "narrative" can be used for either a real or a made-up account. "Narrative" is the less common of the two simply because it is the longer word and therefore has an air of pretentiousness about it.

A word which is used exclusively for made-up items and never for real ones is "fiction," from a Latin word meaning "to invent."

What such magazines contain, then, are stories—or tales—or, most precisely, fiction.

Naturally, fiction can be of different varieties, depending on the nature of the content. If the events recounted deal mainly with love, we have "love stories" or "love tales" or "love fiction." Similarly, we can have "detective stories" or "terror tales" or "mystery fiction" or "confession stories" or "Western tales" or "jungle fiction."

The items that appear in the magazines of our own field deal, in one fashion or another, with future changes in the level of science or of science-derived technology. Doesn't it make sense, then, to consider the items to be "science stories," or "science tales," or, most precisely, "science fiction"?

And yet "science fiction," which is so obvious a name when you come to think of it, is a late development.

Jules Verne's extraordinary voyages were called "scientific fantasies" in Great Britain and the term "science fantasy" is still sometimes used today. "Fantasy" is from a Greek word meaning "imagination," so it isn't completely inappropriate, but it implies the minimal existence of constraints. When we speak of "fantasy" nowadays, we generally refer to stories that are not bound by the laws of science, whereas science fiction stories *are* so bound.

Another term used in the 1920s was "scientific romance." Romance was originally used for anything published in the "Romance languages," that is, in the popular tongues of western Europe, so that it was applied to material meant to be read for amusement. More serious works were written in Latin, of course. The trouble is that "romance" has come to be applied to love stories in particular so that "science romance" has a wrong feel to it.

"Pseudoscience stories" was sometimes used, but that is insulting. "Pseudo" is from a Greek word meaning "false" and while the kind of extrapolations of science used in science fiction are not true science, they are not false science either. They are "might be true" science.

"Superscience stories," still another name, is childish.

In 1926, when Hugo Gernsback published the first magazine ever to be devoted exclusively to science fiction, he called it *Amazing Stories*.

This caught on. When other magazines appeared, synonyms for "amazing" were frequently used. We had *Astounding Stories, Astonishing Stories, Wonder Stories, Marvel Stories*, and *Startling Stories* all on the stands, when the world and I were young.

Such names, however, do not describe the nature of the stories, but their effect on the reader, and that is insufficient. A story can amaze, astound, astonish, and startle you; it can cause you to marvel and wonder; and yet it need not be science fiction. It need not even be fiction. Something better was needed.

Gernsback knew that. He had originally thought of calling his magazine *Scientific Fiction*. That is hard to pronounce quickly, though, chiefly because of the repetition of the syllable "fic." Why not combine the words and eliminate one of those syllables? We then have "scientifiction."

"Scientifiction," though, is an ugly word, hard to understand and, if understood, likely to scare off those potential readers who equate the "scientific" with the "difficult." Gernsback therefore used the word only in a subtitle: *Amazing Stories: the Magazine of Scientifiction*. He introduced "stf" as the abbreviation of "scientifiction" and both abbreviation and word are still used sometimes.

When Gernsback was forced to give up *Amazing Stories*, he published a competing magazine *Science Wonder Stories*. In its first issue (June 1929) he used the term "science fiction," and the abbreviation "s.f."—or "sf" without periods—became popular. Occasionally, the word has been hyphenated as "science-fiction," but that is only done rarely.

The story, however, doesn't end there.

Since 1960, in particular, science fiction has tended to shift at least some of its emphasis from science to society, from gadgets to people. It still deals with changes in the level of science and technology, but those changes move farther into the background.

I believe it was Robert Heinlein who first suggested that we ought to speak of "speculative fiction" instead, and some, like Harlan Ellison, strongly support that move now.

To me, though, "speculative" seems a weak word. It is four syllables long and is not too easy to pronounce quickly. Besides, almost anything can be speculative fiction. A historical romance can be speculative; a true crime story can be speculative. "Speculative fiction" is not a precise description of our field and I don't think it will work. In fact, I think "speculative fiction" has been introduced only to get rid of "science" but to keep "s.f."

This brings us to Forrest J Ackerman, a wonderful guy whom I love dearly. He is a devotee of puns and wordplay and so am I, but Forry has never learned that some things are sacred. He couldn't resist coining "sci-fi" as an analog, in appearance and pronunciation, to "hi-fi," the well-known abbreviation for "high fidelity."

"Sci-fi" is now widely used by people who don't read science fiction. It is used particularly by people who work in movies and television. This makes it, perhaps, a useful term.

We can define "sci-fi" as trashy material sometimes confused, by ignorant people, with s.f. Thus, *Star Trek* is s.f. while *Godzilla Meets Mothra* is sci-fi.

AFTERWORD 3

(*The Name of Our Field*)

After the original appearance of the preceding essay, Forrest J Ackerman was slightly chafed by the last few paragraphs and wrote to me, defending the "sci-fi" abomination.

Relax, Forry, you've won.

There are millions of people who talk about "sci-fi." The newspapers, TV, radio, the nonscience fiction magazines, the general public, all speak of it exclusively as "sci-fi." Even the subscription department of my very own magazine can't seem to use anything but "sci-fi."

The only people who say "s.f." are those few (not more than 100,000 in all, perhaps) who combine incredible intelligence with a deep and thoroughgoing knowledge of science fiction.

Surely, Forry, you can't begrudge the fact that we few, we happy few, we band of brothers, should cling firmly to the right.

(*The Universe of Science Fiction*)

Of late I have taken to the preparation of science fiction anthologies, which is perhaps a sign of literary senescence, though I like to think of it, rather, as putting my mature wisdom and expertise at the service of the science fiction reading public. After all, I am by no means ceasing, or even slowing, my own proper output. Besides, I must admit I generally make use of coeditors, and sweet-talk them into taking care of the more turgid aspects of the job—correspondence, bookkeeping, and so on.

One of these recent anthologies was The 13 Crimes of Science Fiction (Doubleday, 1979) *in which my coeditors were Martin Harry Greenberg and Charles G. Waugh. For the anthology, I wrote an introduction relating science fiction to other specialized fields of writing, especially mysteries, and here it is.*

4. THE UNIVERSE OF SCIENCE FICTION*

Science fiction is a literary universe of no mean size because science fiction is what it is, not through its content but through its background. Let me explain the difference that makes.

A "sports story" must have, as part of its content, some competitive activity, generally of an athletic nature. A "Western story" must have, as part of its content, the nomadic life of the cowboy of the American West in the latter half of the nineteenth century. The "jungle story" must have, as part of its content, the dangers implicit in a forested tropical wilderness.

Take the content of any of these and place it against a back-

* Copyright © 1979 by Isaac Asimov, Martin H. Greenberg, and Charles G. Waugh

ground that involves a society significantly different from our own and you have not changed the nature of the story—you have merely added to it.

A story may involve, not the clash of baseball and bat, or of hockeystick and puck, but of gas gun and sphere in an atmosphere enclosed on a space station under zero gravity. It is still a sports story by the strictest definition you care to make, but it is science fiction *also*.

In place of the nomadic life of a cowboy and his horse, herding cattle, you might have the nomadic life of a fishboy and his dolphin, herding his schools of mackerel and cod. It could still have the soul of a Western story and be science fiction *also*.

In place of the Matto Grosso, you can have the jungle on a distant planet, different in key factors of the environment, with exotic dangers in atmosphere, in vegetation, in planetary characteristics never encountered on Earth. It would still be a jungle story and be science fiction *also*.

For that matter, you needn't confine yourself to category fiction. Take the deepest novel you can imagine, one that most amply plumbs the secret recesses of the soul and holds up a picture that illuminates nature and the human condition, and place it in a society in which interplanetary travel is common, and give it a plot which involves such travel and it is not only great literature—it is science fiction *also*.

John W. Campbell, the late great science fiction editor, used to say that science fiction took as its domain, all conceivable societies, past and future, probable or improbable, realistic or fastastic, and dealt with all events and complications that were possible in all those societies. As for "mainstream fiction" which deals with the here and now and introduces only the small novelty of make-believe events and characters, that forms only an inconsiderable fraction of the whole.

And I agree with him.

In only one respect did John retreat from this grand vision of the limitless boundaries of science fiction. In a moment of failure of nerve, he maintained that it was impossible to write a science fiction mystery. The opportunities in science fiction were so broad, he said, that the strict rules that made the classical mystery story fair to the reader could not be upheld.

I imagine that what he expected was the sudden change of rules without warning in the midst of the story. Something like this, I suppose—

"Ah, Watson, what that scoundrel did not count on was that with this pocket-frannistan which I have in my pocket-frannistan container I can see through the lead lining and tell what is inside the casket."

"Amazing, Holmes, but how does it work?"

"By the use of Q-rays, a little discovery of my own which I have never revealed to the world."

Naturally, there is the temptation to do this. Even in the classical mystery story that is not science fiction there is the temptation to give the detective extraordinary abilities in order to advance the plot. Sherlock Holmes's ability to distinguish, at sight, the ashes of hundreds of different kinds of tobacco, while not perhaps in the same class as the invention of a Q-ray at a moment's notice, is certainly a step in the direction of the unfair.

Then, too, there is nothing to prevent even the strictest of strict mystery writers from using actual science, even from using the latest available findings of science, which the reader may not have heard of. That is still considered fair.

There are dangers to that, however, since many mystery writers know no science and cannot prevent themselves from making bloopers. John Dickson Carr in one book revealed that he didn't know the difference between the element, antimony; and the compound, antimony potassium tartrate. That was only irritating, but in another book, he demonstrated that he couldn't tell the difference between carbon monoxide and carbon dioxide and reduced the plot to a shambles. One of Dorothy Sayer's more grisly short stories involved the effect of thyroid hormones and, though she had the right idea, she made the effects impossibly rapid and extreme.

Writing a scientific mystery, then, has its extraordinary pitfalls and difficulties, how much more so the writing of a science fiction mystery. In science fiction, you not only must know your science, but you must also have a rational notion as to how to modify or extrapolate that science.

That, however, only means that writing a science fiction mystery is difficult; it does *not* mean that it is conceptually impossible as John Campbell thought.

After all, it is as perfectly possible to cling to the rules of the game in science fiction mysteries as in ordinary ones.

The science fiction mystery may be set in the future and in the midst of a society far different from ours; one in which human beings have developed telepathy, for instance, or in which light-speed mass transport is possible, or in which all human knowledge is computerized for instant retrieval—but the rules still hold.

The writer must carefully explain to the reader all the boundary conditions of the imaginary society. It must be perfectly clear what can be done and what can't be done; and with those boundaries fixed, the reader must then see and hear everything the investigator sees and hears, and he must be aware of every clue the investigator comes across.

There may be misdirection and red herrings to obscure and confuse, but it must remain possible for the reader to outdeduce the investigator, however *outré* the society.

Can it be done? You bet! Modestly, I refer you to my own science fiction mysteries, *The Caves of Steel* and *The Naked Sun* which I wrote, back in the 1950s, in order to show John that he was being too modest about science fiction.

FOREWORD 5

(Adventure!)

In the fall of 1978, Davis Publications, Inc., the publishers of my magazine, decided to venture a second magazine, to be called Asimov's SF Adventure Magazine, to which I will refer, henceforward as "my adventure magazine."

The new magazine was to be aimed at a somewhat younger audience than its older sibling and was to emphasize action and adventure. What's more, it was to be of a different size, 8⅜ by 10⅞ inches instead of 5⅛ by 7½ inches.

To introduce the magazine, I included an editorial in the first issue (Fall 1978) that related the adventure story to science fiction.

5. ADVENTURE!*

The adventure story has a long and honorable history.

The history couldn't very well be any longer than it is since it is hard to believe that the stories spun over the campfires of Stone Age people were anything but adventure stories of marvelous hunts and of the cracking of skulls of enemies.

The earliest myths we gather from the various primitive cultures on Earth tell of the daring adventures of the gods and of the battles among them. Even the God of the Bible may have had such a history. There are traces in the Bible of primitive tales recounting how the creation of an ordered universe followed only after a battle to the death with the forces of chaos.

In Psalm 74, we may have an echo of that early cosmic battle: "Thou didst divide the sea by thy strength; thou brakest the heads of the dragons in the waters. Thou brakest the heads of leviathan in pieces."

* Copyright © 1978 by Davis Publications, Inc.

Nor could the history of the adventure story be any more honorable than it is.

The oldest intact works of fiction in Western literature are Homer's *Iliad* and *Odyssey*, and what are they but adventure stories? The former is a rousing war story, the latter a thrilling travel tale.

Don't get me wrong. I don't say that *Iliad* and *Odyssey* are *just* adventure stories. Critics have found a great deal more to them than that. —Still, it is the adventure aspect of each that spelled survival and popularity, even today.

The most popular bits in the *Iliad* have always been the battle scenes—especially the climactic duel between Hector and Achilles, with the audience torn apart because Homer's genius led him to divide audience sympathies almost equally between the two heroes.

And the most popular bits in the *Odyssey* are the macabre adventures that Odysseus recounts at the court of the Phaeacians, particularly that episode in the cave of Polyphemus, the cannibalistic, ogrish Cyclops.

Ever since Homer, adventure tales have fascinated human beings and have therefore endured. The medieval tales of King Arthur—the fantasies of the *Arabian Nights*—the blood and thunder of Shakespeare.

Blood and thunder? Yes, indeed. Shakespeare may be the standard for all that is lofty in literature—but the fact is he wrote for the popular taste and was criticized for that both in his time and afterward. He had fighting and hacking all over the place. In *King Lear*, one of the characters has his eyes gouged out right on stage and in *Titus Adronicus*, we have rape, mutilation, and cannibalism.

Science fiction is no stranger to the adventure story. Verne's stories were primarily tales of high adventure, however careful he might have been to include bits of justifying science lectures.

And, of course, once the science fiction magazines appeared on the scene, adventure reigned supreme for decades. Hugo Gernsback used to argue that science fiction was an educational force and so it is, in my opinion, but only secondarily. What the readers wanted was adventure in the first place and that's what they got.

Although at first *Amazing Stories* and then *Wonder Stories* tried, unsuccessfully, to maintain a certain loftiness, making use of footnotes, science quizzes, and so on, they didn't stay on top of the heap. In 1930 there appeared *Astounding Stories*, which was unabashedly adventure-oriented and which quickly took over the leadership of the field.

In 1937, John Campbell became editor of *Astounding Stories*, changed its name to *Astounding Science Fiction* and moved it away from adventure, but by that time *Wonder Stories* had become *Thrilling Wonder Stories* and had moved toward adventure.

In 1939, there came a science fiction magazine boom, and new magazines of all kinds suddenly made their appearance on the newsstand. In December 1939, *Planet Stories* appeared. It was, in some ways, the best of the adventure science fiction magazines of its time.

But if there are science fiction magazine booms, there are also science fiction magazine busts and, all too often, the higher the boom, the deeper the bust. A particularly intense boom came in the early 1950s, and in the particularly intense bust that followed, both *Thrilling Wonder Stories* and *Planet Stories* discontinued publication in 1955.

With that, somehow, adventure science fiction dwindled. The magazines that survived the viscissitudes of the time, such as *Analog*, *F & SF*, and *Galaxy*, did not concentrate on adventure primarily. Nor does the new, but already clearly successful, *Isaac Asimov's Science Fiction Magazine*.

Why is this?

For one thing, the science fiction readership has changed. Back in the 1920s and 1930s, science fiction readers were almost universally under eighteen, and the magazines were geared to them.

Many youngsters dropped out of science fiction as they grew older but not all did, and the median age of the readership has risen steadily. Increasingly after World War II, the growing percentage of older readers influenced the field so that science fiction had to mature as well.

Secondly, not only were there more older readers but there were fewer younger ones, as first comic magazines and then television came along to compete for the allegiance of the young.

And as an accident of history, false definitions have been made. "Adventure" has come to mean "pulp" and both have come to mean "bad writing."

The early magazines between the two world wars were called "pulp" because of the paper they used. Those pulp magazines needed many stories and paid low rates, so they couldn't be too choosy in what they accepted. Writers had to write many stories to meet the demand and to make a living.

Hurried writing is usually lurid and clumsy and those were the characteristics that left their mark on pulp fiction. Perhaps 90 percent of pulp writing was like that, but then, as Ted Sturgeon said, 90 percent of everything is bad.

But that still leaves 10 percent that is good, and well-written adventure can be very effective indeed.

Then, too, "adventure" has come to mean "kids," because the early magazines were youngster-oriented. Surely, though, it doesn't take much thought to see that well-written adventure stories can be enjoyed by anyone of any age.

It is with that thought in mind that *Asimov's SF Adventure Magazine* is being brought out.

Asimov's SF Adventure Magazine is dedicated to adventure, or it wouldn't bear the name it does, but not to adventure at any cost. As far as we can, it is our intention to supply well-written adventure science fiction by authors who are not ignorant of science. Our stories will have action, but not at the expense of science or of writing skill.

Can we do it?

It would be foolish to guarantee success. These are precarious times for magazines generally and the tightrope is difficult to walk.

We must hope that our distribution is sufficiently efficient; that we can find the writers who will supply the material we need; and that we discover that our estimate of readership is reasonably accurate.

What we know we have are a reliable publisher, an experienced staff, and a great deal of determination.

So we'll start with this first issue and see if we can't use it to convince enough of you that "adventure" and "good" can be adjectives that are not at war with each other; that "adventure" and "intelligent" are adjectives that can be applied to the same story; that "adventure" and "let's have more" can reinforce each other and lead to success.

Afterword 5

(Adventure!)

My adventure magazine was, if anything, better than its older sibling, in my opinion. It had clearer print, terrific artwork, and excellent stories.

But, alas, we didn't make it despite the hopes expressed in the preceding essay.

The large-size science fiction magazines of the last half century have uniformly failed (with the exception of Omni, which had behind it the millions of dollars of Penthouse International, Ltd., and was only one-third science fiction). My adventure magazine proved to be no exception.

It could not get the kind of newsstand distribution that it needed, and when it was on the newsstand, it was buried in innumerable other magazines of the same size.

It hung on for four issues but couldn't quite make the necessary sales, so it was suspended—only temporarily, I hope, and some day, under more favorable conditions, perhaps we can try again.

II

THE WRITING OF
SCIENCE FICTION

(Hints)

I have firmly maintained over the decades that I have no real editorial capacity. Since that is so, I am glad to leave the editorship of my magazine in the capable hands of George and Shawna, and take good care not to interfere.

Among the many reasons I can't really edit a magazine is the fact that I have no judgment in stories. I don't really think I can tell a good story from a bad one except in extreme cases either way (though, like every critic working with blunt tools—I know what I like).

Because of this lack within me, I can never be sure what changes must be introduced to turn a bad story into a good one or a good story into a better one. I can't even do it for the stories I write myself, but have to work by some sort of primitive instinct.

Yet I'm not a complete idiot, either. There are some general rules I have worked out as far as the writing of science fiction is concerned, and I have no hesitation in lecturing the public at large in this respect—particularly since I do have a magazine with my name on it and I want it to be as good as it can possibly be.

Therefore, some of my editorials are given over to advice to aspiring writers as, for instance, the following.

6. HINTS*

Every once in a short while I get a letter from some eager young would-be writer asking me for some "hints" on the art of writing science fiction.

The feeling I have is that my correspondents think there is

* Copyright © 1979 by Davis Publications, Inc.

some magic formula jealously guarded by the professionals but that since I'm such a nice guy I will spill the beans if properly approached.

Alas, there's no such thing, no magic formula, no secret tricks, no hidden shortcuts.

I'm sorry to have to tell you that it's a matter of hard work over a long period of time. If you know of any exceptions to this, that's exactly what they are—exceptions.

There are, however, some general principles that could be useful, to my way of thinking, and here they are.

1) *You have to prepare for a career as a successful science fiction writer—as you would for any other highly specialized calling.*

First, you have to learn to use your tools, just as a surgeon has to learn to use his.

The basic tool for any writer is the English language, which means you must develop a good vocabulary and brush up on such prosaic things as spelling and grammar.

There can be little argument about vocabulary, but it may occur to you that spelling and grammar are just frills. After all, if you write great and gorgeous stories, surely the editor will be delighted to correct your spelling and grammar.

Not so! He (or she) won't be.

Besides, take it from an old war-horse, if your spelling and grammar are rotten, you won't be writing a great and gorgeous story. Someone who can't use a saw and hammer doesn't turn out stately furniture.

Even if you've been diligent at school, have developed a vocabulary, can spell "sacrilege" and "supersede" and never say "between you and I" or "I ain't never done nothing," that's still not enough. There's the subtle structure of the English sentence and the artful construction of the English paragraph. There is the clever interweaving of plot, the handling of dialogue, and a thousand other intricacies.

How do you learn that? Do you read books on how to write, or attend classes on writing, or go to writing conferences? These are all of inspirational value, I'm sure, but they won't teach you what you really want to know.

What *will* teach you is the careful reading of the masters of English prose. This does not mean condemning yourself to years of falling asleep over dull classics. Good writers are invariably fascinating writers—the two go together. In my opinion, the writers of English who most clearly use the correct word every time and who most artfully and deftly put together their sentences and paragraphs are Charles Dickens, Mark Twain, and P. G. Wodehouse.

Read them, and others, but with attention. They represent your schoolroom. Observe what they do and try to figure out why they do it. It's no use other people explaining it to you. Until you see it for yourself and it becomes part of you, nothing will help.

But suppose that no matter how you try, you can't seem to absorb the lesson. —Well, it may be that you're not a writer. It's no disgrace. You can always go on to take up some slightly inferior profession like surgery or the presidency of the United States. It won't be as good, of course, but we can't all scale the heights.

Second, for a science fiction writing career, it is not enough to know the English language, you also have to know science. You may not want to use much science in your stories, but you'll have to know it anyway, so that what you do use, you don't misuse.

This does not mean you have to be a professional scientist, or a science major at college. You don't even have to go to college. It does mean, though, that you have to be willing to study science on your own if your formal education has been weak in that direction.

It's not impossible. One of the best writers of hard science fiction is Fred Pohl and he never even finished high school. Of course, there are very few people who are as bright as Fred, but you can write considerably less well than he does and still be pretty good.

Fortunately, there is much more good popular science writing these days than there were in previous generations, and you can learn a great deal, rather painlessly, if you read such science fiction writers as L. Sprague de Camp, Ben Bova, and Poul Anderson in their nonfictional moods—or even Isaac Asimov.

What's more, professional scientists are also writing effectively for the public these days, as witness Carl Sagan's magnificent books. And there's always *Scientific American*.

Third, even if you know your science and your writing, it is still not likely that you will be able to put them together from scratch. You will have to be a diligent reader of science fiction itself to learn the conventions and the tricks of the trade—how to interweave background and plot, for instance.

2) *You have to work at the job.*

The final bit of schooling is writing itself. Nor must you wait till your preparation is complete. The act of writing is itself part of the preparation.

You can't completely understand what good writers do until you try it yourself. You learn a great deal when you find your story breaking apart in your hands—or beginning to hang together. Write from the very beginning, then, and keep on writing.

3) *You have to be patient.*

Since writing is itself a schooling, you can't very well expect to sell the first story you write. (Yes, I know Bob Heinlein did it, but he was Bob Heinlein. You're only you.)

But then, why should that discourage you? After you finished the first grade at school, you weren't through, were you? You went on to the second grade, then the third, then the fourth, and so on.

If each story you write is one more step in your literary education, a rejection shouldn't matter. The next story will be better, and the next one after that still better, and eventually—

But then why bother to submit the stories?

If you don't, how can you possibly know when you graduate? After all, you don't know which story you'll sell. You might even sell the first. You almost certainly won't, but you just might.

Of course, even after you sell a story, you may fail to place the next dozen, but having done it once, it is quite likely that you will eventually do it again, if you persevere.

But what if you write and write and write and you don't seem to be getting any better and all you collect are printed rejection slips? Once again, it may be that you are not a writer and will have to settle for a lesser post such as that of Chief Justice of the United States.

4) *You have to be reasonable.*

Writing is the most wonderful and satisfying task in the world, but it does have one or two insignificant flaws. Among those flaws is the fact that a writer can almost never make a living at it.

Oh, a few writers make a lot of money—they're the ones we all hear about. But for every writer who rakes it in, there are a thousand who dread the monthly-rent bill. It shouldn't be like that, but it is.

Take my case: Three years after I sold my first story, I reached the stage of selling everything I wrote, so that I had become a successful writer. Nevertheless, it took me seventeen more years as a *successful* writer before I could actually support myself in comfort on my earnings as a writer.

So while you're trying to be a writer, make sure you find another way of making a decent living—and don't quit your job after you make your first sale.

(By No Means Vulgar)

*Of all the requirements for writing good science
fiction stories, the one that is nearest my heart is that
of scientific rationality.*

*Note that I didn't say "scientific accuracy." To re-
main absolutely accurate, one would have to stay on
ground level and science fiction must be able to soar;
that is, the science fiction writer must guess, extrapolate, take liberties. However, no matter how the
writer guesses, extrapolates, and takes liberties with
the present beliefs in science, he or she must know
enough about these beliefs to remain rational in the
use of science in even the wildest flights of imagination.*

7. BY NO MEANS VULGAR*

The Latin word *populus* means "people"; the Latin word
vulgus means "people."

In English we have the word "popular" and the word "vulgar,"
both referring to attributes of the people. We can have, for instance, "popular elections," meaning elections in which the people generally, rather than privileged individuals only, can vote.
We can also have the "vulgar tongue," meaning the language of
the general multitude, rather than the Latin of the learned classes.

Of course you can, by "people," refer to all the population without distinction. You can, on the other hand, refer only to most of
them and apply the word to the "common people" as distinct
from the "better classes"—better through birth, education, or self-
esteem.

You can, if you are of democratic mind, use the adjectives in a favorable sense and think highly of anything characteristic of the people. Or, if snobbish, you can use the adjectives in an unfavorable sense, and assume that anything that pleases many is bound to be inferior since only a long process of cultivation can raise the level of taste to your own refined pitch.

In our English language, we have differentiated these two meanings, and "popular" has come to represent the favorable aspects of the general taste, while "vulgar" represents the unfavorable ones. Thus, Shakespeare has Polonius advise his son: "Be thou familiar, but by no means vulgar."

In French, I believe the distinction is less clear. I have, for instance, been described in French as being involved in the "vulgarization" of science. That would raise my hackles were it not that the surrounding sentences made it clear that praise was intended.

In English, however, it is only possible to say that I am a "popularizer" of science. Should anyone try to say I am a "vulgarizer" of science, he had better be a friend of mine and he had better be smiling when he says it.

Yet I cannot help but feel that to some scientists there is no such thing as "science popularization"; there is only "science vulgarization."

Why? For the usual reason—snobbery.

It is not surprising to find a scientist feeling himself to be a member of an intellectual aristocracy. To reach the level of professionalism in science requires a kind of intelligence, curiosity, dedication, and patient training that is not very common. Because it is not common, there is a tendency to think it is superior.

There are, of course, two ways to react to superiority (real or fancied). You can decide that to possess more of talent or privilege confers upon the possessor special obligations (*noblesse oblige*). The true gentleman, who occupies a favored position in society, has standards of behavior and courtesy not expected or required of a commoner, and these standards must apply, as far as possible, to all and not to other gentlemen only. Similarly, the true intellectual, who has attained a refined understanding of any segment of learning, is required to make that learning available, as far as possible, to all and not to other intellectuals only.

On the other hand, you can react by assuming a wide gulf between yourself and those less favored; one that cannot be crossed at all if the difference is one of caste, or that can be crossed only by heavy exertion on the part of the unfavored one if the difference is one of training or education. In this case, for a favored one to extend a helping hand across the gulf is not done; it is "vulgar" and it gives rise to the suspicion that the helper is perhaps not truly a member of the upper class.

Naturally, my own outlook is that of *noblesse oblige* or I wouldn't be in the profession I occupy.

Nor is this a matter of personal predilection alone. To me, the intellectual *noblesse oblige* has become a matter of life and death for society. Consider:—

1) Science is no longer the private concern of a few ardent souls intent on plumbing the mysteries of the Universe out of personal curiosity. Science cannot be a private concern as long as it depends on the public purse—and these days it does just that. It depends on it directly, through the tax funds granted scientific projects by the government; or, indirectly, through industrial support which is made up for by an appropriate increase in the pricing of goods and services.

2) Science is no longer divorced from the public good or evil, as it once was when it lived in an ivory tower (or fancied it did so). Scientific advance can easily produce something that will, wittingly or unwittingly, serve to destroy civilization—or save it.

3) Science is no longer an activity that can be carried out by a few volunteers. We need many people trained in many levels of scientific accomplishment if our technological civilization is to work well, and these people can be drawn only from the general public and only by active proselytization.

Well, then, if the general public pays for scientific advance, it deserves to know as much about what it is paying for as it can—so that it may choose its manner of support intelligently.

If the general public's destruction or salvation depends on scientific advance, it deserves to know as much about what may destroy it or save it as it can—so that it can more intelligently behave in such a fashion as to guide the advance away from destruction and toward salvation.

If it is from the general public that the scientists and technicians of the future are to be drawn, then it deserves to know as much about the profession as it can—so that it can more intelligently choose a point of entry.

Each scientist is, of course, part of the general public. He or she pays taxes, endures the chance of technological destruction or salvation, suffers the possibility of technological breakdown through lack of trained personnel. Science popularization is therefore as necessary to the scientist as to anyone else, and if any scientist looks upon it as science "vulgarization," he is an ass. —And a dangerous one, too.

It is more than twenty years now since I gave up formal classroom work, and I am sometimes asked if I miss it, or if I feel guilty about having "abandoned" teaching. My answer is "No," for I have abandoned neither my teaching nor my classes. I still teach through my books and lectures, and reach a far larger "class" in more fields than ever I did in the classroom.

I am also asked if I regret "no longer being a scientist." The answer to that is also "No," for I am *still* a scientist. In fact, since I devote my almost every waking hour to teaching all whom I can reach, which I consider the very first duty of any scientist at any moment when not actively engaged in research, I feel myself to be more a *working* scientist than ever.

All this has a sharp application to science fiction. Teaching science may not be the primary function of science fiction, but *mis*-teaching science should be anathema to it.

If you take your spaceship to Titan, there is no need to make your story into a travelog, nor need you feel compelled to give the vital statistics of the world you're landing on. You might do so, if you can weave it into the story skillfully enough, but it is not necessary.

Under no conditions, however, should you describe Titan as a satellite of Jupiter (which it isn't) rather than one of Saturn (which it is).

Mistakes can be made. Writers are only human. We should *not*, however, be among those who say, "Who cares about scientific minutiae? The story's the thing." And you can't have good science fiction stories with bad science.

So, to you aspiring science fiction writers out there—you need not feel you must have a graduate degree to write, but you must learn enough science to bear the load of the particular story you want to write.

(*Learning Device*)

Of course, science fiction writers sometimes find the science in their story becoming awry through no fault of their own. Science advances, corrects itself, sometimes even overturns itself. When that happens, it may be that a story which was filled with a perfectly legitimate scientific background when it was written becomes hopelessly wrong five years later.

That is a forgivable sin for writers; I have suffered from such scientific advances as much as anyone else. In fact, such unavoidable out-of-dateness should not in the least affect the literary value of a story, and may not even affect its scientific usefulness.

8. LEARNING DEVICE*

When Hugo Gernsback first originated magazine science fiction over half a century ago, he considered its purpose that of prediction and education. He may have been serious about its predictive value, for he was a terrific futurist of gadgets (none better, I think). Even late in life, he would, at Christmastime, distribute small booklets in which he would include his latest foresights into the world of future technology.

I believe he was also sincere in feeling science fiction to be of educational value, but I knew that he was a shrewd promoter and there may have been more to it than that. He must have known that the new magazines were bound to be considered sensational nonsense and that parents and teachers would try to keep the youngsters in their charge from reading them. It was only natural, then, that he try to cast a pall of respectability over the stuff.

(After all, my father wouldn't let me read sensational literature and I got him to make an exception in the case of science fiction only by stressing the learning value of its content of science.)

* Copyright © 1979 by Davis Publications, Inc.

One way in which Gernsback tried to establish the educational value of science fiction was by running a science quiz in each issue in those early days, with a page reference for finding the answer. ("What is the nearest star?" page 29.) If you looked up the page reference you would find the answer. ("But, Captain, those vicious pirates have dragged the fair Ilanadee to their lair on the planet, Xybu, that circles Alpha Centauri, the nearest star.")

Those science quizzes drove me crazy. I was nine years old when I persuaded my father that science fiction would educate me, and there were indeed some things I had not yet learned about science, so the questions in the science quiz had the potentiality of intriguing me. What *was* the nearest star? I might ask myself.

The trouble was that if I allowed my curiosity to force me to turn to page 29, I had to read the entire page sometimes to find the answer and that would tend to kill the story for me. I would find out that the fair Ilanadee had been dragged off to the pirate lair (for who knows what fell purpose, and I certainly didn't) and I didn't want to know that in advance.

On the other hand, if I waited till I had read all the stories, the questions no longer interested me. I had the answers.

There are additional problems to the notion of science fiction as a learning device.

First, science advances and science fiction writers sometimes lag behind.

Back in 1940, I referred to element 43 as "masurium" in a story I had written. However, the discovery of masurium, reported in 1925, proved a false alarm. When element 43 was really discovered (it had to be formed in the laboratory, actually, since all its isotopes are radioactive) it was named "technetium." The embarrassing point was that the real discovery was made in 1937, three years before I had written the story, but the news hadn't caught up to me yet.

Of course, in the good old days there was nothing as evanescent as a science fiction story. Here today and gone next month forever, except in the yellowing files of the more ardent science fiction fans. If you made a mistake, it was quickly gone, and the damage was fleeting.

Nowadays, on the other hand, science fiction stories can live on for many years. My *Foundation* stories, for instance, have been before the public and readily available in book form for nearly thirty years now, more or less continuously, and bear considerable promise of outliving their author.

There are sins of omission in it that become more glaring by the decade. My *Foundation* stories span the galaxies in detail and yet nowhere do I mention quasars, pulsars, or black holes. To be sure, none of these objects was known in the 1940s when I wrote the stories, but I'm still uneasy about it.

As for sins of commission, consider my six books about Lucky Starr. Each of them is set in a different world of the Solar system and I did my best to describe those worlds accurately. Those books were written in the 1950s, however, and I described them accurately only as far as the astronomers of the 1950s knew.

Unfortunately for me, the 1950s saw us on the verge of the Space Age and, what with radar astronomy, satellites, and space probes, there was a revolution in our knowledge of the Solar system and virtually every world in it turned upside down and inside out.

Until the 1950s, as an example, it was taken for granted, and was virtually a science fictional convention, that Venus was a warm, waterlogged primitive planet, similar to Earth in its dinosaur-ridden Mesozoic age. Why not? According to the nebular hypothesis of the origin of the Solar system, which held sway throughout the nineteenth century, the planets were formed from the outside in, so that Mars was considered older than Earth, and Venus was considered younger than Earth.

It made for excellent science fiction. If you wanted an advanced, decadent, dying civilization, you went to Mars. If you wanted a primitive dangerous world, you went to Venus. In *David Starr: Space Ranger*, I used the former; in *Lucky Starr and the Oceans of Venus*, I used the latter.

In the Venus book, particularly, I went to town. I had a worldwide ocean filled with all kinds of interesting creatures, and Lucky had terrific adventures there with something that was rather like a mile-wide jellyfish.

Within just a few years after the appearance of the book in

1954, it turned out our notions of Venus were all wrong. It proved to be a nearly red-hot planet without a drop of surface water, with poisonous clouds, with virtually no rotation, but with gale winds, and so on.

Well, the Lucky Starr books are still in print, both in hard-cover (Gregg Press) and soft-cover (Fawcett); but in recent editions, I've had to insist on the publishers including introductory notes in which I bring the readers up-to-date on planetary conditions and explain that the books were written before present-day knowledge of the planets was established. It doesn't seem to hurt the sales, and even if it did, I wouldn't care. I can't mislead young readers; nor can I have them think I am a quarter century behind in my knowledge of the Solar system.

Am I saying, then, that science fiction is useless as an educational device?

It may sound like it, so far, but I am not. All I am saying is that it is untrustworthy as a source of "facts," since these may be wrong, or at least out-of-date. There is nothing wrong, however, with science fiction as a way of arousing interest in science.

There, at least, it doesn't matter whether the scientific background of a science fiction story is accidentally wrong through ignorance, deliberately wrong through the exigencies of the plot, or simply out-of-date through the progress in science. If the story is *interesting*, it can be used.

Let us suppose, for instance, that you have a junior high-school class, or a young boy-scout troop, to whom, for some reason, you want to transmit an understanding of the planet, Venus. You may feel that they are not particularly interested in learning about Venus.

You therefore give them *Lucky Starr and the Oceans of Venus* to read, and we can suppose, for the purpose of argument, that they find it interesting and are enthusiastic about it. You may then pose them questions like:

Do you think it makes sense to suppose that Venus has a world-wide ocean? Why?

Scientists have found that Venus has a surface temperature of over 600° F. What do you suppose causes that? How do you suppose they found out? What happens to the ocean Asimov said Venus had?

—And so on.

I'm quite willing to bet that youngsters would be far more eager to talk about Venus after they have enjoyed a story about it—even a story about an out-of-date Venus—than before.

And *that's* the educational value of science fiction; that is what makes it a learning device. It stimulates curiosity and the desire to know.

(It's a Funny Thing)

From the very start I always tried to write with a certain leavening of humor. On occasion, I even tried to write a story that was funny throughout. I wasn't very successful at first, but I continued to try.

In the end I learned how. My first completely successful humorous story (in my own opinion) was "The Up-to-Date Sorcerer" which appeared in the July 1958 issue of The Magazine of Fantasy and Science Fiction, *so it took me twenty years to achieve my goal.*

Naturally, then, I don't underestimate the difficulty of being funny. Nevertheless, I feel that I now know how to be funny, and I have no hesitation in handing out advice on the subject.

9. IT'S A FUNNY THING*

It's a funny thing, but many beginners try to write humorous science fiction. What makes it funny is that being funny is very difficult, and some extremely good science fiction writers can't handle humor—yet so many beginners think they can.

Why is being funny so difficult?

For one thing, you're not allowed to miss. If you're trying for pathos, you can end up being fairly pathetic and you get a part-score and may even sell the story if it ends up moving the editor, even if not quite to tears. If you try for suspense, you can be moderately suspenseful and sell by at least speeding the editor's heart, even if you don't send it racing madly.

You can hit the outer rings of the target, if not the bull's-eye, in any of the other characteristics sought for in fiction and still make a sale.

* Copyright © 1980 by Davis Publications, Inc.

Except humor. The target for humor is all bull's-eye. There are no outer rings.

Can you imagine something being partly funny? Have you ever heard someone tell a story that is only somewhat humorous? What happens?

Right! Nobody laughs. At best, someone may manage a polite smile.

Yet a funny story, when it *is* funny, is a very good thing and should be encouraged. Good humor, wit, even slapstick, when well done, add to the gaiety of nations and the eupepsia† of individuals.

Still, even the best of us aren't born already knowing how to write humorously. We have to practice a little to begin with to see if we have the talent—and if we do, we have to develop that talent by continuing to practice.

Here are some rules, then, that may be helpful.

1) Keep it brief. Unless you're a born comic genius, a Mark Twain or a P. G. Wodehouse, you are not going to maintain a satisfactory and even level of humor for the length of a novel. In fact, the longer you try to maintain it, the less likely you are to avoid falling off into flatness or zooming upward into painful travesty. My own feeling is that you ought to keep it down to three thousand words or less.

2) Don't try to make every single sentence killingly humorous. In the first place, you'll wear yourself out and die young, and a dead author is no good to anyone. In the second place, you won't succeed. And in the third, continuous humor, even if achieved, is not likely to be effective. The reader will wear himself out laughing early in the game and find the rest of the story tedious. The periodic flashes that give time for the reader to build up his reserves of laughter in between are best.

3) Humor is not, in itself, a story. Humor, if well done, will make a good story better, but it will not make a bad story good. If you're writing a funny science fiction story, make sure then that if

† So look it up. How will you become a writer if you don't develop your vocabulary?

the fun is subtracted, what is left will still be a reasonably good science fiction story in itself.

Now let us consider one particular subdivision of the humorous science fiction story: the "Ferdinand Feghoot."‡ This consists of a story whose only reason for existence is that it ends in an elaborate pun.

There are rules here, too.

1) Since the final pun supports the story, you can see that you mustn't overload the pun with an overlong story, or the anticlimax will arouse murderous rage in even the Gentlest of Editors. Keep it very short, then; I would say not more than five hundred words.

2) Even those five hundred words must make up a reasonable science fiction story and one that does not too obviously strain itself in preparation for the pun. Ideally, the reader should not suspect that a pun is on the way so that he doesn't have time to intensify his feelings of homicidal hostility.

3) Strive for the golden mean. The punning phrase should be long enough to strike the reader as ingenious, but not so long that it wearies him before it is done. Ideally, he should be able to read the entire phrase at a glance.

Again the distance between the pun and the true phrase should be great enough to be ingenious and unpredictable, but not so strained that even after the reader reads it, there is a perceptible period of time in which he doesn't know what you're talking about. Remember that the point of a joke must be caught at once. Even a short pause can be fatal to laughter.

4) A pun is meant for the ear. It's the *sound* that counts, not the appearance. A singer who trips on a dock and falls into the harbor is off-quay in a new way. Never mind that "quay" doesn't look like "key," the pronunciation is identical.

On the other hand, there's no point in saying that an interpreter who doesn't know his etiquette is useless in Warsaw because he "lacks polish." That may be an optical pun, but even in reading silently you hear the words in your mind and "polish"

‡ The name is derived from a series by Grendel Briarton (Reginald Bretnor) about a gentleman with that name. It ran in *F & SF* a number of years ago.

simply doesn't sound like "Polish" and never mind the identity in spelling.

To summarize, the ideal Ferdinand Feghoot, in my own immodest opinion, is my story "Sure Thing" in the Summer 1977 *IASFM*. Reread it and you'll see.

The final point to remember is a sad one. Even a good humorous story, or an excellent Ferdinand Feghoot, isn't guaranteed an acceptance. A magazine must contain variety if it is to be successful, and that variety must reflect, with reasonable accuracy, the general biases and tastes of its readers.

The fact is that many people are not fond of humor and very many nourish a bigoted antipathy toward the harmless pun. So editors must sprinkle the lighthearted tale in a light-handed way over the contents page, while the Ferdinand Feghoot must come into play only when the antennae of the Gentle Editor quiver to him the message that enough of an interval has passed since the last batch, to make the printing of a new one safe.

(The Mosaic and the Plate Glass)

> *I even have the gall to lecture people on style in writing, though I often say I know nothing about such matters. What irks me, however, is that others sometimes say I have no style.*
>
> *I may say what I please about myself but that doesn't mean I yield the right to others.*

10. THE MOSAIC AND THE PLATE GLASS*

I have always been reluctant to give reasoned judgments of individual stories for I have no faith in my ability to see what is good and what is bad and why. Still, I can't help having accumulated thoughts on writing in general in the course of my career and one of those thoughts involves a metaphor I heard first from my good friend, science fiction's indefatigable photographer, Jay Kay Klein.

It seems there are two ways of writing fiction.

In one way, you pay more attention to the language itself than to the events you are describing. You are anxious to write colorfully, to paint a picture of the setting or the background of the events. You wish to evoke a mood in the reader which will make it possible for him to feel the events taking place more intensely than would be possible through a mere recounting.

This is not an easy thing to do well. There have been very many colorful phrases, which have been so frequently employed in the past by other writers, to evoke whatever it is you are trying to evoke that they have been used up and wrung dry. They have lost all capacity to do their work. Sometimes even one use in the past knocks out a phrase if that one use is very famous because it occurs in *Hamlet* or in the Gettysburg Address.

* Copyright © 1980 by Davis Publications, Inc.

The effort to be colorful and yet to avoid the cliché is difficult. Sometimes considerable polishing and repolishing is required to make things just right.

If you succeed, you have written poetically. You have written with style. Everyone admires you—at least everyone with pretensions to literary taste.

And yet, though the phrases may be memorable, though the swing of the sentences may be grand, though the moods and emotions may be effectively evoked—the *story* may be just a little bit hard to understand.

Such writing is like a glorious mosaic built up out of pieces of colored glass. It may be a gorgeous spectacle and wonderful to look at, but if you're interested in seeing what's going on in the street, you're going to have a little trouble seeing through the mosaic.

Don't get me wrong. It is not necessarily important to understand something at once. In fact, brooding over a well-written mosaic of a story and rereading it may, little by little, illuminate you. You may find all kinds of symbolisms, all sorts of understandings on different levels. The fulfillment you will feel at achieving a deep understanding of something cannot be matched by instant surface "understanding."

If you have the time for it.

Let's face it. We're not all people of leisure. And even if we have leisure sometimes, there are many activities competing for the time we have at some particular period, and we may not feel able to spend the time on a work of literature that requires all of our sustained attention. Yet we would like to read a story. What can we do?

There's another kind of writing, too.

In this other kind, words and phrases are chosen not for their freshness and novelty, or for their unexpected ability to evoke a mood, but simply for their ability to describe what is going on without themselves getting in the way. Everything is subordinated to clarity. It is the kind of writing in which the direct sentence is preferred to the involved subordinate clause; the familiar word to the unfamiliar word; and the short word to the long word.

This does not mean there are no involved subordinate clauses and no unfamiliar or long words. It does mean that these devices are used only when it is necessary to do so for clarity. *All things being equal,* you plump for the direct, the familiar, the short.

The result is that you can see what's happening with absolute clarity (if the writing is handled well enough). Ideally, you're not even aware of the writing.

Such writing might be compared to plate glass in a window. You can see exactly what's going on in the street and you're not aware of the glass.

As it happens, many critics value only the mosaics. They are used to achieving an understanding beyond that of less expert readers (or of affecting one, for if there are more bad writers than good writers, there are also more incompetent critics than competent ones) and they become uneasy if something is too clear and simple. If everyone can understand a work of art, after all, what need is there for a critic? Since the critic stands in danger of losing his job (or, worse, his shaky self-respect) in the presence of plate-glass writing, his usual reaction is to dismiss it as "superficial," "without style," "nonsignificant," and a few other carefully memorized adjectives.

Indeed, it might even seem that they are right. If we look first at a good mosaic and then at a good plate-glass window, we would have to be totally lacking in judgment to fail to see that the former is a work of art while the latter is just a utilitarian object.

Yet mosaics of great artistic value were created out of colored glass as long ago as the third century BC, while plate glass was not successfully manufactured until the seventeenth century.

In other words, it took two thousand years to progress from colored glass that made marvelous mosaics, to something as simple and "nothing" as clear glass without streaks, wobbles, or bubbles. Strange that something so "simple" should be so much more technically difficult to manufacture than something "artistic."

And it is so in literature, too. Because one story is written very artistically, very poetically, very stylishly, it is easy to see that it was difficult to write and required great skill in the creation. But because another story is written so simply and clearly that you're not aware of the writing, doesn't mean that there was no trouble in the writing at all. It may well have been more difficult to insert clarity than to insert poetry. There is a great deal of art to creating something that seems artless.

I know one writer (his initials are I.A. and I'm very close to him) who's been told on numerous occasions: "I don't know that you're exactly a writer, but you're a good storyteller."

The jackasses who say this intend to be condescending, but I smile and feel complimented, for it's not easy to tell a story well. If you don't believe that, stop people at random and ask them to tell you a story. If you keep it up for an unbroken period of as little as three hours, you may never recover your sanity.

Writing in such a fashion that the writing is unnoticeable, that the events described pass directly into your brain as though you were experiencing them yourself, is a difficult and a necessary art.

Sometimes you *want* to see what's happening in the street and even the smallest imperfection in the glass in the window will annoy you. And sometimes you *want* to read a story and be carried along with the events rapidly and smoothly, without even the smallest imperfection in the writing to remind you that you are only reading and not experiencing.

Well, then, suppose we have two stories: a mosaic and a plate glass. They are not directly comparable, to be sure, but suppose that they (each in its own way) are equally good. In that case, which should one choose? If it were I making the choice, I would plump for the plate glass every time. It's what I like to write and what I like to read.

But science fiction readers are numerous and their tastes are by no means universally identical to mine. It is up to editors to see that, in this respect and in a number of others, too, a magazine ends with a reasonable mix to satisfy a variety of reading preferences.

A story has to be *good*, but beyond that, what is wanted is variety.

(*The Scientist as Villain*)

Science fiction stories are notoriously weak on characterization as compared with mainstream stories. At least, so the critics say.

I am always struck with impatience at such cavils. Even if it be true, there happens to be a good reason for it. The characters are a smaller portion of science fiction than of the mainstream.

A good science fiction story usually deals with a society distinctly different from the one we are familiar with; a society that does not exist and has never existed; that is completely imaginary. That imaginary society has to be built up in detail and without internal contradiction even while the plot is unfolding. The society can't be skimped; it should (at its best) be as interesting as the plot and catch just as strongly at the reader's attention.

The double task of building the background society and developing the foreground plot is extremely difficult, and it requires an extraordinary amount of the writer's attention. There is that much less attention that is, or can be, paid to the characters. There is, physically, less room in the story for character development.

Nevertheless, that doesn't mean that characterization should be deliberately bad, or that it should not be as good as the author can manage.

11. THE SCIENTIST AS VILLAIN*

The various subclassifications of literature have their characteristic inhabitants. The Western story has its sheriffs, its gamblers, its dance-hall cuties, and its schoolmarms, but the figure who instantly characterizes the story is, of course, the cowboy. The mystery story has, as its indispensable inhabitant, the solver of crimes—whether amateur or professional.

Mind you, it is possible to write a Western in which neither a cowboy nor a horse appears, or a mystery in which no true criminal appears and in which no true solution is found, but these are *tours de force* and not in the mainstream of the genre.

Well, then, while it is possible to write a science fiction story in which there is no professional scientist (or engineer or inventor), it is very common to make a scientist central.

There is, however, a difference. In the vast majority of Westerns, the cowboy (or the sheriff) is the hero in the sense that he brings about a happy resolution of the crisis. In the vast majority of mysteries, the hero is the detective—amateur or professional.

In science fiction stories, however, the scientist is as likely to be a villain as a hero. By a "villain" I mean that the scientist's aims must be defeated to bring about a happy resolution of the crisis.

To be sure, the likelihood of scientist-as-villain varies from author to author. In my own stories, for instance, scientists are very likely to be heroes. Why not? I view technology and science (wisely used—an enormously important condition) as beneficent and as the key to human progress. Why shouldn't the practitioners in the field be heroes then?

On the other hand, it is certainly possible to view technology and science as a major source of the problems that humanity endures. In that case, its practitioners would then be villains. It is a sign of the ambivalence people feel toward science that scientists are so often villains in science fiction.

Not all scientific villains are the same, however. It is easy to divide them up into categories. For instance:

1) *Presumption*—A scientist may dare the unknown and, perhaps, climb to heights or plumb to depths beyond his strength or comprehension. This is a rather old-fashioned notion if one takes the attitude that "there are some things not meant for man to know" because, presumably, they are reserved for God alone. The prototype of such a villain is, of course, Victor Frankenstein, who dared usurp what was considered the divine prerogative of giving life and who paid dearly in consequence. (Of course, Frankenstein was not portrayed as possessing a villainous character. He is, actually, a tragic hero; he meant well.)

However, even if we eliminate the religious angle, it is quite conceivable that a scientist or inventor cannot control his discovery—the situation of the sorcerer's apprentice, for instance.

2) *Madness*—This is a natural offshoot of presumption. Why should someone dare too much unless he is mad or, as a variation, would not someone who dared too much be struck mad? The mad scientist may differ from the presuming scientist in that the former does not even mean well.

A common way of handling this is to suppose that a scientist, who is too daring, arouses intense opposition on the part of his more conservative colleagues. The scientist then grows mad with frustration and rage and is thereafter intent on demonstrating his point in order to show up his enemies, and quite regardless of consequences, too.

3) *Evil*—A scientist need not be mad in the clinical sense, but he might simply be sadistic or take pleasure in doing harm or be intent on using his discoveries to establish his domination over part or all of humanity. Consider Conan Doyle's Moriarty.

4) *Arrogant*—A scientist may be neither mad nor evil and yet be coolly convinced that he knows best. He may refuse to admit the possibility of mistake, and dismiss all opposition as the maunderings of inferior individuals.

5) *Indifference*—Both the evil and the arrogant scientist are often characterized as indifferent to the human qualities of mankind and, indeed, to view them as contemptible weaknesses. Even without evil and arrogance, however, a scientist may simply be

viewed as a reasoning machine, untouched by emotion, who finds
the pursuit of knowledge as the only worthwhile endeavor. Here it
is sheer inability to comprehend human values that may lead to
catastrophe.

Well, then, I have presented five varieties of villainous scientists, and undoubtedly some of you can think of more.

An important point that should be made, however, is that not
one of these five villain-species is satisfactory in itself.

The presumptuous scientist is an outgrowth of Faust and is
most at home in a world of the supernatural.

The mad scientist is a cliché that went out with the early 1930s.

The evil scientist is embarrassing to sophisticated readers and is
now usually found only in comic strips.

The arrogant or the indifferent scientists lack juice. The fact
that they eschew human weakness means they lack human interest.

Well, then, does this mean that it is impossible to have scientists as villains? Of course not. If they are one-dimensional, however, if they are nothing but presumptuous or mad or evil or arrogant or indifferent, they are not successful villains and you are
very likely to be writing an unsuccessful story.

(Nor does this apply to villains only. Any character who is one-
dimensional is a source of literary weakness.)

It helps, in other words, to introduce complexities and thus add
dimensions. Heroes should have their flaws, villains their admirable aspects.

It is because Milton's Satan is indomitable in defeat and has an
occasional pang of pity that he is interesting, while it is because
Milton's God is never permitted to be less than perfect that he is
so dull.

Again Shakespeare's Richard III has courage; Shakespeare's
Iago has a sense of humor; Shakespeare's Shylock has pride and
will not truckle—and all three are monumentally successful villains.

In science fiction, A. Conan Doyle's Professor Challenger is almost a mad scientist, but *not quite*. Driven to rage by opposition
from his inferiors, he behaves so eccentrically that he is considered

mad—but presented to the reader, he turns out to have his reasonable and even his humane and gentle moods.

Again, Mr. Spock of "Star Trek" is almost a caricature of the indifferent scientist. He is literally nonhuman since he is half Vulcan, and his stock-in-trade is his refusal to show emotion and to meet all crises with superrational calm. Yet he steals the show. To be sure, calm rationality is admirable but, by itself, it would rather repel. However, and this is the key, that is not all there is to Spock. The viewers see clearly that he *does* feel emotion, and though he tries to keep it hidden, it is evident that he loves his shipmates and will risk his life for them even though that might seem irrational.

There is a moral to all this. A science fiction writer (or any writer) in fashioning his villains (or any character) must strive to supply more than one motive that will serve to drive their actions. Furthermore, it must not be predictable, or even always clear, which motive of several possible ones might prevail under a particular set of circumstances.

Why? Because that is the way people behave in real life, and the more closely fictional characters imitate the behavior of real ones, the more we like them and the more effectively they interest and move us.

(*The Vocabulary of Science Fiction*)

> *Words and etymology are among my favorite passions and I can rarely pass up a chance to discuss such things. Science fiction is a happy hunting ground for made-up words, and of all the words that science fiction has donated to the world at large (and, as far as I know, into every language of the world), "robot" is the most important.*

12. THE VOCABULARY OF SCIENCE FICTION *

Like every specialized occupation, science fiction writing has a vocabulary of its own, and the more advanced writers assume the reader understands that vocabulary. Occasionally, this sets up a barrier against the new reader, who finds difficulty in understanding what's being said.

Thus, a reader once wrote to ask the difference between "android" and "robot," saying, "I have been trying to find out, but so far have gotten no satisfactory explanation."

Well, this is the right shop for explanations. The only difficulty is that I don't like to explain anything briefly, so be patient—

The Greek word "anthropos" means "human being," and from that comes the adjective "anthropoid." Since the suffix "-oid" is from the Greek word for "form," "anthropoid" means "human-form" or "resembling a human being in form."

"Anthropoid" entered the ordinary language in recent centuries, when Europeans became particularly conscious of the apes of Africa and Southeast Asia. The word "ape" was originally given to the tailless Barbary ape of North Africa. The new species—chimpanzee, gorilla, orangutan, and various gibbons—are also apes, since they are tailless, but they are much more human in appear-

* Copyright © 1979 by Davis Publications, Inc.

ance than the Barbary apes are. The newly discovered apes were, therefore, distinguished from the longer-known one by being called "anthropoid apes."

Since, in English, there is a continuous drive toward shortening and simplifying the language, there is a tendency to drop a noun in any oft-used adjective-noun combination and to use the adjective alone as the noun. This is frowned upon by careful users of the language but it is constantly being done. For instance, I have heard apes referred to as "anthropoids" in absolute contradiction of the actual meaning of the word.

The proper word for "apelike" is "pithecoid" from "pithekos," the Greek word for "ape."

The Greek word "andros" means "man," as used for a male human being rather than for the species generally. The word "android" means "malelike," but it is usually defined as "manlike" with the careless unconcern that marks the male chauvinism of the English language.

Now, then, if a scientist were to produce an artificial device that has the shape and appearance of a human being and imitates the functioning of a living being, the proper name for it would be "an anthropoid device" or, using the adjective only, "an anthropoid."

This term is not used, probably because of the apelike flavor of the word. Instead, the artificial human being is "an android device" or "an android."

Strictly speaking, an android should be an artificial device with the appearance of a male human being. One with the appearance of a female human being would be a "gynoid," from the Greek word "gynē" meaning "woman." However, I have never seen the word "gynoid" used for any artificial device of human appearance. "Android" is used for artificial devices that mimic either sex—or, for that matter, that are neuter.

But if an android is an artificial human being, where does "robot" come in?

In 1920, the Czech playwright, Karel Capek, published a play† named *R. U. R.*, which was first performed in 1921 and first

---

† Odd that the word "robot" should have been invented in the year of my birth. Pure coincidence!

translated into English in 1923. The initials "R. U. R." stand for "Rossum's Universal Robots." Rossum is the name of the Englishman who, in the play, mass-produced a line of mechanical human beings intended to do the work of the world.

Why "robot"? Because it is from a Czech word "robota" meaning one who is engaged in involuntary servitude; in other words a "slave." In translating the play into English, it would have been appropriate to translate "robot" into "slave." "Slave," however, is a word commonly used for human beings and it would make it difficult to distinguish between the natural and the artificial variety. "Robot," not being an English word, could fairly be left untranslated and be used for the artificial variety, to distinguish it from the natural.

Capek's play is, in my own opinion, a terribly bad one, but it is immortal for that one word. It contributed the word "robot" not only to English but, through English, to all the languages in which science fiction is now written.

Strictly speaking, "robot" and "android" both refer to artificial human beings and might be synonymous. However, in the many robot stories that appeared in the science fiction magazines from 1926 onward, the robots were almost always described and pictured as being constructed of metal. Consequently, "robot" has come to refer specifically to an artificial human being built largely or entirely of metal.

Any artificial human being built of substances more closely resembling human tissues retains the older name "android." —And that is the distinction between the two words.

There is an irony here. Capek in the play, R. U. R. in which the word "robot" was invented, described artificial human beings that were *not* robots in the present-day sense. They were androids.

We're not through. Consider the Greek word "automatos," which means "self-acting." Any device that is self-acting and does not require constant human direction is said to be an "automatic device."

We might imagine an artificial human being would be called an automatic device and then, through noun-dropping, an "automatic." However, "automatic" is obtained through noun-dropping from "automatic pistol" and refers to a self-loading handgun.

Instead, the related word "automaton" is used for an artificial human being. However, "self-acting" seems to imply moving according to a fixed plan without much, if any, leeway for modification. Consequently, "automaton" would be used for an android or robot (or, if it comes to that, for a human being) without much, if any, intelligence. Science fiction robots are usually pretty intelligent, so "automaton" is not much used.

How about Latin? The word "homo" in Latin means "man" and from "homo" is derived the adjective "humanus." This gives us our own adjective "human." We can speak, therefore, of "human beings" or, dropping the noun, "humans." Well, then, would not an artificial object of human shape be a "humanoid"?

Yes, indeed, but "android" fills that niche. Instead, in science fiction writing, "humanoid" is usually used for a *living* creature of human shape, one that has been born or has evolved and *not* one that has been made—but one that has been born or has evolved on some planet other than Earth.

The Latin word for "Earth" is "Terra." Any living species that has evolved on Earth is a "terrestrial being"; any living species that has evolved on some planet other than Earth is an "extraterrestrial being" (where "extra" is a Latin word meaning "on the outside"). In the case of "extraterrestrial beings," it is quite common, in science fiction, to drop the noun and speak of "extraterrestrials."

Strictly speaking, any species that has evolved on some planet other than Earth is an extraterrestrial, but in science fiction, the term is usually restricted to intelligent species. If the species should happen to be human in appearance, it is also humanoid.

The Latin word "monstrum" means "an omen that warns against misfortunes" from "monere" meaning "to warn." Animals or human beings who are born misshapen are considered divine warnings of misfortune to come and in English they are called "monsters."

Mary Shelley applied the term to the large, misshapen being that Frankenstein formed out of bits and pieces of dead body parts, and it was "Frankenstein's monster." Because of the influence of that book, the word "monster" is used for any living object that is unusually large and terrifying. Hence, the subcategory of "monster movies."

The word "golem" in Hebrew represents a shapeless mass not yet given life; in that meaning it is close to "monster" in the Frankenstein sense. The related Arabic word "ghulam" means "servant" and in that sense the word is close to "robot." A "golem," I think, would be a robot that is given life through religious spells rather than through scientific principles.

And there you are.

(Try to Write!)

Some of the essays in this section of the book stress the difficulty of writing and I don't want to seem to be turning people away. On the contrary, for if the difficulties are great, the rewards of surmounting those difficulties are greater.

Therefore, I would like to include in this section the most upbeat essay I ever wrote on the subject. It was written as an untitled editorial for the second issue of my magazine (Summer 1977) with the deliberate intention of encouraging submissions.

When it appeared, there were a number of horrified predictions from people in the field that we would be instantly buried in crud, and, to be sure, the slush pile swelled and some of it was pretty terrible. But then, the terrible stuff can be very quickly recognized.

What we also got were some pretty good stories from people who might not have tried to write if I had not made it plain that the magazine was open to beginners. Every such story we can locate is a blow on the side of the angels.

13. TRY TO WRITE!*

Let's consider the life blood of science fiction magazines—which happens to be the stories. And for the stories, we depend on you, the readers.

Yes, you.

There's a class of human beings called "science fiction writers." I assure you, I know this well. I'm one of them and I've been one for mumblety-mumble years, and we are all of us the finest people in the world.

However—and this is the crucial point—there isn't a single one

* Copyright © 1977 by Davis Publications, Inc.

of us who was born a science fiction writer. Every single one of us was a science fiction reader first. I was. I was a science fiction reader for nine years before I sold a science fiction story and became a science fiction writer.

Let's look at it from the other direction. Is it possible to be a science fiction reader without at least *wanting* to be a science fiction writer? Of course, when I say "science fiction reader," I don't mean someone who just watches a few "Star Trek" reruns now and then, or who occasionally picks up an s.f. novel. —I mean someone for whom science fiction is a more or less steady diet, who subscribes to magazines, who combs the book and magazine racks, to whom the various authors are household names.

Like you!

Anyone who's that kind of reader *must* want to be a science fiction writer. I've been through that and I remember it well.

And you can *do* it, too. You can become a science fiction writer. You want to, don't you?

What's stopping you? Is it that it's hard?

Well, yes and no. Writing *good* science fiction is indeed hard for the beginner. Doing anything that requires a great deal of skill is hard for the beginner.

But just writing science fiction is easy. Forget the "good" part. Just putting paper in the typewriter and banging out words on it till you've got a rotten science fiction story in front of you is a snap.

What's the point of writing a rotten story?

Ask yourself what's the point of taking general science in junior high school? What's the point of playing scales? What's the point of spring training?

Writing is a skill that must be learned, and that's how you learn.

You can read books about writing and listen to people lecture on how to write, and attend writers' conferences, and subscribe to writers' magazines, but none of that is going to make a writer out of you.

Only one thing ever invented has made a writer out of anybody. Writing!

It's the writing that teaches you. It's the rotten stories that make it possible for you to write the good stories eventually. Do you think the story I wrote at the age of eleven was any good? Of course not. I had to keep writing after that, on and off, for ten years before I could write "Nightfall."

Is that too long a time to struggle? Look, it takes longer than that to learn to be a good surgeon, and being a good surgeon isn't nearly as exciting as being a good writer.

Of course, once you write your stories, your tendency will be to show them to your wife or husband, or your parents or children, or your teachers or neighbors. Don't do it. It's a waste of time. They'll all tell you the story is great and you'll be no further along at all.

You may also have the urge to send it to some favorite author and ask him to look it over and give you the few necessary hints that will make the story great. Don't do it. Authors are generally busy people who don't know how to deal with any stories but their own.

What's left? Easy. Send your stories to editors. If you have written a science fiction short story, send it to the editors of science fiction magazines.

Are you afraid of rejections? Don't be. It's the common coin of response for all beginning writers, and editors send them out without hostility or hatred, I assure you.

Some writers, of course, make a sale their first time out. Robert A. Heinlein did. If you're another Robert A. Heinlein, you may, too. If you're nothing more than another Isaac Asimov, however, then relax. I received twelve rejections before I made my first sale, and I received a lot of rejections after I made my first sale, and I occasionally get rejections even now.

Nobody likes rejections. I certainly never did, and when I get one nowadays, I hate it, but I just go on to write something else, and you should, too.

Besides, suppose you get enough rejections to paper your apartment? That will just make the triumph of the first sale all the sweeter. The intensity of triumph will be something those unlucky Heinleins who never get rejections will never feel.

So I'm urging all of you who feel like writing science fiction to do so, and to send the results to this magazine. —And why am I doing this? Wouldn't we like to have stories from the old tried and true professionals?

Sure we would, as many as possible. —But old writers die, old writers retire, old writers move on to other things, old writers can even grow weary and stale. We need new writers to infuse the field with fresh vigor, and to keep the old writers on their toes. (There's nothing that will keep you running harder than some rotten young kid pounding up behind you.)

And do we really want to receive all those rotten stories, almost all of which will be unreadable. Yes, we do, because editors never know when they'll pick up a manuscript by someone they never heard of and find they have a new Arthur C. Clarke, for instance —or find someone who will be a new Clarke with a little grooming.

III
THE PREDICTIONS
OF
SCIENCE FICTION

(How Easy to See the Future!)

To people who don't read science fiction, the most amazing thing about the field is its apparent ability to predict the future. Sometimes one would think they see nothing in science fiction beyond that.

Actually, there is very little in the vast output of science fiction, year after year, which comes true, or which is ever likely to come true. I don't think time travel or faster-than-light travel will ever come true, for instance. I think galactic empires have a near-zero chance of ever coming to pass.

Nevertheless, successful prediction can take place. Intelligent science fiction writers attempt to look at world trends in science and technology for plot inspiration and, in doing so, they sometimes get a glimpse of things that later turn out to be near the truth.

14. HOW EASY TO SEE THE FUTURE!*

If one were to glance over the thousands of years of history of Homo sapiens, we might make the following generalizations:

1) As time passed, the human way of life continually changed.

2) The change has generally resulted from a technological advance: a new tool, a new technique, a new energy source.

3) As each technological advance broadened the base of human technological capacity, further advances became more frequent and were made in a greater number of directions, so that the rate of change has, in the course of history, continually increased.

Until modern times, the rate of change was so slow as to make the process unnoticeable in the course of any one person's lifetime. It was therefore the illusion of mankind that change did not

* Copyright © 1975 by the American Museum of Natural History

take place. When, in the face of that illusion, a change had clearly taken place, the response was to view it as something that should not have taken place, as something that represented a degeneration from the "good old days."

The steadily increasing rate of change reached the stage, at about 1800, of becoming clearly visible to many thoughtful individuals. The Industrial Revolution was beginning, and those affected by it could detect change in the course of their own lifetimes.

For the first time, some people grew to understand that not only was change taking place, but that it would continue to take place after their deaths. It meant there would come to be changes still greater than a person had lived to see, changes that he would never see. This gave rise to a new curiosity—perhaps the first really new curiosity developed in historic times—that of wondering what life on Earth would be like after one was no longer alive. The literary response to that new curiosity was what we now call "science fiction."

Science fiction can be defined as that branch of literature which deals with the reaction of human beings to changes in science and technology.

The reference can be to *any* changes, of course, and the science fiction writer chooses those which provide him with a dramatic situation out of which he can weave an exciting plot. There is usually no deliberate attempt to predict what will actually happen, but a science fiction writer is a creature of his times, and in trying to imagine a change in science and technology he is quite likely to base it on those changes he already sees in embryo.

Often this means an extrapolation of the present, an extrapolation that is so clear and obvious as to forecast something that is inevitable. When this happens, the science fiction writer *does* make a successful prediction. Usually, this astonishes almost everyone, for mankind generally, even today, takes it for granted that things do not change.

Here is an example. As the twentieth century opened, oil was coming into use as a source of energy and, thanks to the internal-combustion engine, was beginning to gain on coal.

Now oil, like coal, is a fossil fuel. There is only so much of it in the ground—even if our entire planet were solid coal and oil, there is only so much of it in the ground—and new supplies are being formed at an entirely trivial rate. If oil and coal are being constantly burned, then someday the natural supply present in the ground will be used up. That is not a matter of argument at all; it is inevitable. The only question is, When?

Mankind, generally, assuming that since there is oil in the ground today, there will be oil in the ground forever (the doctrine of no change), is not concerned with the matter. The science fiction writer, however, avidly seeking out change as a matter of artistic necessity, takes up the possibility of an end of our fossil-fuel supply. It then becomes possible for a science fiction writer to say:

"Coal is the key to metallurgy and oil to transit. When they are done we shall either have built up such a fabric of apparatus, knowledge, and social organization that we shall be able to manage without them—or we shall have travelled a long way down the slopes of waste towards extinction— Today, in getting, in distribution, in use, we waste enormously— As we sit there all the world is wasting fuel—fantastically."

That certainly sounds familiar these days, but it wasn't said these days. The writer was H. G. Wells, and the book is *Secret Places of the Heart* (not even science fiction, strictly speaking) and the year of publication is 1921.

Imagine Wells foreseeing the energy crunch half a century before it happened! Well, don't waste your admiration. He saw the obvious and foresaw the inevitable. What is really amazing, and frustrating, is mankind's habit of *refusing* to see the obvious and inevitable until it is there, and then muttering about unforeseen catastrophes.

The science fiction writer, Laurence Manning, wrote a story called "The Man Who Awoke" about a man who invented a potion that would place him in suspended animation for three thousand years. He would then awake and see the world of the future. When he carried this through, he found the world of three thousand years hence was energy-poor. They explained the reason to him as a result of what they called the Age of Waste. They said,

"But for what should we thank the humans of three thousand

years ago? For exhausting the coal supplies of the world? For leaving us no petroleum for our chemical factories? For destroying the forests on whole mountain ranges and letting the soil erode into the valleys?"

The story appeared in the March 1933 issue of *Wonder Stories* and I read it when it appeared and I had just turned thirteen. Science fiction, everyone said, was "escape literature." Reading it was disgraceful, for it meant turning away from the hard realities of life into a never-never fantasy land of the impossible.

Who lived in a never-never fantasy land? I, who began worrying about our oil and coal in 1933 as a result of Manning's story? Or the rest of mankind who, as always, were convinced that tomorrow would be exactly like today and who waited for the day when the long lines at the gas station came before deciding that there might some day be long lines at the gas station.

Yes, science fiction can have its fantasy aspects. I have written stories about galactic empires, about faster-than-light speeds, about intelligent robots which eventually became God, about time travel. I don't consider that any of these have predictive value; they weren't intended for that. I was jusy trying to write entertaining stories about the might-be, not at all necessarily about the would-be.

But sometimes—

In the July 1939 issue of *Astounding Science Fiction*, there appeared one of my stories. It was called "Trends" and it dealt with the first flight to the Moon (silly escape literature, of course). I got all the details childishly and ludicrously wrong, including having it happen ten years later than it really did happen.

However, even at the age of nineteen, I was aware that all those technological advances in the past that had significantly ruffled the current of human custom had been attacked by important segments of the population who, for one reason or another, found it difficult to accept change. It occurred to me, then, that this would surely be true of the development of space flight as well. My story "Trends," therefore, dealt primarily with opposition to space flight.

It was, as far as I know, the first description of ideological opposition to mankind's advance into space. Until then, all those who had looked forward to the new development had either ignored the reaction of humanity, or had assumed it would be favorable. When there did indeed arise ideological opposition, in the late 1960s, I found myself accepting credit as a seer, when I had merely foreseen the inevitable.

Once uranium fission was discovered, a nuclear bomb was an easy extrapolation, and through the World War II years, the science fiction stories dealing with nuclear bombs nestled as thickly as snowflakes in the pages of the science fiction magazines. One of them, "Deadline" by Cleve Cartmill, which appeared in the March 1944 issue of *Astounding Science Fiction*, came so close to the actual facts that both the author and the editor of the magazine were interviewed by suspicious intelligence agents. But when the bomb dropped on Hiroshima, the world was astonished.

More remarkable still was a story "Solution Unsatisfactory" by Anson Macdonald (a pseudonym of Robert A. Heinlein), which appeared in the May 1941 issue of *Astounding Science Fiction*. Written and published before Pearl Harbor, Heinlein described a vast gathering of scientists called together to develop a nuclear weapon. The weapon was invented, used to end World War II, and a nuclear stalemate developed thereafter.

It all made sense, you see, in the light of what was already known in 1940, but who else foresaw it but science fiction writers?

Today we face the most predictable of all disasters, that of the consequences of overpopulation. The population of Earth is now 4,200,000,000 and that population is increasing at the rate of 1.6 percent a year, which means that each day there are 185,000 more mouths to feed than the day before.

In the course of the last thirty years, when population has risen by 1,500,000,000, the food supply has managed to keep up; thanks to the spreading use of farm machinery and irrigation pumps; of fertilizers and pesticides; and of an extraordinary run of good weather.

But now weather is taking a turn for the worse, and the energy shortage is slowing the machinery and raising the price of fertilizers and pesticides. The food supply will not be increasing anymore; it will probably go down—and with the population going up at a rate of 185,000 per day, isn't it the easiest and surest thing in the world to predict great and spreading famines?

Yet whenever I do, I am greeted with amused disbelief. After all, people look around and see no famine today, so why should there be famine tomorrow?

Now let's consider this: If science fiction writers foresee the problems and catastrophes that will come to face mankind, do they also foresee solutions?

Not necessarily! Science fiction writers foresee the inevitable, and although problems and catastophes may be inevitable, solutions are not. Science fiction writers are all too often forced to pull solutions out of thin and implausible air—or leave the matter with no solution and end the story in dramatic disaster.

The best way to defeat a catastrophe is to take action to prevent it long before it happens. To conserve the oil and work for alternate sources of energy in time. To consider the international effects of the nuclear bomb before ever it is invented. To lower the birthrate before the population grows dangerously high.

To do that, one must foresee the catastrophe in time, and science fiction helps one do so.

(The Dreams of Science Fiction)

In the last few years, popular science magazines have proliferated on the newsstands. As is to be expected, more were planned than actually appeared.

One that was planned was intended to have a strong futuristic outlook and, for that reason, the publishing house asked me to come up with two dozen or so themes for the future that were often dealt with in science fiction. I did as requested but, unfortunately, for reasons that had nothing to do with my manuscript, the magazine never appeared and I did not have the chance to see what they would do with my comments.

I include it here because I consider it a good summary of the futuristic (and, possibly, predictive) aspects of science fiction, so that it may possibly be helpful to aspiring writers in the audience.

15. THE DREAMS OF SCIENCE FICTION *

1) *Population Control*—An indefinite population increase will surely bring about starvation and ruin the environment irretrievably. The human population on Earth cannot continue to increase for much longer, and the only way to prevent such an increase humanely, without bringing about the very death and destruction that will ruin our civilization (perhaps permanently), is to reduce the birthrate. Perhaps we can work out some chemical or hormonal control of reproduction that will have no undesirable side effects, or perhaps we can develop some benign social manipulation to reduce the birthrate.

2) *World Government*—It is quite clear that as long as the nations of the world spend most of their energy, money, and emo-

* (Not previously published.)

tional strength in quarreling with words and weapons, a true offensive against the common problems that threaten human survival is not very likely. A world government that can channel human efforts in the direction of the great solutions seems desirable, even essential. Naturally, such a world government should be a federal one, with regional and local autonomy safeguarded and with cultural diversity promoted.

3) *Permanent Energy Sources*—The Industrial Revolution was supported on the back of the fossil fuels, first coal and then oil—but both, especially the latter, are in temporary supply. If we are to continue advancing, we need energy sources that are permanent, safe, and copious. There are two clear alternatives: Earth may someday be run by nuclear fusion and solar power. A particularly advanced possibility is that Earth's energy would be supplied by a chain of solar-power stations in space along the equatorial plane. In this way energy would be a global matter and the nations of the world would be encouraged to unite in the common goal of maintaining an adequate energy supply.

4) *Weather Control*—Most of the great natural disasters involve weather extremes: heat waves and cold waves; droughts and floods; hurricanes, tornadoes, and blizzards. We already air-condition buildings and the time may come when the planet as a whole is air-conditioned, so to speak. Weather may have different patterns in different parts of the globe, but never to an extreme damaging to life. One possible way of insuring this would be to have our population centers retreat underground, where there is no weather, and where time-passage need not be fixed by the uncontrollable alternation between day and night.

5) *Robots*—Throughout history, human beings have used animals and other humans to do the brute manual labor of the world. Machines have now replaced muscle in many cases, but why not develop machines with an approach to human versatility and for that matter human appearance? Robots can be the new servants—patient, uncomplaining, incapable of revolt. In human shape they can make use of the full range of technological tools

devised for human beings and, when intelligent enough, can be friends as well as servants.

6) *Computers*—Artificial intelligence need not be developed, as in robots, only for the purpose of physical labor and social service. Intelligence may reach the point where computers or artificial brains approach the human in capacity, or even surpass it. To be mentally equal, however, may not be the same as mentally equivalent. Computers, starting from a different point, developing along different lines and for different purposes, will have abilities and deficiencies that human beings don't have. Together, the strong points of each will supplement the weak points of the other, and, in cooperation, the two types of intelligences can advance more rapidly than either would alone.

7) *Computerized Education*—The advance of computers makes the thought of a global computerized library a tenable one. It would be one from which any item of human knowledge could be retrieved. If communications satellites and laser beams are used to give each human being a private television channel, each human being can use his own computers to hook up to the computerized library, so that he will have an advanced teaching machine. Each individual could study whatever he wants at his own pace and in his own time, and the result could be that education can be efficient, pleasurable, and lifelong.

8) *Mass Transference*—It is very difficult to accelerate objects possessing mass. Radiation, however, on the very instant of creation, moves at the speed of light—186,282 miles per second. Is it conceivable that an object with mass, such as a loaded truck or a human being, be turned into radiation, beamed outward, received and turned back into a loaded truck or a human being? If so, all earthly distances could be traversed in fractions of a second and you could get to the Moon in a second and a quarter.

9) *Global Village*—We can already communicate at the speed of light and have done so since the invention of the telegraph in 1844. With the development of communications satellites and holography, we may use individual television channels in such a way that our three-dimensional image, rather than ourselves,

travels in order to indulge in business meetings. There can be long-distance transmission of documents, long-distance control and supervision of factories, and so on. Combine this with mass transference, and with plentiful energy from space stations, and the whole planet shrinks to a global village in which any individual can interact with any other individual with no more trouble than if they lived on the same block. Such a situation makes a world government much more useful and practical.

10) *Cloning*—It is possible that eventually a new option may be developed for reproduction; one in which a given individual can have his gene content reproduced as such, without the admixture of other genes as is inevitable in sexual reproduction. Such cloning would have its uses. Endangered species might be saved by cloning. A clone might be developed in such a way as to form not a complete individual but merely specific organs. In this way, a bank of organs could be created that are genetically compatible with the individual whose cell nucleus had been used. Organ transplantation and replacement would become much more practical.

11) *Bionic Human Beings*—Failing or damaged organs could be replaced by other organs, perhaps through cloning. Another alternative, however, would be the use of mechanical devices that would perform the function of various living organs, but might have advanced capabilities and be more durable. In a sense this would be a roboticization of human beings, and if robots could be made steadily more human in structure, the two types of intelligence might approach some more or less identical intermediate form that would be better than either the totally human or the totally robot.

12) *Genetic Engineering*—Individuals are, to some extent, the product of their genes and the time may come when scientists are able to determine the gene pattern of an individual at birth or before. Embryos may be developed in the laboratory instead of in the womb and gene defects could then be observed and corrected. If not correctable, the embryo could be disposed of. In this way, congenital disease may be avoided or corrected and a stronger

human species developed. And women may be freed of the absolute necessity of turning their bodies into a baby-making machine periodically.

13) *Control of Evolution*—With increasing development of genetic engineering, it could become possible to alter genes or to direct those combinations that would produce desired characteristics. Microorganisms could be developed with enhanced chemical abilities that would be useful to humanity—to produce desired hormones or other biochemicals, to fix atmospheric nitrogen, to consume particular wastes, and so on. Human beings might be endowed with new abilities that would tend to increase health and happiness and would move us in the direction of an abler and more intelligent species.

14) *Immortality*—The whole trend of medicine has been to eliminate disease, produce more vigorous individuals at every age level, and to prevent premature death. Nothing yet has been able to abort old age, however, or death through final senile failure of the body. Yet old age, too, may be viewed as a disease. If the cause of aging is discovered and is halted, or even reversed, then human beings would be able to live indefinitely with mature vigor —or at least until some accident ends life, or they choose of their own accord to end it.

15) *Telepathy*—The shortcomings of communication seem to hold back the progress of the human species. Different languages make some of us imcomprehensible to others and introduce differences that serve as handles for hate and suspicion. Even among people speaking the same language, different accents can make trouble. And at best, language is an imperfect way of expressing thoughts. Might not a way be discovered eventually to allow mind to melt into mind directly, thought into thought, so that a telepathic society can result. Other "wild talents" such as telekinesis (moving things at a distance) or precognition (foreseeing some aspects of the future) might be developed, too.

16) *Interspecies Communication*—Homo sapiens is the only species on Earth that has developed a civilization, but can there be other species intelligent enough to carry on a conversation with

us? The dolphins and their relatives seem the best hope here, and the time may come when, without leaving the Earth, we can discuss our dreams, problems, and philosophies with other minds sufficiently different from our own to cast fresh light upon all of these things. (And our minds can cast fresh light upon cetacean thought and problems.)

17) *Exploitation of Near Space*—Space supplies us with many things we do not have enough of, or at all, on Earth. We can collect solar energy in space more efficiently than we can on Earth's surface. The Moon is a new and untouched source of vast mineral supplies. Space itself offers us an infinite supply of hard vacuum, both high and low temperatures, hard radiation, gravity-free conditions—all of which are useful in various industrial processes. We could have whole industries, laboratories, observatories in orbit about the Earth run on Lunar material and Solar energy. This would free Earth of the various disadvantages of industrialization and return it to the benefits of an agricultural/pastoral/wilderness pattern, while not depriving it of the benefits of science and industry that would be only a few thousand miles away—straight up.

18) *Space Settlements*—If near space is the site of industries, laboratories, and observatories, there will have to be human beings in space to build, maintain, and run these various structures. They could live in artificial structures capable of supporting tens of thousands or even tens of millions of people apiece. Each would have an independent self-supporting ecology, and while their existence would never completely obviate the need for population control, space settlements would allow for further expansion and growth when Earth itself will have reached its limits.

19) *Low-gravity Flying*—In space settlements, there are bound to be regions of low or even zero gravity. This would represent an environment we cannot have on Earth, and advantage can be taken of it. With low gravity and an adequately dense atmosphere, human beings can be outfitted with properly designed wings and will fly through the power and manipulative ability of

their own muscles. A whole new class of sports and entertainment would become possible.

20) *Interplanetary Travel*—With near space exploited and the Moon being used for its mineral wealth, it will be inevitable that human beings will try for the various other worlds of the Solar system. Eventually, human spaceships will be penetrating the Solar system to its farthest reaches, and permanent settlements will be established on a number of worlds.

21) *Terraforming*—None of the worlds of the Solar system, other than Earth, are now hospitable to human life. To settle such worlds, human beings would have to live under pressurized domes or underground. Earthlike conditions would have to be developed in relatively small regions. Why not, however, transform whole worlds into new Earths by importing water, or air, adjusting temperature, altering rotation rates, and so on? Human beings would then have the freedom of the surface and could move about without space suits.

22) *Gravitational Control*—Gravitation is the predominant force in the Universe as a whole; the force that has been longest known is least understood and is the most intractable. If, somehow, a method for insulating gravitational force can be devised, travel through space would become much easier and cheaper. So would much of the work of the world.

23) *Interstellar Communication*—Even the nearest stars are thousands of times as far away from us as even the farthest planets of our own Solar system. On planets round those stars, however, there may be intelligent species more advanced than ourselves, and they may be sending out signals, or they may perhaps be routinely communicating with each other. We might, on some occasion, be able to receive those signals or eavesdrop on the communication. We might even be able to interpret the messages, enter the communications ourselves, gain much knowledge, and advance rapidly to higher levels of understanding.

24) *Interstellar Travel*—The vast distances separating us from the stars may be conquerable. Gravity control may make matters

easier and so may faster-than-light travel if that can be developed. Alternatively, huge starships might be built on which many generations of human beings can live and die during the trip to the stars. Or else, the space settlements themselves, which we would have built in the Solar system, would take off on the far journey. Alternately, other civilizations may visit us, coming, we hope, in peace so that we can learn from them and they from us.

25) *Black Holes*—Black holes represent portions of mass so great and so condensed that nothing can escape from them. If we can reach them and if we have gravity control, then it may be possible to enter them. According to some theories, it might be possible to pass through black holes and cover vast distances in short periods of time. Black holes may therefore be the key to interstellar travel. In addition, they may offer sources of energy greater than anything else in the Universe and even nuclear fusion and solar power would shrink in comparison.

26) *Galactic Empires*—However, interstellar travel may be achieved, human beings may someday occupy many planetary systems in the Galaxy, either living on planetary surfaces directly or on artificial settlements within the system. With faster-than-light communication, the Galaxy might become a single economic unit, albeit with endless varieties of individual cultures. In fact, it may not be entirely human in nature; there may be hundreds or even millions of other intelligences, all cooperating in a brotherhood of the mind.

27) *Time Travel*—Might we some time gain the ability to travel through time as we can travel through space? Travel into the past may be of great use in historical, sociological, archeological, and paleontological research. Travel into the future may bring us back knowledge that will offer us shortcuts to further heights of development.

28) *Alternate Time Paths*—Time travel might not be of a nature that would confine us to observation only. We might be able to participate in the times we visit. If so, we would surely be tempted to interfere with events. Why not prevent Lincoln's assassination, or the start of World War I, or the rise of Nazism?

Why not order events now so as to prevent a specific catastrophe we have seen in the future? Time travel might make it possible to pick and choose between alternate time paths and adjust history to the greatest advantage of humanity.

NOTE: Some of these dreams, such as gravitational control or time travel, are probably impossible even in theory. Others, such as the use of black holes or mass transference or galactic empires or telepathy, would seem to be unlikely in the extreme.

Some dreams are mutually incompatible, for if we develop a complex society of space settlements, there isn't much reason to indulge in terraforming.

Almost any dream can turn into a nightmare. A world government may become a universal, oppressive dictatorship. Immortality may produce a boring world of sameness that completely stultifies humanity. Control of evolution may produce a race of mediocrities. Computers may reduce human beings to helplessness or even obsolescence. Telepathy may end the last vestige of privacy.

—Nevertheless, what is life without dreams?

IV
THE HISTORY
OF
SCIENCE FICTION

(The Prescientific Universe)

> *To every history there is a prehistoric period. In the case of science fiction, the prehistory lingers on even today in some of the aspects of the field.*
>
> *But what of that? Just as Ice Age art can hold up its head with any form of art produced by sophisticated modern man, so can the prehistoric aspects of science fiction prove an accomplished literary form.*

16. THE PRESCIENTIFIC UNIVERSE*

I have often made the point that true science fiction is a creature of the last two centuries. Science fiction cannot exist as a picture of the future unless, and until, people get the idea that it is science and technology that produce the future; that it is advances in science and technology (or, at the very least, changes in them) that are bound to make the future different from the present and the past, and that thereby hangs a tale.

Naturally, no one could possibly get that idea until the rate of scientific and technological change became great enough to be noticed by people in the course of their lifetime. That came about with the Industrial Revolution—say, by 1800—and it was only thereafter that science fiction could be written.

And yet there must have been something that came before science fiction, something that was not science fiction and yet filled the same emotional needs. There must have been tales of the strange and different, of life not as we know it, and of powers transcending our own.

Let's consider—

The respect that people have for science and for scientists (or the fear that people have or a combination of both) rests on the certain belief that science is the key to the understanding of the Universe and that scientists can use science to manipulate that key. Through science, people can make use of the laws of nature to control the environment and enhance human powers. By the steadily increasing understanding of the details of those laws, human powers will be greater in the future than in the past. If we can imagine the different ways in which they will be greater, we can write our stories.

In previous centuries, however, most men had but a dim understanding, if any at all, of such things as laws of nature. They did not know of rules that were unbreakable; of things-as-they-must-be that could serve neither to help us nor to thwart us but that might allow themselves to be ridden to glory, if we but knew how.

Instead, there was the notion that the Universe was the plaything of life and the will; that if there were events that seemed analogous to human deeds but that were far greater in magnitude, they were carried through by life-forms resembling those we know but greater in size and power.

The beings who controlled natural phenomena were therefore pictured in human form, but of superhuman strength, size, abilities, and length of life. Sometimes they were pictured as superanimal, or as supercombinations of animals. (The constant reference to the ordinary in the invention of the unusual is only to be expected, for imaginations are sharply limited, even among the best of us, and it is hard to think of anything really new or unusual—as Hollywood "sci-fi" constantly demonstrates.)

Since the phenomena of the Universe don't often make sense, the gods are usually pictured as whimsical and unpredictable; frequently little better than childish. Since natural events are often disastrous, the gods must be easily offended. Since natural events are often helpful, the gods are basically kindly, provided they are well-treated and that their anger is not roused.

It is only too reasonable to suppose that people would invent formulas for placating the gods and persuading them to do the right thing. Nor can the validity of these formulas be generally disproven by events. If the formulas don't work, then undoubtedly someone has done something to offend the gods. Those who had invented or utilized the formulas had no problems in finding guilty parties on whom to blame the failure of the formula in specific instances, so that faith in the formulas themselves never wavered. (We needn't sneer. By the same principle, we continue to have faith in economists, sociologists, and meteorologists today, even though their statements seem to match reality only erratically at best.)

In prescientific times, then, it was the priest, magician, wizard, shaman (again the name doesn't matter) who filled the function of the scientist today. It was the priest, etc., who was perceived as having the secret of controlling the Universe, and it was advances in the knowledge of magical formulas that could enhance power.

The ancient myths and legends are full of stories of human beings with supernormal powers. There are the legendary heroes, for instance, who learn to control winged horses or flying carpets. Those ancient pieces of magic still fascinate us today, and I imagine a youngster would thrill to such mystical methods of aeronavigation and long for the chance to partake in it, even if he were reading the tales while on a jet plane.

Think of the crystal ball, into which one can gaze to see things that are happening many miles away, and magic shells that can allow us to hear the whispering of humans many miles away. How much more wonderful than the television sets and the telephones today.

Consider the doors that open with "Open sesame" rather than by the click of a remote-control device. Consider the seven-league boots that can transport you across the countryside almost as quickly as an automobile can.

Or, for that matter, think of the monsters of legend, the powerful travesties of life invented by combining animal characteristics: the man-horse Centaur, the man-goat Satyr, the woman-lion Sphinx, the woman-hawk Harpy, the eagle-lion Gryphon, the snake-woman Gorgon, and so on. In science fiction we have extraterrestrials that are often built up on the same principle.

The goals of these ancient stories are the same as those of modern science fiction—the depiction of life as we don't know it.

The emotional needs that are fulfilled are the same—the satisfaction of the longing for wonder.

The difference is that the ancient myths and legends fulfill those needs and meet those goals against the background of a Universe that is controlled by gods and demons who can in turn be controlled by magical formulas either in the form of enchantments to coerce, or prayers to cajole. Science fiction, on the other hand, fulfills those needs against the background of a Universe that is controlled by impersonal and unswervable laws of nature, which can in turn be controlled by an understanding of their nature.

In a narrow sense, only science fiction is valid for today since, as far as we can tell, the Universe *does* follow the dictates of the laws of nature and is *not* at the mercy of gods and demons.

Nevertheless, there are times when we shouldn't be too narrow or haughty in our definitions. It would be wrong to throw out a style of literature that has tickled the human fancy for thousands of years for the trivial reason that it is not in accord with reality. Reality isn't all there is, after all.

Shall we no longer thrill to the climactic duel of Achilles and Hector because people no longer fight with spears and shields? Shall we no longer feel the excitement of the naval battles of the War of 1812 and of the Napoleonic Wars because our warships are no longer made of wood and are no longer equipped with sails.

Never!

Why, then, shouldn't people who enjoy an exciting science fiction adventure story not enjoy a rousing mythological fiction adventure story? The two are set in different kinds of Universes but follow analogous paths.

So though I am sufficiently stick-in-the-muddish to be narrow in my definition of science fiction and would not be willing to consider sword-and-sorcery examples of science fiction, I am willing to consider it the *equivalent* of science fiction set in another kind of Universe—a prescientific Universe.

I don't even ask that they be wrenched out of context and somehow be made to fit the Universe of reality by being given a scientific or pseudoscientific gloss. I ask only that they be self-consistent in their prescientific Universe—and that they be well-written and exciting stories.

(*Science Fiction and Society*)

What with one thing and another, I have been asked on a number of occasions to write a short history of science fiction, and I generally tend to oblige. I alter the approach and style to suit the audience but the content cannot vary to any great extent.

For that reason, I cannot include them all in this book. In fact, I had to choose only one of them, and the one I chose (because it is the most embracing) follows.

17. SCIENCE FICTION AND SOCIETY*

Science fiction came into being in the early nineteenth century as a literary response to a new curiosity that did not truly exist in all of man's earlier history.

Through almost all of man's history, there was never any visible change in the basic manner of life as far as the individual human being was concerned. There was, indeed, change. There was a time when fire was tamed, when agriculture was developed, when the wheel was invented, when the bow and arrow were devised. These inventions, however, came at such long intervals, established themselves so gradually, spread outward from the point of origin so slowly that the individual human being, in his own lifetime, could see no change.

There was therefore, until modern times, no literature that dealt with the future since there seemed nothing about the future that could not be dealt with in terms of the present. There were fantasies, to be sure, dealing with supernatural worlds of gods and demons; fantasies of faraway mythical lands such as Atlantis, or

---

* Copyright © 1973 by the American Medical Association

unattainable lands such as the Moon, but all was described as taking place in the present or the past.

Those changes which did take place (however slowly) were invariably the result of technological advance. This was true even in the cases where what happened seems at first glance to have no connection with technology.

Many a military victory was won by a general who knew how to use some technological advance; that's obvious.

Less obvious is the fact that the transition from the Dark Ages to the culture of the High Middle Ages after AD 1000 might not have taken place without the increased food supply made possible by the development of the moldboard plow which more efficiently broke up the heavy soils of northern Europe; and the invention of the horsecollar which made it possible to hitch the horse to that plow.

Again, the Protestant Reformation succeeded, where previous movements of the sort had failed, because of the invention of the printing press. Martin Luther, an accomplished pamphleteer, spread his printed words across the length and breadth of Europe faster by far than those words could be suppressed.

Even the Scientific Revolution of 1550–1650 would probably have been impossible without the printing press, which spread the news of discoveries rapidly and which, for the first time, created a continent-wide scientific fraternity.

The rate of advance in technology increased steadily over the centuries as each group of advances built on those that had gone before. By 1800, the rate had increased to the point where an Industrial Revolution was taking place in Great Britain and where this Revolution was spreading outward from its point of origin with unprecedented speed. And wherever the Industrial Revolution took hold, the rate of change increased to the point where it became noticeable in the single lifetime of an individual human being.

Mind you, change is not a pleasant thing. People grow accustomed to a way of life and to break the caked custom that has built up about them is painful, even when the change might seem, to the dispassionate, to be for the better. Or as Thomas

Jefferson said in his immortal Declaration, "all experience hath shewn that mankind are more disposed to suffer, while evils are sufferable, then to right themselves by abolishing the forms to which they are accustomed."

Consequently, while some looked forward to the advance of science and technology as the means by which a Utopia might be produced on the Earth, others feared the consequences of change and foresaw nightmare. From the beginning, then, science fiction has swung between the two poles of optimism and pessimism.

Consider the first novel which might be defined as true science fiction, for instance—*Frankenstein,* by Mary Shelley, published in 1818 in Great Britain, the home of the Industrial Revolution. It dealt with the creation of life not by magic or the supernatural, but by the reasoned application of scientific techniques (which Mrs. Shelley was cautious enough to leave undescribed). And it dealt with the evil consequences thereof. As we all know, the Monster that was created destroyed Frankenstein, his creator.

The nineteenth-century mood, however, rapidly became one of optimism. The developing Industrial Revolution fastened a factory system on Great Britain that was one of the nightmare horrors of history, but the middle and upper classes, who alone were articulate, benefited greatly. Great Britain's empire spread, and other nations, as they industrialized, grew in power and in (unevenly distributed) wealth.

It is not surprising, then, that the French writer, Jules Verne (the first professional science fiction writer, in the sense that he was the first to make the major portion of his livelihood out of tales we now recognize to be science fiction), breathes optimism in his tales. His heroes probe the air and the sea depths; they penetrate indeed to the height of the Moon and to the depth of the Earth's center; and always with a glory in achievement that carries us along with them. There are barriers to be hurdled, and the hurdling's the thing.

We must realize, of course, that no science fiction story with thought behind it—whether as pessimistic as Shelley or as optimistic as Verne—is unrelated to the society in which it is produced. The writer's imagination, though it soar its mightiest, is tethered

perforce, however long the thread, to the life the author lives and
knows.

Thus, Shelley's dead-tissue-made-alive was based on the discovery of the Italian anatomist, Luigi Galvani, twenty years earlier,
that an electric shock would cause dead muscles to twitch as
though they were alive. And Verne's tales were written in the era,
and permeated with the spirit, of the great nineteenth-century inventors—Thomas Alva Edison, most of all.

Even when a man like Herbert George Wells divorced himself
from the immediate effects of technology and allowed himself unlimited range of imagination, he left himself tied to his own
society.

In *The Time Machine* (1895), the very first true time-travel
story, and Wells's first success, Wells made use of a device that
could take men through time at will, something for which the
technology of his time (and of ours, too) holds out no promise.
The time traveler finds a far future in which men are divided into
two classes, one beautiful but decadent, the other ugly and de-
praved. This is an obvious reflection on the possible consequences
of a class society such as the Great Britain of Wells's time still
was.

In *The War of the Worlds* (1898), which was the first tale ever
written dealing with interplanetary warfare, Wells was inspired by
the discovery of markings on Mars, twenty years earlier, which
were interpreted as canals and which gave rise to speculations concerning the presence of an advanced civilization on Mars; one
which was fighting, desperately, to survive on a dying world.

Wells's picture of Martians landing in Great Britain and remorselessly taking over the land without any regard for the native
Earthmen, whom the invaders clearly pictured as inferior beings
with no rights that needed to be respected, was, however, as
clearly inspired by the fact that the British themselves, and, to a
lesser extent, other European nations, had just completed the
takeover of the African continent under precisely similar conditions.

Whereas Verne was almost invariably optimistic, Wells's vision
of the future was tempered by pessimism, as might be expected,
since the opening decade of the twentieth century was filled with

the booming of war drums that were steadily growing louder. Wells's view of future wars was as fearsome as it was accurate, and it is in Wells's works, half a century before the reality, that we come across what he calls "the atomic bomb."

When World War I did come, it put an end to the almost childlike optimism of the nineteenth century. It was seen that civilized nations could make war in fashion worse than barbarians and that science—the great force that was to bring all mankind to a Utopia—could introduce unprecedented horrors in the form of advanced explosives, bombing from the air, and, worst of all, poison gas.

In 1920, immediately after the end of the war, the Czech playwright, Karel Capek, wrote *R. U. R.* ("Rossem's Universal Robots") concerning the mass production of artificial living creatures called "robots," the Czech word for "slaves." By the end of the play, the robots, intended by science to bring Utopia, brought instead the end of humanity.

In 1926, science fiction entered a new phase when Hugo Gernsback, a Luxemburg-born American, published *Amazing Stories*, the first magazine ever to be devoted to science fiction exclusively. At first, Gernsback had to reprint stories by Verne, Wells, and other writers of the past to fill his pages, but slowly he attracted American writers of a new generation, who took to the new field.

The stories, as always, were sometimes pessimistic and sometimes optimistic. On the whole, though, despite the experience of World War I, magazine science fiction opened a new era of optimism in science fiction. There are reasons for this.

The United States, in which the new magazine science fiction rose to prominence, had suffered least in World War I, and had carried the Industrial Revolution to its highest extreme. There seemed nothing Americans could not do in the booming 1920s, and the "superscience story" originated in consequence.

The first of these, *The Skylark of Space* by Edward E. Smith, appeared in *Amazing Stories* in three parts beginning in the August 1928 issue—at the very height of the boom. In this story and in others of the sort that followed, engineers conceived new inventions, constructed and put them to use at once, and in the space of a few years conquered the Galaxy.

There were many who followed Smith's lead, notably John W. Campbell, Jr., and for several years this variety of science fiction carried all before it.

But the Great Depression began at the end of 1929, and optimism shrank steadily in the world generally and in the United States in particular. The new pessimism was reflected in Aldous Huxley's *Brave New World*, published in 1932 at the depth of the Depression. In it science was portrayed as a dehumanizing agent.

Even in the adventure-centered magazines, the loss of optimism took place. One of the first of the magazine writers to feel the new mood was Campbell who, in 1934, when the Depression in the United States had begun to yield to Franklin Delano Roosevelt's New Deal, began a new deal of his own. He abandoned superscience stories and, under the pseudonym of Don A. Stuart, started to deal with human beings at closer range and with technology at more plausible focus.

In 1938, he came to be in editorial control of *Astounding Stories*, at that time the most successful of the science fiction magazines. He at once altered its name to *Astounding Science Fiction*, and its outlook as well. Campbell, who had received an education in physics, began to search for writers who had an understanding of science and scientists and who could write believably about them. In the process, he discovered and helped develop many of the science fiction writers who now, a generation later, still dominate the field.

The verb "to affect" is double-edged. Society, while affecting science fiction was, in its turn, affected.

For one thing, while science fiction magazines had relatively small circulations, the youngsters who read those magazines in the 1920s and 1930s were, for the most part, keen-minded, imaginative, and feverishly interested in science. They might have made up no more than a tenth of one percent of the population, but they grew up to form far more than a tenth of one percent of the scientists, engineers, and, in general, the intellectual leadership of the nation.

There was also a kind of fallout. There were comic strips such as "Buck Rogers," "Flash Gordon," and "Superman" which presented a dilute science fiction to all levels of the population. The concept of scientific advance became a dim part of the general consciousness, therefore, so that when the time came, for instance, to reach the Moon, enough romance had been created around that theme to make the concept acceptable to the general population.

To be sure, in the 1930s science fiction had been stigmatized, by those who took refuge in haughty ignorance, as childish escape literature. This escape was, in many cases, an escape to reality.

The science fiction stories of the 1930s dealt with the energy crunch, with overpopulation and atomic energy, with television and computers, with mutations and organ transplantation—the kind of escape it would have been better to force on all the world.

Under John Campbell's leadership, *Astounding* began to depict societies that were plausibly and accurately extrapolated from new discoveries. As soon as uranium fission was discovered and announced in 1939, atom-bomb stories came to be written, some of them with amazing prescience.

With the coming of the atom bomb, society could no longer look upon science fiction as childish escape literature. The science fiction writer had seen too much to which others were blind.

It was clear by then, moreover, that the rate of change of society, sparked by technological development, had been continuing to increase throughout the nineteenth and twentieth centuries, and had now reached the point where decisions could no longer be made on the basis of present conditions only. In order to make intelligent decisions, the future would have to be foreseen.

As a consequence, what had been science fiction has now become "futurism," a respectable specialty highly thought of by those, in government and industry, who must, everyday, make decisions by guessing the future; decisions that affect millions of people and billions of dollars.

And this has, in turn, profoundly affected science fiction. By 1960, the Campbell era was about over, for Campbell had been too successful. The real world of the 1960s proved to be so like the science fiction world of the 1940s that writers, in search of tales that would not be so readily overtaken by fact, moved away from the hardware of technology and toward the more difficult software of the human being.

Secondly, a growing disillusion with science and scientists had begun to sweep the world in the wake of World War II, and by the 1960s, there was an antiscience mood among the young sufficiently deep to be reflected in science fiction.

This second effect was intensified by a third, the general decline of fiction in the wake of World War II. The rate and importance of change was so great that fiction dealing with the here-and-now seemed increasingly irrelevant. Magazine markets for fiction withered; novels appeared in smaller numbers and were, generally, less successful.

Young writers, looking about, found almost no flourishing fiction market, except science fiction. As a result, the 1960s saw the rise of new writers who lacked knowledge of science and even sympathy for science, but who wrote science fiction because that was all there was.

The overall result was the New Wave, as some call it, in which the most pronounced characteristic is that of stylistic experimentation, a heavy infusion of sex and violence, and, most of all, a mood of deep pessimism.

In its extreme form, the New Wave has not been successful, but it has succeeded in making its point, and in science fiction, generally, the deeds of the engineers sink into the background and the present-day frustrations of human beings take the stage.

To take one example out of very many, consider "When It Changed" by Joanna Russ, which won the Nebula Award as the best science fiction short story in 1972. It pictures a planet, far out in space, from which the males have disappeared and on which the women have been left alone. They manage to devise and maintain an interfertile homosexual society and to find joy in it, and then, before that society can be made strong enough to defend itself, the planet is rediscovered. Men arrive—and all is changed.

It is the ultimate Women's Lib story, one that can be told only in a science fiction milieu—but like almost all science fiction, though it seems to concern itself with human beings and worlds of the far distance and far future, it also concerns itself with the here and the now.

(Science Fiction, 1938)

A crucial year in the history of science fiction was 1938, since that was the year in which John Campbell first gained effective control of Astounding Stories, *renamed it* Astounding Science Fiction *and began the "Golden Age."*

As it happened, 1938 was also the year in which I began to submit science fiction to the magazines and made my first sale. Frederik Pohl, who was to edit the 1980 edition of Nebula Award Stories, *asked me to contribute a reminiscence of that year and the following is the result.*

18. SCIENCE FICTION 1938 *

Science fiction in 1938, by modern standards, virtually did not exist. Suppose we call the roll—

There were three pulp magazines: *Astounding Stories, Amazing Stories,* and *Thrilling Wonder Stories.* The first two paid a cent a word; the last paid half a cent a word.

Only *Astounding* might be considered a quality magazine. *Thrilling Wonder Stories* featured action stories intended to appeal to younger and less sophisticated readers. *Amazing,* which passed under new management that year, was getting set to feature fringe nonsense. It was the oldest of the magazines, being fully thirteen years old.

There were a few comic books that might be classified as very simplistic science fiction. "Flash Gordon" was to be found in the newspaper strips.

There were a few books published that were science fiction, but

* Copyright © 1980 by the Science Fiction Writers of America

they were put out by houses that were at best semiprofessional; their sales were low and their earnings lower.

There were occasional movie serials that seemed to aspire to a science fiction quality not quite as high as those of the comics. Even more occasional serious motion pictures appeared now and then that might be classified as honest science fiction. *The Shape of Things to Come* springs to mind.

Out of it all, almost nothing was at more than childish level. What kept it from sinking through the subbasement and into moronic oblivion was the unremitting labor of one quixotic and idiosyncratic man, John W. Campbell, Jr., who, in 1938, took over full editorial responsibilities for *Astounding Stories* and promptly changed its name to *Astounding Science Fiction*.

It was in that year, 1938, that I sold my first science fiction story and broke into the field. Why on earth did I bother?

Science fiction fans of today, accustomed to multimillion-dollar extravaganzas in the movies and on television, to novels that earn block-busting advances in six figures, to endless racks of paperbacks may think of the impoverished era of the 1930s with disbelief, and pity those of "First Fandom" who grew up with science fiction in those days.

Don't! The pity is misplaced. What we had, the fans of today will never have.

In the first place, there were few fans, and, in such cases, less can be more.

There were many readers, to be sure. The magazines had circulation figures that were as high then as they are now (though magazines were the entire field then and are only a small proportion of it now). Most of the readers were casuals, however, who came and went and were content to be silent. They contributed their dimes and that was the extent of their importance.

There were, however, a few fans, who not only bought the magazines but kept them; who not only read the stories, but discussed them; who not only enjoyed the stories but sought out others with whom to share the enjoyment.

So restricted was the experience of science fiction, so narrow were the limits within which it was familiar, so few were those who knew the language, the subject matter, the unending excitement of it that it was as though we had a secret world that no one knew. We all lived in a tree house in a trackless forest, in a cave in an unapproachable cliff wall, in a burrow in the hidden center of a vast labyrinth. We had a universe of our own and the world was well lost.

We few—we happy few—we band of brothers—

Well, we weren't a band of brothers exactly, for discussions degenerated to arguments sometimes, and we were all young enough to know that we were right and that there was no such thing as compromise. We were also sufficiently articulate—all of us—to shake the walls of the Cosmos with even our lesser adjectives. Those were the days when Hitler's speeches ruled the headlines, but for fervor and extremity of utterance he could have come for lessons to any of us.

The magazines cooperated. They ran pages and pages of letters in microscopic print in which every one of us could be a lordly critic dismissing some stories with a blister, praising others with a hallelujah, spreading salvation and damnation at whim.

That was not enough, so some of us began fan clubs with memberships of five, six, even ten. There was the place where we developed our taste for *power*. There, we competed for leadership and dreamed of political coups that would leave the club in our hands, and organized splinter groups of two or three to burrow from within.

There were many who felt, "Today, the Astoria Science Fiction Club; tomorrow, *all of fandom*." I doubt that anyone dreamed that the day after tomorrow might bring the world itself to heel. If one could control fandom, the mere world would be an anticlimax.

Fans from different cities began to visit each other. They were all young, all virtually penniless, so getting from one place to another was an adventure and called for ingenuity.

No one could foresee in those happy infant days that in one more year the first "World Convention" would be held; that this would be followed by the hibernation of World War II and then the explosion of the atom bomb and the coming of a suffocating blanket of respectability. People out there would begin to take us seriously. The world would flood in, and gone forever would be joy and innocence.

But in 1938, the last year of our delight, there was no hint of such a thing.

Remember, too, that aside from the fact that we fans had each other, we had the world of science fiction, the *whole* world. It was perfectly easy to read every issue of every science fiction magazine and in that way stay abreast of all of science fiction. I mean *all* of it, every word.

The fan could know all the authors and everything each one of them wrote. For years, for instance, I kept a catalog in which I listed every story that was published. I don't mean lots of them. I mean *every* story. I listed them alphabetically by title and by author; I rated each one and gave my comments. I made lists of the better stories.

You could wake me up in the middle of the night and whisper a title to me and I would give you, without perceptible pause, the author, the plot, my opinion of the quality, and sometimes the exact issue of the exact magazine in which it appeared.

Try to do that now.

The most assiduous reader of science fiction must allow innumerable novels and short stories to get past him; must find that writers will win Hugos and Nebulas and that somehow he has never heard of them; occasionally discovers that his favorite author has written twenty items he has never read and cannot locate; finds something he considers wonderful and is lost in frustration because no one he knows has read it or heard of it.

You may read science fiction today, but you can't *know* science fiction; no one can.

We could.

In those days, most fans dreamed of being writers, of selling stories to the professional magazines. I don't think we worried much about making money. Money was nice but it was not to be compared to the glory of seeing your byline in the magazine, of becoming a god in the tiny microcosm of science fiction. (Even your name on a letter in the back of the magazine was the equivalent of archangeldom.)

Seeing my name on a story in *Astounding* was my dream, too.

And we could make it, for standards weren't high. Anyone who could really write, *anyone*, would try for other markets that paid better and had higher hopes of advancement. Only fanatics (of which "fan" is a short form) insisted on writing science fiction, and as long as the sentences hung together at least loosely, you might very well sell. Then, for a time, you could make a few hundred dollars a year in money, and a few million dollars a year in glory and adulation in the only place that counted—fandom.

Nowadays, the standards are enormously higher, the difficulties of breaking in massively greater. I couldn't possibly sell the equivalent of my early stories in today's market.

And the expectations are greater now, too. Having once sold a novel, if you sell your second for an advance of less than fifty thousand dollars, you fire your agent and take to drink.

In the old days your story was off the stands and unavailable exactly one month after it appeared, and you had to write another one for another one-month stand. That was all there was. Nowadays, if your books go out of print, you fire the whole world and build a tent to retire to and sulk in.

—Well, how much of all this is nostalgia for vanished youth?

A lot of it, I suppose. I wouldn't want to go back; I'm spoiled. I can't bring myself to want to exchange wealth for poverty and celebrity for nonentity. I, too, have tried rich and poor; and I, too, find that rich is better.

And yet—

So much for the field as an abstract entity. What about the people who ran it in those days?

To begin with, there was the founding father, Hugo Gernsback. He invented magazine science fiction in 1926 when he published *Amazing Stories*, the first magazine to be devoted to science fiction exclusively.

He received the worshipful respect any founding father should get. The "Hugo," fandom's award for the best of this and that, given out at the World Science Fiction Conventions, is named in his honor.

He was, however, an irritating person. He had a constitutional aversion, it would seem, to paying his authors. Heaven knows he paid tiny sums and keeping them could not improve his financial situation, but he kept them anyway as long as he could. It was his quirk.

He also persisted in imagining that the purpose of science fiction was to predict the gadgetry of the future, and this led to his filling his magazines with science quizzes and to undervaluing writing quality.

He was forced to relinquish *Amazing* in 1929 and started *Science Wonder Stories* and *Air Wonder Stories* (later combined to *Wonder Stories*) instead. He finally passed from the scene of science fiction publishing in 1936, but by that time his loss was little felt.

He tried to make a comeback in the early 1950s with *Science Fiction Plus*, a large-size magazine that pretended it was still 1929. Naturally, it didn't survive long.

I met him only twice and that was in the early 1960s. The first time was at a talk he gave at MIT. He handed out papers before the talk and, having nothing better to do, I read it while waiting for him to begin. So did everyone else. It turned out to be the speech Gernsback was going to give. He painstakingly read the talk we had all just read.

The second time we had lunch together for some purpose that turned out to be of no importance. He walked me a mile to get to the dining place, but I walked eagerly for I heard he was fond of gourmet food and I expected he would take me to some small and elegant dining place. He finally found a distant cafeteria and ordered a ham sandwich. I did the same. It was a mediocre ham sandwich. Gernsback was still a careful man with a dime.

Through the 1930s, after Gernsback left *Amazing*, the editor of that magazine was T. O'Conor Sloane, an elderly gentleman who created a furore among the fans by stating in one of his editorials that he didn't believe in the possibility of space travel. *Amazing* changed hands in 1938, and Sloane left the field at the age of eighty-six. I had never had any opportunity of meeting him.

Replacing Sloane was Raymond A. Palmer, a four-foot-tall hunchback who was only twenty-eight years old at the time. As soon as he became editor, he turned the magazine around with enormous energy. He pushed the quality of the stories down and the circulation up.

I remember reading the June 1938 issue of *Amazing*, the first under Palmer (who had to work so quickly there was no time to get cover art so that he was forced to use a photograph) and being heartsick over the comic-book quality of the stories.

Palmer, however, continued on his way and as the stories grew worse, the circulation continued to go up. In the 1940s, he published stories by a man called Shaver, pure nonsense, which took on the dimensions of a cult and briefly made *Amazing* more successful than any other science fiction magazine before or since. Eventually, Palmer abandoned science fiction for flying saucers and the occult.

I began to submit stories to the science fiction magazines in the very month Palmer became editor. It was Palmer who bought the very first story I sold, "Marooned Off Vesta," and it appeared in the March 1939 *Amazing*. What's more, my second story to be published was "The Weapon Too Dreadful to Use" and that appeared in the May 1939 *Amazing*.

The closest I ever came to meeting Palmer was in 1952 when I visited the offices of a magazine he was editing in Evanston, Illinois. He was not there. I saw his associate, Bea Mahaffey (incredibly better-looking) so I didn't feel too bad.

Editing *Wonder Stories* in the 1930s, under Hugo Gernsback, was Charles D. Hornig, who, like Palmer, was a fan before he was an editor. This is really not so unusual. In order to get someone who has any judgment about science fiction, you have to get either a writer or a fan, and if you are anxious to pay five bucks a week, or thereabouts, it has to be a fan—and a young one, at that. Charles Hornig was nineteen when he took the job.

When *Wonder Stories* came under new management in 1936 and reappeared as *Thrilling Wonder Stories*, men such as Leo Margulies and Mort Weisinger were in charge. I never met either one at the time, but in the last few years of their lives, we were friendly. Indeed, Weisinger, a couple of years ago, made up the following story: "Isaac Asimov was asked how Superman could fly faster than the speed of light, which was supposed to be an absolute limit. To this Asimov replied, 'That the speed of light is a limit is a theory; that Superman can travel faster than light is a fact.' "

I assure you it never happened and I never said it, but it will be repeated, I am quite certain, indefinitely, and it will probably be found in Bartlett's quotations a century from now, attributed to me, after all my writings have been forgotten.

Running *Astounding Stories* in the 1930s was F. Orlin Tremaine. Where Gernsback and Sloane tended to be stodgy, Tremaine was innovative. He did not care at all for the Gernsbackian notion of the "educational" value of science fiction, but was on the lookout for unusual plots.

He pioneered the "Thought Variant" story, which was intended to be as far-out as possible and which caught the imagination of the science fiction fans. The quintessential thought-variant story was Jack Williamson's "Born of the Sun" in the March 1934 *Astounding*, a tale which dealt with the concept of the stars as living organisms and the planets as their eggs.

Under Tremaine, *Astounding* rapidly took the lead in circulation and quality. I myself worshiped Tremaine and his magazine and, in those days, in fact, I neglected *Amazing* and *Wonder*, for it seemed to me that all the science fiction worth reading was in *Astounding*. That was almost right, but not quite—it meant I missed "A Martian Odyssey" when it appeared.

I never met Tremaine when he was the most important man in the field. He left *Astounding* in 1938, and I met him some two years later when he was trying to make a comeback with a magazine called *Comet Stories* and didn't succeed.

The end of the decade of the 1930s saw a rash of new magazines, all of them on small budgets and almost all of them edited by young fans who were friends of mine.

Editing *Science Fiction* and *Future Fiction* on a tiny budget was Robert W. Lowndes, plump, smiling, moustached, soft-spoken, and incredibly literary. He was the author of the first letter to an editor that praised my stories. I have never forgotten this.

He also bought two of my very early stories.

Editing *Astonishing Stories* and *Super Science Stories* on just as tiny a budget was Fred Pohl, who was my closest science fiction friend in those days. He was skinny, solemn, smooth-shaven, soft-spoken, and multitalented. As far as I could judge, he succeeded in every intellectual endeavor to which he turned. He was editor before he was twenty, and though his magazines could not possibly succeed considering the small capital investment the publishers were willing to make, he turned out an amazingly good product.

He bought no less than seven of my early stories. He bought my first positronic robot story after Campbell had rejected it. He was the first to give my name on a cover and the first to publish a lead novel, with a cover illustration, by me.

Editing *Stirring Science Stories* and *Cosmic Stories* on no budget at all (so that neither lasted more than a very few issues) was Donald A. Wollheim, tall, homely, loud-spoken, articulate, sardonic, and very nearly as talented as Fred. He was forced to buy stories for nothing and published one of my early stories (paying me five dollars out of his own pocket—with a loud outcry—in order that he might use my name rather than a pseudonym).

Yes, those were exciting times. Penurious, but exciting.

I have not mentioned John Campbell. He was not of that era. He created the era that followed.

(How Science Fiction Came to Be Big Business)

Usually, when I write about science fiction I talk about the magazines and books, both hard-cover and soft-cover. In other words, I deal with the printed medium.

To the outside world in the 1970s and thereafter, however, science fiction evoked "sci-fi," the world of the visual media. There is no question that economically and popularly, the world of printed s.f. is microscopic compared to that of visual "sci-fi."

19. HOW SCIENCE FICTION CAME TO BE BIG BUSINESS*

When I first began to write science fiction, over forty years ago, there were only three science fiction magazines. Only one of them, *Astounding Stories* was any good, and it paid a penny a word.

That meant that a writer could earn $50 for a short story and $600 for a novel-length, three-part serial. That was *all* he could make, too, for there were no science fiction books to speak of, nor any anthologies nor any reprint houses. A story would be available for a month and then would disappear forever, except in the attics of the few magazine collectors.

And now?

A magazine as slick, as expensive, as elaborate as *Omni* features several science fiction stories in every issue.

Science fiction novels appear in book form by the dozens each year and in paperback form by the scores. Go to any paperback bookstore and you will find rack upon rack of science fiction. There are even science fiction bookclubs and science fiction book-

---

* Copyright © 1980 by World Book-Childcraft International, Inc.

stores, and science fiction writers can sometimes get advances of over $100,000 for a new novel.

As for movies and television, science fiction is not only big business; it is, at the moment, the biggest business.

What happened?

The world happened.

When I began writing science fiction, the subject matter that interested science fiction writers seemed laughable and ridiculous to most "sensible" people. Science fiction stories dealt with flights into outer space, with television, robots, intelligent machines, atomic bombs, overpopulation, and so on.

The first clear indication that it was the people who wrote and read science fiction who lived in the real world, and everyone else who lived in a fantasy, came on August 6, 1945, when the world discovered that an atomic bomb had been exploded over Hiroshima.

That didn't mean that everyone suddenly began to read science fiction, but it did mean that, once and for all, science fiction lost its appearance of being nonsense. Science fiction became respectable and it could no longer be laughed at. In fact, science fiction was more advanced than people realized when the atom bomb first hit world headlines. Even before the bomb fell, science fiction stories were dealing not only with the bomb itself, but with the nuclear stalemate, with peaceful uses of nuclear fission, and with the possible radiation dangers of nuclear fission.

The effect of the new respectability of science fiction made itself apparent quickly. Within a year of Hiroshima, large and elaborate hard-cover anthologies of science fiction appeared, published by such respectable houses as Crown and Random House. In 1949, Doubleday & Company initiated a special line of science fiction hard-cover novels. In the early 1950s, there was a huge boom in science fiction magazines as dozens of new titles appeared.

If science fiction grew respectable, it had to prove worthy of respectability, and this did not happen automatically.

There was science fiction in the nineteenth century, written by such men as Jules Verne, H. G. Wells, and others—and such science fiction included thoughtful tales involving the possibilities, the hopes, the dangers of scientific advance, written in good, contemporary style.

Magazine science fiction, however, when it began in 1926 was a pulp-fiction phenomenon.

The pulp magazines (so-called because they were printed on cheap paper from wood pulp, unglazed and rough-edged) filled the racks by the dozen in those days. They came in all varieties and categories—love stories, detective stories, Western stories, war stories, jungle stories, sports stories, and so on. They featured super-heroes like the Shadow and Doc Savage.

They paid their writers very little, but they offered an endless market for stories that did not require great sophistication or polished writing. Scores of young people, filled with the ambition to write, had their chance in the pulp magazines.

The science fiction magazines were part of the pulp magazine phenomenon and perhaps the least successful part of it, but they didn't stay part of it.

That they didn't is to the credit of one man, John W. Campbell, Jr., who, in 1938, became the editor of *Astounding Stories*. He had been one of the best-known writers of the early 1930s, and there had been a great deal of pulp-writing to his stories. He knew that and he wanted something better.

He changed the name of the magazine to *Astounding Science Fiction* and began to look for writers who knew science and understood scientists, who had an idea of engineering and what made engineers tick. He found such writers and bullied and cajoled them into writing stories that dealt with reasonable advances in technology and concerned themselves with just what such advances might mean to society.

He developed a stable of writers that dominated the field for decades and whose names still ring bells today—Robert A. Heinlein, Arthur C. Clarke, Lester del Rey, Theodore Sturgeon, A. E. van Vogt, Hal Clement—even Isaac Asimov.

Many of the old Campbell writers, now gray-haired and elderly, are still in the forefront of the field today. The so-called "Big

Three" who have topped the polls for two decades—Heinlein, Asimov, and Clarke—are all Campbell authors.

Were it not for Campbell, when the time came that science fiction could be viewed as respectable, the field would not have deserved it. But he was there, and that made all the difference.

The pulp magazines did not last forever. In the late 1930s, the comic books came along and began drawing off the younger readers of the pulp magazines. The trend deepened and accelerated and by the late 1940s, the pulp magazines vanished. The only relic of the pulp-magazine phenomenon that remained were the science fiction magazines, for they alone had graduated from the field (so had one or two mystery magazines).

In fact, the science fiction magazines continued to gain respectability as science continued to advance in the direction marked out by the stories in *Astounding*. The nuclear bomb became a far more dreadful thing with the development of the hydrogen bomb in the middle 1950s. The invention of the transistor in 1948 made it possible to devise all sorts of compact electronic devices from pocket-sized radios to desk-top computers (the "intelligent machines" of science fiction). Jet planes and television also seemed cases of science fiction coming true.

Most of all, scientists were beginning to talk of orbiting artificial satellites. On October 4, 1957, the first artificial satellite actually went into orbit around the Earth, and people began to work toward the goal of putting human beings in orbit, and even of reaching the Moon. How science fictional could you get?

Throughout the 1950s, therefore, magazine science fiction, with Campbell and his writers in the lead, probed more and more deeply into scientific gadgetry, staying, sometimes, not very far ahead of actual science.

Everything changes, however, and Campbellesque science fiction had to change, too, and for several reasons.

First, Campbell was, if anything, too successful. The world was becoming too much like the world of Campbell-type science fiction. Science fiction that stayed too close to the nuts-and-bolts of scientific advance read too much like the science columns of the New York *Times*. It made science fiction seem a little dull.

Second, the world was becoming disillusioned with some of the directions taken by science. The nuclear bomb was an ever-more-frightening threat and scientists seemed more and more to be mercenaries in the service of the military establishment. That put Campbell's essentially optimistic view of scientific advance out of touch with popular feeling.

Third, there was an increasing freedom of expression which made sex and vulgar language more acceptable in print, and Campbell's own puritanical editing began to seem out of date.

Fourth, and most important, it was not only pulp fiction that had died. In the 1950s, the world of printed fiction was shaken to its foundations by the rapid growth of television. Many people abandoned their addiction to popular fiction in books and magazines in order to watch television fiction—the Westerns, the crime shows, the situation comedies.

This meant that all magazine fiction, except for science fiction, was dwindling. Fiction books of every variety, except science fiction, were published in fewer numbers.

This meant also that young people who were filled with the urge to write could no longer find a market for writing—except science fiction.

What a change that introduced! In previous decades the only writers who tried science fiction were those who were fanatical devotees of the field, who were excited over science and technology, and were therefore writing it by choice. Many of the new writers, from 1960 on, were writing science fiction for lack of other outlets and were not very interested in science; were, in some cases, actually antagonistic to science.

As a result of all this, the early 1960s saw the beginning of a revolution in science fiction as important as Campbell's earlier revolution. The term used for the new type of stories that were written was "the New Wave."

These involved stories that were not so much about science and scientists as about ordinary people affected by science. In many cases the science was far in the background, scarcely noted. The New Wave was also much more experimental in style and content; more generous in its use of sex and violence; not as clearly possessing a beginning, a middle, and an end; not as obviously telling a story.

It roused violent passions, both for and against, among science fiction readers and, in its more extreme form, did not succeed, but on the whole, the New Wave was a good thing. It broke the Campbell mold that was beginning to fit too tightly about science fiction and made for freer expression even for those science fiction writers who continued to work on "hard science fiction," that is, on the variety which continued to stress gadgetry and the physical sciences.

There were several interesting side effects of the New Wave era.

First, it brought non-American science fiction to the fore. To begin with, of course, there had been a very strong European component in science fiction. After all, Verne was a Frenchman and Wells was an Englishman. Then, too, American magazine science fiction was founded, in 1926, by Hugo Gernsback, an immigrant from Luxemburg; and the first issues of his *Amazing Stories* featured reprints of European science fiction.

Soon, however, new writers, almost entirely American, began to come forward; and for thirty years afterward, the United States dominated the field. Magazines in other nations were not usually successful and survived largely by reprinting American science fiction. Writers who weren't American, nevertheless, tried to publish in American magazines which were, after all, the best paying.

American readers tended to view the field as purely American. When, in the late 1930s, "World Science Fiction Conventions" began to be annual affairs, it was taken for granted that they would be held in various cities of North America.

(And yet the field was never as American as Americans thought. Of the "Big Three," Arthur C. Clarke is an Englishman, I was born in the Soviet Union, and only Robert Heinlein is a native-born American.)

This changed with the New Wave. The British, as it happened, were less enamored of technology than the Americans were and were more nearly in the forefront of the new experiments in style.

It was in Great Britain that the New Wave began, and it was the English writer Brian Aldiss, who was its great exemplar.

It couldn't help but become noticeable thereafter that science fiction was an international phenomenon. Although articles published in the Soviet Union shortly after World War II made it seem that the Soviets viewed science fiction as a medium of capitalist imperialist propaganda, this proved to be not so. Not only did science fiction flourish in the Soviet Union, but much American science fiction was translated into Russian. Science fiction writers from behind the Iron Curtain made their names known, and Stanislaw Lem of Poland is one of the most admired science fiction writers in the world.

The American-sponsored World Science Fiction Conventions began to be held on other continents: in London, in Brighton, in Melbourne. In 1970, the Convention was held for the first time in a non-English-speaking city—Heidelberg, Germany. Important international conventions in the field of science fiction and fantasy are now held annually under European sponsorship in Ireland, Italy, and France.

The broadening of scope that the New Wave encouraged in science fiction had the effect of accelerating another change that was overtaking the field.

Through the 1950s, science fiction had been predominantly a masculine field of endeavor. The editors, the writers, the readers, were almost all men and, for the most part, young men. If women were introduced into the stories at all, they were passive characters whose function was to complicate the plot and give the male characters something to win or rescue. Even the few women who wrote science fiction in the 1930s and 1940s—notably Catherine L. Moore and Leigh Brackett—tended to write in this fashion.

With the New Wave, however, the change in style and content (and the growing lack of alternate forms of fiction) encouraged more and more women to begin reading and writing science fiction. This, in turn, meant a broadening and deepening of the manner in which women were portrayed in the stories.

Nor did the women entering the field need to accept minor positions. In 1970, a woman, Ursula K. LeGuin, won the coveted "Hugo" for the best novel of the year. Anne McCaffrey has written phenomenally successful science fiction. There are even militant feminists such as Joanna Russ, who use science fiction as a medium for advancing their views.

The broadening of science fiction meant also that it was approaching the "mainstream" (those novels written for the well-educated public generally) in style and content. It also meant that increasing numbers of mainstream novelists were recognizing the importance of changing technology and the popularity of science fiction, and were incorporating science fiction motifs into their own novels. Thus, Michael Crichton's *Andromeda Strain* made the best-seller lists.

Science fiction writers found their own books becoming popular with the general public, taught in schools as courses in science fiction erupted in every college and in many high schools, and treated almost as cult objects. Heinlein's *Stranger in a Strange Land*, Frank Herbert's *Dune*, Clarke's *Childhood's End*, my own *Foundation Trilogy* are examples.

Science fiction writers even became international celebrities in some instances, featured in national magazines, asked both in print and on television for their views on almost any conceivable topic and, in some cases, proved in growing demand as after-dinner speakers. Ray Bradbury, the one great writer of the 1940s who was not a Campbell discovery, led the way, but others followed. Arthur C. Clarke has even been profiled in *The New Yorker*.

Nor would it occur to scientists these days to be ashamed of their liking for science fiction or of the debt they might owe it. A scientist of the stature of Carl Sagan has written of his science fiction enthusiasm for the Sunday New York *Times Magazine*.

All this represents science fiction only in the printed media. Of overwhelming importance to far more people than read science fiction is the version of science fiction that appears in motion pictures and television. This visual science fiction is quite different from printed science fiction.

A science fiction hard-cover novel can be profitable if it sells in the thousands. A science fiction magazine can be profitable if it sells in the tens of thousands. A science fiction paperback can be profitable if it sells in the hundreds of thousands.

In contrast, science fiction in the visual media can be profitable (such is the expense of its manufacture) only if it attracts viewers in the tens of millions.

One way of getting round this difficulty is to produce low-budget films that require almost nothing in the way of acting or writing and are aimed primarily at children. Such quickie films are at the level of comic books in quality, and since even they are seen by many more people than read science fiction, the quality (or lack of it) of those films lends a spurious imbecility to the whole field.

There were honorable exceptions, of course, such as the film made of H. G. Wells's *The Shape of Things to Come* released in 1936. In 1950, there was *Destination: Moon* on which Heinlein worked, but the level of acting and cinematography was still low.

The real breakthrough in visual science fiction came in 1966 with the appearance on television of "Star Trek," a brainchild of Gene Roddenberry. There, an attempt was made to present real characters interacting warmly and facing problems of importance not only to themselves but, by clear analogy, to ourselves as well.

The tales of the Starship *Enterprise*, on its tour of the Galaxy, did not win an enormous audience and, as the first season waned, it was clear that "Star Trek" would not be renewed. It was then that a most unexpected phenomenon took place. The viewers of "Star Trek" might not be huge in numbers but they were savage in their dedication to the program. The television network was bombarded by protests the like of which they had never seen and, in astonishment, they continued the program a second year and even a third.

At the end of three years and seventy-eight episodes, it was discontinued at last, but it was not forgotten. Enthusiasm grew, rather, and was fed on the reruns. Ten years after the program had gone off the air, there were more "Trekkies" than ever there had been during its actual lifetime. "Star Trek" conventions were convened to which fans flocked by the tens of thousands, including many who weren't old enough to have watched and understood the program in its lifetime.

In motion pictures, a turning point came with the appearance of *2001: A Space Odyssey*, which Arthur C. Clarke helped write. Its realistic portrayal of space travel attracted a wide following and it was the first science fiction movie to be a true hit.

Why is it, though, that so many watch "Star Trek" and *2001: A Space Odyssey*, when so few, in comparison, read science fiction? Nor was there an enormous spillover. Of the tens of millions who were introduced to visual science fiction, only a handful began to read science fiction.

Clearly, visual science fiction offered something printed science fiction did not. What visual science fiction offered was, of course, the visual "special effects," usually the sight of vast destruction, of alien or monstrous beings, of unearthly abilities that come with zero gravity or wild talents.

This emphasis on special effects makes visual science fiction almost a different species from printed science fiction, something that is even demonstrated by the difference in the abbreviations used for the field. Printed science fiction has, for decades, been referred to as "s.f." by its devotees. The term that grew up in Hollywood for the science fiction productions there is "sci-fi." This latter term is looked down upon, and even abhorred, by science fiction readers.

Special effects hit the big time in terms of profits with the motion picture *Star Wars*, released in 1977. The motion picture itself, as far as content is concerned, was very much like the Flash Gordon serials of the 1930s. It was, however, immeasurably superior cinematographically, made inspired use of a pair of robots, and was good-humored throughout.

The result was enormous popularity, unprecedented profits, and, immediately, a host of imitations.

As usual, the imitations were not as good as the object imitated. Some were too slavish in the imitation. Most chose those elements they saw as money-makers—the special effects—and eliminated what they did not see as contributing—the cleverness and good humor.

What about the future of science fiction?

Printed science fiction (s.f.) is not likely ever to become wildly or enormously popular. Good science fiction has, perforce, a fairly high intellectual content, for it must consider science and people and their interaction and do so in a plausible and knowledgeable manner. This limits the readership to a fairly thoughtful segment of the population—but to a very faithful one as well, so that there seems every possibility that printed science fiction will continue to climb at a moderate speed in the near future.

The shakiest portion of the field of printed science fiction are the magazines, which forty years ago were all there were. They have lost ground steadily to anthologies and paperbacks, but they remain viable. The late 1970s even saw the appearance of new and successful magazines including *Isaac Asimov's Science Fiction Magazine* and, of course, *Omni*. The value of the magazines is that they permit the appearance of short stories and represent the natural opening targets of new young science fiction writers.

As for visual science fiction (sci-fi), that may have a more dramatic future. If it clings to special effects as the all-in-all, each must exceed its predecessors if it is to be a blockbuster and the public will be quickly jaded. This is especially so since the vast expense of special effects encouraged the movie producers to exercise stringent economy as far as the writing and acting is concerned. Thus "Battlestar Galactica" a weekly program on TV that closely imitated *Star Wars* began at a high pitch of viewer popularity, quickly faded, and was canceled at the end of the first season.

If, however, it occurs to the producers of visual science fiction to add to their mindless devotion to special effects such things as thoughtful content, some interesting plotline, some characterization in depth; then it is possible that visual science fiction may graduate from sci-fi to s.f. and gain a new and reasonably permanent plateau of popularity.

(*The Boom in Science Fiction*)

It sounds great to have science fiction become big business as I described in the previous essay. What's more, when I wrote the previous essay I tried my best to be objective about it, and to allow it to sound great.

However, I am not really objective about it. There are aspects to the boom concerning which I feel jaundiced indeed.

20. THE BOOM IN SCIENCE FICTION*

I am frequently asked by reporters: "How does the current boom in science fiction affect you?"

The answer is: "Not at all and in no way. The boom in science fiction to which you refer is in the movies and television. My own science fiction is in the magazines and books. The latter is doing well, thank you, but it is the former which is having its boom and the two are of different species. They bear the same name but that is where the similarity ends."

That always surprises the reporters and it may even surprise you, so let me explain. In order to do so, I must give the two species different names in order to avoid confusion.

In the movies and television, science fiction deals primarily with images, so we might call it image-science-fiction. Since the show-business people and journalists who talk about image-science-fiction refer to it, abominably, as sci-fi, suppose we call image-science-fiction i-sci-fi or, better yet, eye-sci-fi.

The science fiction of magazines and books we can simply call what we have always called it: science fiction, or possibly s.f.

To begin with, then, eye-sci-fi has an audience that is fundamentally different from that of science fiction. In order for eye-sci-fi to be profitable it must be seen by tens of millions of people; in order for science fiction to be profitable it need be read only by tens of thousands of people. This means that some 90 percent (perhaps as much as 99 percent) of the people who go to see eye-sci-fi are likely never to have read science fiction.

The purveyors of eye-sci-fi cannot assume that their audience knows anything about science, has any experience with the scientific imagination, or even has any interest in science fiction.

But, in that case, why should the purveyors of eye-sci-fi expect anyone to see the pictures? Because they intend to supply something that has no essential connection with science fiction, but that tens of millions of people are willing to pay money to see. What is that? Why, scenes of destruction.

You can have spaceships destroying spaceships, monsters destroying cities, comets destroying the Earth. These are called "special effects" and it is what people go for. A piece of eye-sci-fi without destruction is, I think, almost unheard of. If such a thing were made, no one would go to see it; or, if it were so good that it would indeed pull a small audience, it would not be thought of as science fiction of any kind.

The overriding necessity for having special effects in order to make sure a piece of eye-sci-fi can make money means that such movies are incredibly expensive. This puts the producers in a bind. They may possibly make so much money that any expense is justified—but how can they know in advance the movie will make that kind of money? They don't, so there is always a tendency to cut down on expenses, and *cheap* special effects are incredibly bad.

Then, too, even if a producer decides to spend freely on special effects, he is quite likely to skimp on other aspects of the picture, and first in line for skimping is always the writing. The result is that the plot and dialogue of any piece of eye-sci-fi is generally several grades below poor. Once a character has managed to say "Oh, wow!" as a spaceship explodes, he is usually a spent force.

Still further, once people get used to special effects and destruction, they quickly get jaded. The next picture must have more and better special effects, which means more expense, and rottener everything-but-special-effects.

Finally, the producers of eye-sci-fi have the "bottom line" psychology—that is, they consider only the final bookkeeping calculation that tells whether one has made a profit or a loss and how much of either.

Naturally, we all have a bottom-line psychology. I write for money; and you do whatever you do for money. Still, the larger the sum of money you invest and the larger the profit or loss you may come out with, the more the bottom line tends to swallow up everything else. My own books, essays, and stories represent such small profits or losses, individually, that I can afford to go my own way, aim for the unusual now and then, take a chance on quality once in a while, shrug off the occasional failure. You, undoubtedly, can do the same. A movie or TV producer can't. One failure may wipe him out. One success may make him a millionaire.

With the intense bottom-line psychology that comes when one throw of the dice is the difference between pauperdom and affluence, it is impossible for a producer to deal with anything that he doesn't think is sure-fire. In eye-sci-fi only the special effects approach being sure-fire. Everything else, therefore, receives no attention. Even if some minor facet of the production can be changed in such a way as to greatly improve it without either trouble or expense to speak of, it won't be done. Why should the producer take the time or make the effort to do so when it doesn't matter to him, and when all his concentration must be on the sure-fire?

Well, then, do I see no good in eye-sci-fi at all? No, I am not a complete curmudgeon in this respect. Some eye-sci-fi can be amusing if it contains humor and has the grace not to take itself too seriously. That's why I enjoyed *Star Wars* and why I expect to enjoy *Superman* when I get around to seeing it. Then, too, if something is outright fantasy and if cartoon techniques take some of the pressure off the special effects, the results can be tolerable.

Besides that, a small percentage of those who are introduced to eye-sci-fi may happen to know how to read, and these may be impelled by curiosity to read science fiction, something they might not otherwise have thought of doing. Thus a boom in eye-sci-fi means our audience can grow somewhat even if it doesn't quite go along with the boom.

It may seem to you that I haven't made the difference between eye-sci-fi and science fiction clear. After all, consider the science fiction magazines.

Are some of them not primarily devoted to adventure science fiction, to scenes of action, to destruction?

Yes, they want action, and if it is necessary to destroy a spaceship, they destroy it—but destroying a spaceship in words is no more costly or difficult than doing anything else in words, so it doesn't take up all the mind and effort of all of us. Writers have time and will and active desire to add other things as well—plot, motivation, characterization, and some respect for science.

Since we who write for the magazines are all only human, we may fall short in these added qualities out of sheer lack of ability, but it is *never* out of a contempt for our audience or out of indifference to anything but the bottom line.

We are not nobler than the people in Hollywood; if we were exposed to their pressures, we might do just as they do.

But we are not in Hollywood, we are here; and so we need only please one thousandth the size of audience that they do. We like to think that our thousandth part of the audience happens to be the best thousandth. It is an audience that can read, that likes its adventure with good writing stirred in, that has a respect for science even when it doesn't have a professional understanding of it.

(*Golden Age Ahead*)

Even the literature of the future should have a future, and I wouldn't be much of a futurist if I didn't occasionally think of what might come to be in my own field.

Most people who know nothing about science fiction tend to think that "science is catching up with science fiction" and that science fiction writers will soon have nothing to write about. Words cannot describe the contempt I feel for such idiocy.

21. GOLDEN AGE AHEAD*

It seems to be an almost unvarying habit among human beings to find golden ages in the past, both in their own personal lives and in their societies.

That's only natural. In the first place, there's something to it—at least in our personal lives. To those of us who are elderly (or even in their late youth, as I am), there is no question but that there are memories of a time when we were younger and stronger and thinner and more vigorous and less creaky and could perform more frequently and grow tired less frequently and so on. And if that isn't golden, what is?

In general, this is naturally extrapolated to the point where whatever society was like in our teenage years is our view of what society *ought* to be like. Every change since then is viewed as a deterioration, a degeneration, an abomination.

Then, too, there are the falsities of memory, which cast a delicious haze over the past, eliminating the annoyances and frustrations and magnifying the joys. Add to that the falsities of history which inevitably produce a greater emphasis on heroism, on dogged determination, on civic virtue; while overlooking squalor, corruption, and injustice.

And in the subuniverse of science fiction, isn't this also true? Doesn't every reader who has been reading for a decade or two remember a "golden age"? Doesn't he complain that science fiction stories aren't as good as they used to be? Doesn't he dream of the classics of the past?

Of course. We all do that. I do it, too.

There is one "Golden Age of Science Fiction" that has actually been institutionalized and frozen in place; and that is the period between 1938 and 1950, which was dominated by John Campbell.

Let's, however, take a closer and unimpassioned look at the Golden Age.

To begin with, how was it viewed in its own time? Did all the readers sit around, saying, "Golly, gee, wow, I'm living through a Golden Age!"?

You'd better not believe it. Sure, the young readers who had just come into the field were fascinated, but the older readers who had been reading since the late 1920s were not. Instead, they frequently talked of the "good old days" and longed for *their* golden age of the Tremaine *Astounding*, which ran from 1933 to 1938.

I was one of the old fossils, as a matter of fact. Much as I liked the stories of the Campbell era and much as I enjoyed contributing to them myself, it was of the earlier 1930s that I dreamed. It wasn't Heinlein that was the epitome, to me, of science fiction (though I recognized his worth)—it was Jack Williamson's *The Legion of Space*; it was E. E. Smith's *Galactic Patrol*; it was Nat Schachner's "Past, Present, and Future"; it was Charles R. Tanner's "Tumithak of the Corridors."

Even at this very day there is an organization called "First Fandom" (to which I belong), and only those can belong to it who were science fiction fans *before* 1938.

And if there were golden ages before the Golden Age, there were also golden ages to still younger readers *after* the Golden Age. Indeed, Terry Carr has just published an excellent anthology of stories from 1939 through 1942 entitled *Classic Science Fiction: The First Golden Age*.

How many more have there been? I should guess that there has been one for every three-year interval since—to one group of readers to another.

Think again? Were the stories of your golden age really golden? Have you reread them lately?

I have reread the stories of my own golden age and found the results spotty indeed. Some of the stories I slavered over as a teenager turned out to be impenetrable and embarrassing when I tackled them again. A few ("Tumithak of the Corridors," for one) held up very well, in my opinion.

It was clear to me, though, that the general average of writing forty years ago was much lower than the general average later. That, in fact, seems to me to have been a general rule. Magazine science fiction over the last half century has steadily risen above and away from its pulpish origins.

That means me, too. I imagine that many people who drooled over *Nightfall, The Foundation Trilogy,* and *I, Robot* in their teens find some of the gloss gone when they reread them in their thirties. (Fortunately for myself, a substantial number do not—and there are always new teenagers entering the field and ready to be dazzled.)

Why has the quality of writing gone up?

For one thing, the competition to science fiction has gone. The pulp magazines are gone. The slick magazines scarcely publish fiction. Whereas, some decades back, science fiction magazines, with their small circulation and even smaller financial rewards, could not compete in the marketplace and could gain only raw enthusiasts, there is now comparatively little else for a beginning writer to do, few other places for him to go.

The competition for space in the science fiction magazines is therefore keener, so that better natural talents reach their pages—and set higher standards for other novices to shoot at.

I doubt, for instance, that I could possibly have broken into science fiction in 1979 with nothing more than the talent I had when I broke into the field in 1939. (Nor need this discourage new writers—they are learning in a better school in 1979 than I did in 1939.)

There is also greater knowledge of science today.

The writers of my own golden age knew very little science that they didn't pick up from the lurid newspaper stories of the day (equivalent to learning about sex in the gutter).

Nowadays, on the other hand, even those science fiction writers who are not particularly educated in science, and who don't particularly use science in their stories, nevertheless know much more about science and use it far more skillfully (when they do) than did the creaky old giants of the past. The new writers can't help it. We now live in a society in which science saturates every medium of communication and the very air we breathe—and the growing ranks of capable science writers see to it that the communications are of high quality.

What do we face then?

We will have stories by better writers, dealing with more exciting and more subtle themes in a more intelligently scientific manner.

Need we worry that it will all come to an end? That science is outpacing science fiction and putting us all out of a job?

No! What the scientists are doing is exactly the reverse. They are providing us with fresh, new gimmicks daily; new ideas; new possibilities.

In just the last few days, I have read about the discovery of gases in Venus's atmosphere which seem to show that Venus could not have been formed in the same way Earth was. I have read about the possibility of setting up a modulated beam of neutrinos that could allow communication *through* the Earth instead of around it. I have read that the Sun may have a steadily ticking internal clock with the irregularities of the Sunspots a superficial modification—but what the clock is and why the modification, we do not know.

Each of these items can serve as the starting point for a story that might not have been possible to write last year, let alone thirty years ago. And they will be written with the skill and expertise of today.

These are exciting times for society, for science, for science fiction, for science fiction writers, for science fiction readers.

There's a Golden Age ahead!

(Beyond Our Brain)

Back in 1976, Saturday Review was planning a special issue on the brain. They wanted to know how the brain and its various aspects were treated in science fiction, and they asked me to tell them. Feeling the need for assistance, I dragooned my good friend, Ben Bova, who was then editor of Analog, *into helping me. The following essay is the result.*

22. BEYOND OUR BRAIN*

(with Ben Bova)

It is not until very recently in human history that people have become proud of the human brain. If we look back into the near past and then as far back as we can see, we find that human beings have taken it for granted that they were not the most intelligent of living things nor the most powerful.

In a world in which the laws of nature are not understood, such powerful phenomena as storm, flood, drought, and earthquake must, it seems, have intelligence behind them. Death itself was personified and puzzled over, as well as feared. It was natural to assume the existence of superhuman intelligences, malevolent at worst and whimsical at best, to account for the things over which puny humans had no control.

As a result, the myths and legends of all peoples dealt with imaginary beings, with gods and demons. Usually, despite their power over space and time, these mythical entities shared the passions and weaknesses of humankind. In the human image were created the gods. And those undoubted human beings who showed themselves to be of heroic mold were often categorized as the son or daughter of one god or another.

In a world in which human beings were at the mercy of the great predators, the beasts of claw and fang, and where the slightest hiccup in the orderly processes of nature could destroy humanity, the legends are full of dread and danger. Even the djinn rescued from the bottle would turn and destroy you; even the pretty fairies who carried you off to their land for a day of feasting and dancing would return you a hundred years later in the world's time.

What could humanity do, faced with these powers who could be such deadly enemies? Learn how to control them, perhaps. Learn how to cajole and placate them into obedience, or learn how to find their weaknesses and use powerful magic to bind and control them.

In either case, learning to understand and control the superhuman powers, whether by might or by indirection, was equivalent, in prescientific times, to our modern learning to understand and put to use the laws of nature. But the power to control was a strange, fearful, and possibly deadly power. If the demon was feared, how much more ought the wizard who controlled him be feared.

What was feared was *knowledge*. It was the eating of the fruit of the tree of knowledge that was the sin of Adam and Eve, and this theme of knowing-too-much runs through much legendary literature. Actaeon accidentally sees Artemis and is turned into a stag to be torn by his own hounds, Semele sees Zeus in his glory and is shriveled by the radiance. Lot's wife looks back to see the work of the Lord and becomes a pillar of salt. Faust, the seeker after knowledge, finds that his search leads him naturally to the devil.

This suspicion of intelligence, this view of wisdom-as-villain, has never left us. Indeed, today's modern generation, coming across this oldest of all suspicions, takes it up and inveighs against modern science as though it had discovered something new.

Nor is science fiction immune from it. Though, simplistically, science fiction would appear to be devoted to the triumphs of science, to the predictions of even greater glories, it is, in actual fact, ambivalent to science. *Frankenstein*, by Mary Shelley (1818), is very Faustian in its attitude toward knowledge. The anatomy student, Henry Frankenstein, learns enough about the machinery of life to put together dead organs and imbue them with consciousness, creating the Monster which eventually kills him. Moral: There are some things we are not meant to know!

Beginning with *Frankenstein*, the mad scientist (often equipped with a beautiful daughter) became a staple of science fiction. The scientist might mean well at the start, as did the one in H. G. Wells's *The Invisible Man* (1897), but the lust for knowledge leads inevitably on to a mad lust for power. The supervillains, the Fu Manchus and the Dr. Nos, were intelligent; the heroes who defeated them were younger, handsomer, stronger, and far more stupid. It was brawn over brains every time.

There were, of course, benevolent intelligences, the Dr. Huers and Dr. Zarkovs of the comic strips, for instance, but they were merely the tools of the Buck Rogerses and the Flash Gordons. It was the latter who were the real heroes, and the scientists merely played Merlin to King Arthur.

In 1938, John W. Campbell, Jr., became editor of *Astounding Science Fiction* (now called *Analog*), and he put an end to this as far as the more sophisticated branches of science fiction were concerned. He insisted that scientists and engineers in fiction be at least recognizably similar to those in real life (a point the movie and TV industry has yet to reach). Campbell generated stories that pitted intelligence against the universal sea of ignorance and danger. For a quarter of a century, intelligence was hero. With the 1960s, however, pessimism began to gain ground once more.

In 1859, Charles Darwin published his watershed book, *On the Origin of Species*. For the first time it occurred to people that superhuman brains need not have been created *de novo*, but could be developed from ordinary human brains or even from subhuman brains by natural evolutionary processes. The notion of man-to-superman entered world literature, even in the works of such titans as Friedrich Nietzsche and G. Bernard Shaw.

This made it possible to find a new way of handling the intelligence-as-villain motif. While attempts to portray the future had usually concentrated on social institutions rather than on human physiology, as in Edward Bellamy's *Looking Backward* (1887) and Wells's *The Time Machine* (1895), science fiction writers discovered the pitiless superbrain that is to come. Facing the superbrain was the relatively brainless (but brave) hero, who, of course, would win out.

One interesting consideration of such future evolution is to be found in the short story "The Man Who Evolved," by Edmond Hamilton (1931). In that story, a scientist (monomaniac where his specialty was concerned as so many fictional scientists were in those days) experiments on himself with cosmic rays in order that his evolution might be speeded. (The science is wretched, but never mind.) He evolves first to a glorious specimen of physical and mental excellence, more eager than ever to examine the future stages of evolution. Then he becomes a wizened fellow with a hypertrophied brain, with no emotions but contempt; then a thing nearly all head anxious to conquer the world (intelligence is dangerous); then nothing but a giant brain far beyond even the dreams of conquest; and then, finally, a giant lump of undifferentiated protoplasm. The process had come full circle.

In the 1950s, science fiction writers were beginning to examine the possibilities of evolution from a much stronger scientific background.

In Theodore L. Thomas's short story, "The Far Look" (1956), two-men teams of astronauts live and work on the Moon in thirty-day shifts. The harsh lunar environment forces them to a new understanding and appreciation of human cooperation. Each astronaut returns to Earth with the knowledge that his life is inextricably linked with the lives of all human beings. The astronauts begin to go into new fields of social endeavor, especially politics. Their minds, their outlooks, their attitudes have been irrevocably altered (evolved, in a way) by their lunar experience.

Theodore Sturgeon's *More Than Human* (1953) deals with a collectivistic evolution. A group of five individuals link minds to form a superhuman entity, a group-mind, that is capable of many feats no individual human being can perform. This group-entity is not evil and is, for that very reason, often at the mercy of normal human greed and stupidity.

To concentrate on evolved intelligence is, of course, rather unsophisticated. The human brain has tripled in size with almost explosive speed on an evolutionary scale, but that explosion took about a million years just the same, and that is rather too long for fictional drama.

Why not a *manufactured* intelligence beyond that of the human?

An obvious raw material for the purpose is the human brain itself. In Isaac Asimov's novel *Pebble in the Sky* (1950), use is made of a device that increases the speed of nerve impulses across the synapses joining individual brain cells and this (in the fevered imagination of the author) made telepathy possible.

Frank Herbert in *Dune* (1963) had his characters use a drug that not only opened their minds to the complete racial memory of their species but also permitted adepts to foresee the future.

A particularly skillful treatment of the theme is to be found in *Flowers for Algernon* by Daniel Keyes (1960). That is the story of a retarded adult who is surgically stimulated in such a way as to cause his intelligence slowly to intensify to the genius level. The treatment, however, is temporary and he, as slowly, recedes to what he was before.

New biological capabilities, such as cloning and engram imprinting, have begun to make their mark on science fiction in the 1970s. In Gary Alan Ruse's short story "Nanda" (1972), a Latin American dictator has a supply of cloned bodies stored in deep frozen sleep. The sleeping "copies" of the dictator are imprinted daily with the day's experiences. When the dictator is assassinated, a clone body is revived and immediately takes over for the dead man. Thus the dictatorship is immortal.

In Ben Bova's novel *The Multiple Man* (1976), the President of the United States is actually a clone group of seven "brothers," each of them an expert in one field of required presidential lore, such as foreign policy or finance. Thus, a sort of group-mind serves as Executive, in secret, while the clone member, who has specialized in being the public "face" for the group, is supposed to be the only man in the White House.

An older and more common theme in science fiction is that of a *completely* artificial human or superhuman intelligence, with nothing but inert material as the starting point.

The notion of "mechanical humans," or "artificial intelligence," is as old as literature. To begin with, such devices were of divine or magical origin. The Greek god Hephaistos is described in the *Iliad* as having artificial women of gold (what other substance would be good enough for a god?) to help him around the house. A brazen giant, Talos, was supposed to guard the shores of Crete.

The medieval rabbinical legend of Rabbi Löw of Prague and his "golem" was magical too, for the golem came to life only when the ineffable name of God was placed on his forehead and was dead again when the name was torn away.

The modern attitude toward mechanical intelligence received its first important launching with the play *R. U. R.*, by Karel Capek (1920). Here we have the picture of a kind of wholesale Frankenstein. The industrialist Rossum did not impart life to dead tissue, he manufactured living tissue in a biochemical production line and created untiring, loyal beings to do the work of humans. Each of his creations was a "slave" or, in the Czech language in which Capek wrote, a "robot." (R. U. R. stands for "Rossum's Universal Robots.") Through an interesting semantic evolution, the word "robot" has now come to mean a mechanical object (usually of metal) that mimics the actions of men and resembles the human form. In modern science fiction parlance, Capek's biochemical, humanoid creations would be called "androids."

Rossum's intentions were good, as were Frankenstein's, but his robots, like the Monster many-times amplified, destroyed not only their creator but the whole human race. This theme was borrowed four decades later by Pierre Boulle to serve as the basis for his novel *Planet of the Apes* (1963). Again we see the danger of a too-intrusive curiosity and the dubious rewards of intelligence.

Capek set a fashion and throughout the 1920s and 1930s robots were dangerous objects who turned on their creators with dismal regularity. This came to an end with Asimov's creation, in 1941, of "positronic robots," rigidly controlled by "the Three Laws of Robotics" which kept robots from ever harming human beings. For the first time, robots were considered as machines with built-in safeguards.

Sometimes the safeguards worked too well, as in Jack Williamson's "With Folded Hands" (1947), where robots took over *all* human tasks and left the human race with nothing to do. Sometimes the safeguards are so strong, as in Lester del Rey's "Instinct" (1952) that in the far future, when the human race is extinct and the surviving robots feel bereft of purpose, the machines create a human being that they might bow low and serve.

Yet the disillusioned days of the 1960s saw a retreat from this attitude and a return to earlier fears, as witness the robots-gone-wrong of movies such as *Westworld*.

A form of mechanical intelligence, which dispenses with the bodily attributes of the robot and keeps only the brain, is the computer, which did not play a big part in science fiction until it finally appeared in real life.

An approach to this sort of thing, in science fiction, had pictured the human brain itself, immobilized and kept alive artificially. In Hamilton's series of novels about Captain Future (which began in 1940), such a brain, encased in metal and bathed in nutrient fluids, played the role of the benevolent scientist.

More subtly, there were human or even animal brains, so immobilized and kept alive in order that they might run complicated machinery as in "Integration Module," by Daniel B. James (1973), or "The Ship Who Sang," by Anne McCaffrey (1961). Sometimes these brains evolved, through long introspection, into superhuman intelligences who then served as advisors and mentors to normal human beings. The electronic mind, however, carrying arithmetical steps to completion at light-speed, eluded science fiction writers for the most part. It is as though they dismissed the chance of getting drama out of a superb adding machine.

Once the computer appeared, however, there was an instant extrapolation to computers of human and even superhuman intelligence. There is the computer on the Starship *Enterprise* in TV's "Star Trek," for instance, which occasionally speaks in a sexy female voice to the embarrassment of the noble Captain Kirk. There is the computer named HAL, in Arthur C. Clarke's movie *2001: A Space Odyssey*, which goes very humanly insane and must be dismantled before it kills everyone on the spaceship.

On the other hand, in Asimov's "The Last Question" (1956), the history of both humanity and computer is traced over the next trillion years. Both grow ever more complex, both rise steadily superior to the inanimate Universe and, in the end, the final computer becomes God—and starts the whole process over again.

Science fiction writers quickly learned that the interaction between human beings and computers can be the source of high drama. Robert A. Heinlein, in his novel *The Moon Is a Harsh Mistress* (1966), and Poul Anderson, in his story "Sam Hall" (1953), both had computer-created personas leading rebellions against repressive political regimes. In *Colossus: The Forbin Project*, mammoth computers in the military systems of the U.S.A. and the U.S.S.R. join forces and take over the world. In Bova's novel *Escape!* (1970), a young convict tries to outwit the computer that runs his juvenile prison.

And, of course, there can be combinations of man and machine, beginning from either end and working toward the other. There are visions of men who must be mechanized in one fashion or another if they are to withstand the hostile environment of space or of other worlds. An example is "Scanners Live in Vain" by Cordwainer Smith (1950). In *The Dueling Machine* by Bova (1969), men are linked mentally to each other, through a computerlike device, for the purpose of satisfying their aggressions by fighting savage duels with each other—completely in their imaginations. Samuel R. Delaney's works have explored many facets of man-machine combinations, most notably in his novel *Nova* (1968).

But there are visions of robots that lead not in the direction of superhumanity but, more subtly and movingly, in the direction of humanity. Lester del Rey began the making of his formidable reputation with "Helen O'Loy" (1938) in which a robot resembling a female is made more and more female until we forget she is a robot. More recently, the theme of robot becoming human was dealt with in Asimov's *Bicentennial Man* (1976).

The human brain need not be advanced in sheer overall intellect. It can have special powers that the ordinary brain does not have—"wild talents" is the phrase commonly used in science fiction.

This sort of story descends from the legendary tales in which some divine or semidivine power grants a chosen human being the fulfillment of a wish or three wishes. Invariably the lucky recipient chooses badly—for knowledge is dangerous, after all.

Thus, Midas of Phrygia asked that everything he touched be turned to gold, which meant he could not eat and that he turned his beloved daughter into a small golden statue. He was happier over the prayed-for loss of his wild talent than over his having acquired it.

In the same way, H. G. Wells's "Man Who Could Work Miracles" (1895)—by wishing—ended by nearly destroying the Earth.

Frank M. Robinson's novel *The Power* (1956) has an ordinary man pursued by a superhuman being who uses wild mental talents for his own evil pleasures. The hero wins only by finding that he, too, has wild talents. The implication is that the hero will prove just as self-serving as his erstwhile enemy was.

Modern science fiction generally accepts wild talents more calmly. They are removed from the divine, shifted into the physiological, and, in many cases, incorporated into science. Heinlein's *Magic, Inc.* (1950) is an example of that, with witches and magicians approaching their task with the cool analytical attitude of scientists. Randall Garrett's long series of "Lord D'Arcy" stories also uses magic in the same way, and for the same diverse purposes that we use science.

L. Sprague de Camp and Fletcher Pratt in "The Roaring Trumpet" (1940) and its sequels also attempted to turn magic into a set of natural laws parallel to our own, with people able to travel from one fictional world to another by appropriately adjusting their own concept of mathematics. Indeed the first sequel to the story was called "The Mathematics of Magic" (1940).

Campbell, the influential editor of *Astounding/Analog*, was extremely partial to stories of wild talents and verged perilously close to mysticism in his excitement over telepathy and related subjects. It is therefore strange that perhaps the best of all wild talent stories did not appear in his magazine.

This is *The Demolished Man* by Alfred Bester (1952) in which a murder mystery is played out against the background of a society in which telepathy is an established method of communication. The social consequences of this are artfully drawn, as is the strategy of the criminal who must commit his crime despite the fact that his thoughts can be read.

On Earth there are no brains to compete with the human brain, except for the dubious case of the dolphin. But elsewhere?

The concept of other worlds has been part of literature for at least two thousand years. There were tales of people traveling to the Moon and finding intelligent beings there as long ago as Roman times. It was with the coming of the telescope, however, and of Galileo's discovery of mountains, craters, and even "seas" on the Moon that it dawned on people generally that there were literally, and not only fancifully, other worlds.

It was always taken for granted, right down into the twentieth century, that all worlds were inhabited, not only by living things but by intelligent living things. Even Wells, when he had his heroes visit the airless, waterless Moon in *The First Men in the Moon* (1901) had them find intelligent life there.

For the most part, extraterrestrial intelligences were, at first, pictured as harmless. They remained on their own worlds until human beings came to discover them as they had earlier discovered the natives of America, Australia, and the Pacific Islands. If the aliens came to visit us, they were merely observers, content to comment on our faults. Thus, Voltaire, in his *Micromegas* (1752), had a creature from Sirius, eight miles high, together with a smaller being from Saturn, stare in astonishment at human folly.

A new and more dramatic view was ushered in with Wells's *War of the Worlds* (1898). It was written when some astronomers were describing canals on Mars and maintaining that these were the products of a great engineering civilization that was fighting off inevitable desiccation. Wells had his Martians coming to Earth to colonize a more fruitful world. And since Europe had just succeeded in partitioning Africa for its own benefit, with little regard for the Africans, Wells had his Martians treating Earth (and particularly England) in just that same fashion.

War of the Worlds was the first tale of interplanetary warfare, and it opened a new chapter in science fiction. World War I showed the true horror of war once science was applied to destruction, and in the decades that followed, Earth was (science fictionally) invaded from space countless times.

Often the invaders were farther advanced in science, technology, and even in intelligence than Earthpeople were. This made sense, since they reached us and not vice versa. Then, too, advanced science and intelligence went along (as almost always) with evil, so that the invaders would destroy Earthmen without compunction.

Perhaps the most vicious invaders were those in Heinlein's *The Puppet Masters* (1951), sluglike parasites that fastened themselves on a human's back and took over control of his brain and body. Certainly the most devastating are Fred Saberhagen's "Berserkers." In a series of stories featuring these, human explorers and colonists, spreading through interstellar space, meet an implacable foe—lifeless, automated giant warships that are directed by self-contained computer intelligences programmed to wipe out all life, wherever they find it. This is the man-machine struggle carried to the ultimate.

In the end, since it is we human beings who tell the stories, the aliens are usually defeated. This might be through no direct action by human beings but through the force of circumstance as when the Martian invaders in *War of the Worlds* prove not to be immune to Earthly decay bacteria. The defeat could also come through the action of parasites deliberately deployed by human beings as in de Camp's "Divide and Rule" (1939) or through sheer heroism as in "Tumithak of the Corridors" by Charles R. Tanner (1932).

Campbell was sufficiently Earth-centered, in fact, to insist that human beings *must* win in the end and would not allow a human defeat. Unwilling to accept this limitation, Asimov evaded it by dealing with a Galaxy that had only a single intelligence, the human being, in his *Foundation Trilogy*, the first portion of which was published in 1942. It was the first time an all-human galaxy was portrayed.

There were also attempts to portray extraterrestrial intelligences as friendly, even in some cases forming a brotherhood-of-intelligence with Earthpeople. This was most dramatically the case in Edward E. Smith's *Galactic Patrol* (1937) and its sequels, where intelligent beings of all sorts were combined in support of humane civilization against another combination-of-intelligences that was destructive.

In Smith's Manichaean view of the Universe, knowledge in itself was not evil and, when used for good, will win. Just as in the Judeo-Christian Universe, God is more intelligent than Satan and therefore prevails, so the God-surrogate in Smith's stories is more intelligent than the forces of evil and must prevail.

Smith also pioneered in presenting his extraterrestrials as not necessarily human in form. Only too often, an extraterrestrial, except for a few superficial differences (green skin, antennae, two navels), is clearly a primate and usually merely a new species of anthropoid ape.

This tendency becomes an overwhelming necessity in the movies and TV, where, whatever the shape of an extraterrestrial intelligence, it is a human actor who must be converted into that shape.

Smith, however, with the greater freedom of the printed word, had intelligent dragons, intelligent featureless cylinders, intelligent gaseous beings. Since then, science fiction writers have branched out in both directions. We have had intelligent astronomical objects in Fred Hoyle's *The Black Cloud* (1957) and intelligent protozoa in James Blish's "Surface Tension" (1952).

About a quarter of a century ago, Arthur C. Clarke commented that human intelligence may, itself, be but an evolutionary step on the road to machine intelligence: self-aware, fully intelligent computers that can think at the speed of light. In a yet-to-be-published novel, physicist-writer Gregory Benford postulates that biological intelligent species may be inherently short-lived, on the evolutionary time scale of the stars, but that metal-and-electronic machine intelligences may last for eons.

Thus it may be that when we actually do find intelligent species among the stars, they will not be remotely human. They may not even be biological entities.

(The Myth of the Machine)

The subject of the treatment of artificial intelligence in science fiction, which I dealt with, to some extent, in the previous essay, was something I was asked to make central by Patricia Warrick, a remarkably intelligent and charming academician.

She was doing an anthology called Science Fiction: Contemporary Mythology, *and each group of stories was to be preceded by a rather philosophical commentary by some well-known science fiction personality. I was asked to do the commentary on the section entitled "The Machine and the Robot."*

23. THE MYTH OF THE MACHINE*

To a physicist, a machine is any device that transfers a force from the point where it is applied to another point where it is used and, in the process, changes its intensity or direction.

In this sense it is difficult for a human being to make use of anything that is not part of his body without, in the process, using a machine. A couple of million years ago, when one could scarcely decide whether the most advanced hominids were more human-like than apelike, pebbles were already being chipped and their sharp edges used to cut or scrape.

And even a chipped pebble is a machine, for the force applied to the blunt edge by the hand is transmitted to the sharp end and, in the process, intensified. The force spread over the large area of the blunt end is equal to the force spread over the small area of the sharp end. The pressure (force per area) is therefore increased, and without ever increasing the total force, that force is in-

tensified in action. The sharp-edged pebble could, by the greater
pressure it exerts, force its way through an object, as a rounded
pebble (or a man's hand) could not.

In actual practice, however, few people, other than physicists at
their most rigid, would call a chipped pebble a machine. In actual
practice, we think of machines as relatively complicated devices,
and are more likely to use the name if the device is somewhat removed from direct human guidance and manipulation.

The further a device is removed from human control, the more
authentically mechanical it seems, and the whole trend in technology has been to devise machines that are less and less under direct
human control and more and more seem to have the beginning of
a will of their own. A chipped pebble is almost part of the hand it
never leaves. A thrown spear declares a sort of independence the
moment it is released.

The clear progression away from direct and immediate control
made it possible for human beings, even in primitive times, to
slide forward into extrapolation, and to picture devices still less
controllable, still more independent than anything of which they
had direct experience. Immediately we have a form of fantasy—
which some, defining the term more broadly than I would, might
even call science fiction.

Man can move on his feet by direct and intimate control; or on
horseback, controlling the more powerful animal muscles by rein
and heel; or on ship, making use of the invisible power of the
wind. Why not progress into further etherealization by way of
seven-league boots, flying carpets, self-propelled boats? The power
used in these cases was "magic," the tapping of the superhuman
and transcendental energies of gods or demons.

Nor did these imaginings concern only the increased physical
power of inanimate objects, but even increased mental power of
objects which were still viewed as essentially inanimate. Artificial
intelligence is not really a modern concept.

Hephaistos, the Greek god of the forge, is pictured in the *Iliad*
as having golden mechanical women, which were as mobile and as
intelligent as flesh-and-blood women, and which helped him in his
palace.

Why not? After all, if a human smith makes inanimate metal

objects of the base metal iron, why should not a god-smith make far more clever inanimate metal objects of the noble metal gold? It is an easy extrapolation, of the sort that comes as second nature to science fiction writers (who, in primitive times, had to be myth-makers, in default of science).

But human artisans, if clever enough, could also make mechanical human beings. Consider Talos, a bronze warrior made by that Thomas Edison of the Greek myths, Daedalus. Talos guarded the shores of Crete, circling the island once each day and keeping off all intruders. The fluid that kept him alive was kept within his body by a plug at his heel. When the Argonauts landed on Crete, Medea used her magic to pull out the plug and Talos lost all his pseudoanimation.

(It is easy to ascribe a symbolic meaning to this myth. Crete, starting in the fourth century, before the Greeks had yet entered Greece, had a navy, the first working navy in human history. The Cretan navy made it possible for the islanders to establish an empire over what became the nearby islands and mainland. The Greek barbarians, invading the land, were more or less under Cretan dominion to begin with. The bronze-armored warriors carried by the ships guarded the Cretan mainland for two thousand years —and then failed. The plug was pulled, so to speak, when the island of Thera exploded in a vast volcanic eruption in 1500 BC and a tsunami weakened the Cretan civilization—and the Greeks took over fifty years later or so. Still, the fact that a myth is a sort of vague and distorted recall of something actual does not alter its function of indicating a way of human thinking.)

From the start, then, the machine has faced mankind with a double aspect. As long as it is completely under human control, it is useful and good and makes a better life for people. However, it is the experience of mankind (and was already his experience in quite early times) that technology is a cumulative thing, that machines are invariably improved, and that the improvement is always in the direction of etherealization, always in the direction of less human control and more auto-control—and at an accelerating rate.

As the human control decreases, the machine becomes frightening in exact proportion. Even when the human control is not visibly decreasing, or is doing so at an excessively low rate, it is a simple task for human ingenuity to look forward to a time when the machine may go out of control altogether, and the fear of that can be felt in advance.

What is the fear?

The simplest and most obvious fear is that of the possible harm that comes from machinery out of control. In fact, any technological advance, however fundamental, has this double aspect of good/harm and, in response, is viewed with a double aspect of love/fear.

Fire warms you, gives you light, cooks your food, smelts your ore—and, out of control, burns and kills. Your knives and spears kill your animal enemies and your human foes and, out of *your* control, are used by your foes to kill you. You can run down the list and build examples indefinitely and there has never been any human activity which, on getting out of control and doing harm, has not raised the sigh among many of, "Oh, if we had only stuck to the simple and virtuous lives of our ancestors who were not cursed with this newfangled misery."

Yet is this fear of piecemeal harm from this advance or that the kind of deep-seated terror so difficult to express that it finds its way into the myths?

I think not. Fear of machinery for the discomfort and occasional harm it brings has (at least until very recently) not moved humanity to more than that occasional sigh. The love of the uses of machinery has always far overbalanced such fears, as we might judge if we consider that at no time in the history of mankind has any culture *voluntarily* given up significant technological advance because of the inconvenience or harm of its side effects. There have been involuntary retreats from technology as a result of warfare, civil strife, epidemics, or natural disasters, but the results of that are precisely what we call a "dark age," and the population suffering from one does its best over the generations to get back on the track and restore the technology.

Mankind has always chosen to counter the evils of technology, not by abandonment of technology, but by additional technology. The smoke of an indoor fire was countered by the chimney. The danger of the spear was countered by the shield. The danger of the mass army was countered by the city wall.

This attitude, despite the steady drizzle of backwardist outcries, has continued to the present. Thus the characteristic technological product of our present life is the automobile. It pollutes the air, assaults our eardrums, kills fifty thousand Americans a year and inflicts survivable injuries on hundreds of thousands.

Does anyone seriously expect Americans to give up their murderous little pets voluntarily? Even those who attend rallies to denounce the mechanization of modern life are quite likely to reach those rallies by automobile.

The first moment, when the magnitude of possible evil was seen by *many* people as uncounterable by *any* conceivable good, came with the fission bomb in 1945. Never before had any technological advance set off demands for abandonment by so large a percentage of the population.

In fact, the reaction to the fission bomb set a new fashion. People were readier to oppose other advances they saw as unacceptably harmful in their side effects—biological warfare, the SST, certain genetic experiments on micro-organisms, breeder reactors, and so on.

And even so, not one of these items has yet been given up.

But we're on the right track. The fear of the machine is not at the deepest level of the soul if the harm it does is accompanied by good, too; or if the harm is merely to some people—the few who happen to be on the spot in a vehicular collision, for instance.

The majority, after all, escape and reap the good of the machine.

No, it is when the machine threatens all mankind in any way so that each individual human being begins to feel that he, *himself*, will not escape, that fear overwhelms love.

But since technology has begun to threaten the human race as a whole only in the last thirty years, were we immune to fear before that—or has the human race always been threatened?

After all, is physical destruction by brute energy of a type only now in our fist, the only way in which human beings can be destroyed? Might not the machine destroy the essence of humanity, our minds and souls, even while leaving our bodies intact and secure and comfortable?

It is a common fear, for instance, that television makes people unable to read, and pocket computers will make them unable to add. Or think of the Spartan king who, on observing a catapult in action, mourned that that would put an end to human valor.

Certainly such subtle threats to humanity have existed and been recognized through all the long ages when man's feeble control over nature made it impossible for him to do himself very much physical harm.

The fear that machinery might make men effete is not yet, in my opinion, the basic and greatest fear. The one (it seems to me) that hits closest to the core is the general fear of irreversible change. Consider:

There are two kinds of change that we can gather from the Universe about us. One is cyclic and benign.

Day both follows and is followed by night. Summer both follows and is followed by winter. Rain both follows and is followed by clear weather, and the net result is, therefore, no change. That may be boring, but it is comfortable and induces a feeling of security.

In fact, so comfortable is the notion of short-term cyclic change, implying long-term changelessness, that human beings labor to find it everywhere. In human affairs, there is the notion that one generation both follows and is followed by another, that one dynasty both follows and is followed by another, that one empire both follows and is followed by another. It is not a good analogy to the cycles of nature since the repetitions are not exact, but it is good enough to be comforting.

So strongly do human beings want the comfort of cycles that they will seize upon one even when the evidence is insufficient—or even when it actually points the other way.

With respect to the Universe, what evidence we have points to a hyperbolic evolution; a Universe that expands forever out of the initial big bang and ends as formless gas and black holes. Yet our emotions drag us, against the evidence, to notions of oscillating, cyclic, repeating universes, in which even the black holes are merely gateways to new big bangs.

But then there is the other change, to be avoided at all costs— the irreversible, malignant change; the one-way change; the permanent change; the change-never-to-return.

What is so fearful about it? The fact is that there is one such change that lies so close to ourselves that it distorts the entire Universe for us.

We are, after all, old, and though we were once young we shall never be young again. Irreversible! Our friends are dead, and though they were once alive, they shall never be alive again. Irreversible! The fact is that life ends in death and that is not a cyclic change and we fear that end and know it is useless to fight it.

What is worse is that the Universe doesn't die with us. Callously and immortally it continues onward in its cyclic changes, adding to the injury of death the insult of indifference.

And what is still worse is that other human beings don't die with us. There are younger human beings, born later, who were helpless and dependent on us to start with, but who grow into supplanting nemeses and take our places as we age and die. To the injury of death is added the insult of supplantation.

Did I say it is useless to fight this horror of death accompanied by indifference and supplantation? Not quite. The uselessness is apparent only if we cling to the rational, but there is no law that says we must cling to it, and human beings do not, in fact, do so.

Death can be avoided by simply denying it exists. We can suppose that life on Earth is an illusion, a short testing period prior to entry into some afterlife where all is eternal and there is no question of irreversible change. Or we can suppose that it is only the body that is subject to death and that there is an immortal component of ourselves, not subject to irreversible change, which might, after the death of one body, enter another, in indefinite, cyclic repetitions of life.

These mythic inventions of afterlife and transmigration may make life tolerable for many human beings and enable them to face death with reasonable equanimity—but the fear of death and supplantation is only masked and overlaid; it is not removed.

In fact, the Greek myths involve the successive supplantation of one set of immortals by another—in what seems to be a despairing admission that not even eternal life and superhuman power can

remove the danger of irreversible change and the humiliation of
being supplanted.

To the Greeks it was disorder (Chaos) that first ruled the Universe, and it was supplanted by Ouranos (the sky), whose intricate
powdering of stars and complexly moving planets symbolized
order (Kosmos).

But Ouranos was castrated by Kronos, his son. Kronos, his
brothers, his sisters, and their progeny then ruled the universe.

Kronos feared that he would be served by his children as he had
served his father (a kind of cycle of irreversible changes) and
devoured his children as they were born. He was duped by his
wife, however, who managed to save her last-born, Zeus, and spirit
him away to safety. Zeus grew to adult godhood, rescued his sib-
lings from his father's stomach, warred against Kronos and those
who followed him, defeated him, and replaced him as ruler.

(There are supplantation myths among other cultures, too,
even in our own—as the one in which Satan tried to supplant God
and failed; a myth that reached its greatest literary expression in
John Milton's *Paradise Lost*.)

And was Zeus safe? He was attracted to the sea nymph Thetis
and would have married her had he not been informed by the
Fates that Thetis was destined to bear a son mightier than his father. That meant it was not safe for Zeus, or for any other god, either, to marry her. She was therefore forced (much against her
will) to marry Peleus, a mortal, and bear a mortal son, the only
child the myths describe her as having. That son was Achilles,
who was certainly far mightier than his father (and, like Talos,
had only his heel as his weak point through which he might be
killed).

Now, then, translate this fear of irreversible change and of
being supplanted into the relationship of man and machine and
what do we have? Surely the *great* fear is not that machinery will
harm us—but that it will supplant us. It is not that it will render
us ineffective—but that it will make us obsolete.

The ultimate machine is an intelligent machine and there is
only one basic plot to the intelligent-machine story—that it is
created to serve man, but that it ends by dominating man. It can-

not exist without threatening to supplant us, and it must therefore be destroyed or we will be.

There is the danger of the broom of the sorcerer's apprentice, the golem of Rabbi Löw, the monster created by Dr. Frankenstein. As the child born of our body eventually supplants us, so does the machine born of our mind.

Mary Shelley's *Frankenstein,* which appeared in 1818, represents a peak of fear, however, for, as it happened, circumstances conspired to reduce that fear, at least temporarily.

Between the year 1815, which saw the end of a series of general European wars, and 1914, which saw the beginning of another, there was a brief period in which humanity could afford the luxury of optimism concerning its relationship to the machine. The Industrial Revolution seemed suddenly to uplift human power and to bring on dreams of a technological Utopia on Earth in place of the mythic one in Heaven. The good of machines seemed to far outbalance the evil and the response of love far outbalance the response of fear.

It was in that interval that modern science fiction began—and by modern science fiction I refer to a form of literature that deals with societies differing from our own specifically in the level of science and technology, and into which we might conceivably pass from our own society by appropriate changes in that level. (This differentiates science fiction from fantasy in which the fictional society cannot be connected with our own by any rational set of changes.)

Modern science fiction, because of the time of its beginning, took on an optimistic note. Man's relationship to the machine was one of use and control. Man's power grew and man's machines were his faithful tools, bringing him wealth and security and carrying him to the farthest reaches of the universe.

This optimistic note continues to this day, particularly among those writers who were molded in the years before the coming of the fission bomb—notably, Robert Heinlein, Arthur C. Clarke, and myself.

Nevertheless, with World War I, disillusionment set in. Science and technology, which promised an Eden, turned out to be capable of delivering Hell as well. The beautiful airplane that fulfilled the age-old dream of flight could deliver bombs. The chemical techniques that produced anesthetics, dyes, and medicines produced poison gas as well.

The fear of supplantation rose again. In 1921, not long after the end of World War I, Karel Capek's drama *R. U. R.* appeared and it was the tale of Frankenstein again, escalated to the planetary level. Not a single monster was created but millions of robots (Capek's word, meaning "slave," a mechanical one, that is). And it was not a single monster turning upon his single creator, but robots turning on humanity, wiping them out, and supplanting them.

From the beginning of the science fiction magazine in 1926 to 1959 (a third of a century or a generation), optimism and pessimism battled each other in science fiction, with optimism—thanks chiefly to the influence of John W. Campbell, Jr.—having the better of it.

Beginning in 1939, I wrote a series of influential robot stories that self-consciously combated the "Frankenstein complex" and made of the robots the servants, friends, and allies of humanity.

It was pessimism, however, that won in the end, and for two reasons:

First, machinery grew ever more frightening. The fission bomb threatened physical destruction, of course, but worse still was the rapidly advancing electronic computer. Those computers seemed to steal the human soul. Deftly they solved our routine problems and more and more we found ourselves placing our questions in the hands of these machines with increasing faith, and accepting their answers with increasing humility.

All that fission and fusion bombs can do is destroy us, the computer might supplant us.

The second reason is more subtle, for it involved a change in the nature of the science fiction writer.

In the 1950s, competition with TV gradually killed the magazines that supported fiction, and by the time the 1960s arrived the only form of fiction that was flourishing, and even expanding, was science fiction.

This meant that in the 1960s and 1970s, young writers began to write science fiction not because they wanted to, but because it was there—and because nothing else was there. It meant that many of the new generation of science fiction writers had no knowledge of science, no sympathy for it—and were in fact rather hostile to it. Such writers were far more ready to accept the fear half of the love/fear relationship of man to machine.

As a result, contemporary science fiction, far more often than not, is presenting us, over and over, with the myth of the child supplanting the parent, Zeus supplanting Kronos, Satan supplanting God, the machine supplanting humanity.

—But allow me my own cynical commentary at the end. Remember that although Kronos foresaw the danger of being supplanted, and though he destroyed his children to prevent it—he was supplanted anyway, and rightly so, for Zeus was the better ruler.

So it may be that although we will hate and fight the machines, we will be supplanted anyway, and rightly so, for the intelligent machines to which we will give birth may, better than we, carry on the striving toward the goal of understanding and using the Universe, climbing to heights we ourselves could never aspire to.

(Science Fiction from the Soviet Union)
(More Science Fiction from the Soviet Union)

In 1962, Collier Books published a collection of six stories by Soviet science fiction writers, and then five more in a separate collection.

I had nothing to do with the choice of the stories, but Collier Books asked me to write an introduction to the first, and when that worked out well (from their standpoint), they asked me to write an introduction to the second as well.

As it happened, I came up with some thoughts on the historical development of science fiction that I had not worked out previously, so here are both introductions.

24. SCIENCE FICTION FROM THE SOVIET UNION*

Science fiction from the Soviet Union?

It seems strange, somehow—and yet why should it seem strange? To me, especially! I am, myself, a prominent science fiction writer (so I am told) here in the United States, and yet I was born in the Soviet Union. Presumably, then, there is nothing in the fact of being born on Soviet territory that of itself militates against the ability to write science fiction.

Yet it still seems strange and let me explain why.

A series of my stories were translated into German once, and I remarked to the editor who had supervised the task that it read well except for the jarring notes introduced by the names of the characters, particularly one named Mike Donovan.

"Since the particular names of the characters play no part in the story, why not make them German?" I asked.

"Never," said the editor. "If I did, it wouldn't sound like science fiction. To a European, science fiction needs American characters to sound like the real thing."

And there you are. Science fiction is a peculiarly American phenomenon; so American that foreigners can have their own brand only by imitating us closely.

The Soviets, however, kept free of American science fiction until very recently (anthologies of American science fiction stories are now appearing in the Soviet Union). How, then, can there be any Soviet science fiction?

Perhaps the answer is that in its origins, science fiction was not peculiarly American. To be sure, science fiction in the modern sense was invented by an American in the 1830s. At the time, the steam engine was bringing on the abolition of home industry and of sailing vessels, balloons were carrying man into the sky, and the power of science was beginning to be everywhere evident.

Therefore Edgar Allan Poe began to extrapolate. He wrote a story in which a balloon carried man not only into the atmosphere, but clear to the Moon. It was not very seriously meant, but many of its details were carefully and rationally worked out. This alone made the story completely different from earlier stories of Moon voyages (dating as far back as the Roman Empire, and commonly miscalled science fiction), in which no rationality was involved or even attempted, but in which social satire and moral teachings were the only objects in view. Poe wrote other pieces that would be called science fiction, too, but these were all relatively minor efforts, and he was (and still is) far better known for his Gothic horror tales.

When Poe's works were translated into French by Baudelaire, they attracted the attention of a young Frenchman named Jules Verne. He, too, took to writing of *voyages extraordinaire*," of submarines under the ocean, of trips to the supposedly hollow center of the earth, of flights out of a giant cannon and to the moon. It was these tales by Jules Verne that first introduced science fiction to a wide audience not only in France but in other countries as well, notably in the United States and in the Russian Empire, for Verne was (and still is) enormously popular both in English and in Russian.

Even as late as 1926, the most famous science fiction writer of all times, here in America, was still the Frenchman Jules Verne, with the Englishman H. G. Wells in second place. Our own Poe was nearly forgotten, as far as science fiction was concerned. The most popular twentieth-century American science fiction writer was then Edgar Rice Burroughs, who wrote for a juvenile audience.

How was it, then, that in one generation, science fiction came to be considered a peculiarly American phenomenon, not only here in the United States, but throughout Europe?

It came about because, in 1926 in the United States, a man named Hugo Gernsback founded a magazine called *Amazing Stories*, the first periodical published anywhere in the world to be devoted exclusively to works of science fiction.

At first, so few were the American writers in the field, Gernsback had to fill his magazine with H. G. Wells reprints and with translations of German science fiction novels. Gradually, however, American writers were developed. With a small but steady (and rather noncompetitive) market, young writers, many still in their teens, found they could put their science enthusiasms onto paper, indulge their powers of speculation to the limit of their bent, and actually be paid small sums for doing it. By the middle 1930s, science fiction had at its disposal three magazines and several tens of thousands of devoted readers, mostly in their teens and twenties.

Nothing like this took place in western Europe, except for a small and belated English venture. When, in the 1950s, science fiction magazines struggled to life on the Continent, in nations such as France, Italy, Germany, and Sweden, the initial Gernsback phenomenon was reversed. These foreign magazines depended for their contents on translations of American stories and are often little more than foreign editions of this or that American magazine.

To one European nation, however, the supply of American science fiction was useless and that nation was, of course, the Soviet

Union. American science fiction is usually permeated with American modes of thought and this does not tend to make the stories palatable to the Soviets. In fact, in the early days of the Cold War, an important Soviet literary publication published an article denouncing American science fiction as militarist, racist, and fascist. By selecting with great care the stories they cited, they made a rather plausible case.

It was widely felt, at the time, that this strong condemnation included science fiction as a whole, and that the Soviets completely eschewed this form of literature. Yet—surprise, surprise— they haven't. Here in this present volume are a half-dozen science fiction stories written by a half-dozen Soviet writers, representative, presumably, of a much larger whole. Obviously there *is* such a thing as Soviet science fiction.

Now, with the wisdom of hindsight, we can see that it had to be so and that the Soviet condemnation of science fiction could only have been intended for *American* science fiction. After all, the Soviets have stressed the importance of science, for almost two generations now, far more than we ourselves have. Students have been encouraged to go into science, by all means, and a scientific career, if it can be managed, is the gateway to as much comfort and luxury as the Soviet Union can afford to hand out. In a society so science-centered, it isn't reasonable to suppose that a form of literature which makes science and scientists the peculiar heroes of the time would not be developed.

In fact, if there was any doubt that the Soviet Union was science fiction oriented before Sputnik I went off like an alarm in the night, surely there was no doubt afterward.

To the science fiction fan, there is something peculiarly fascinating about Soviet science fiction. What can it be like? Of all national varieties of science fiction, it can least have felt the American influence. It descended (like our own, but independently) from Jules Verne. At best, our science fiction and their science fiction are cousins.

What differences have resulted, then, if any?

Well, in order to decide, let me begin by explaining that even in the single generation of American science fiction since Gernsback first put out his magazine, there has been time for three stages to develop.

The first, from 1926 to 1938, saw science fiction largely in the hands of young writers, usually without much formal scientific education. The stories were still "extraordinary voyages." They were primarily adventure stories, but under the exotic conditions of outer space and distant worlds. Science was secondary and generally sounded as though it were gleaned from the Sunday supplements.

In 1938, however, John W. Campbell, Jr., became editor of *Astounding Stories* and promptly brought a new and fresh atmosphere into science fiction. Himself technically trained, he insisted on reasonably accurate science and reasonably plausible extrapolation. The science fiction readers had themselves grown older and more sophisticated and were no longer content with the bang-bang that permeated early science fiction. New writers, with technical training and scientific education, were encouraged. It was in *Astounding,* therefore, that accurate forecasts of the atomic bomb and of several other soon-to-be phenomena appeared.

In 1950 came the third stage. A magazine named *Galaxy Science Fiction* appeared under the editorship of Horace L. Gold. Almost at once it began to emphasize the social structures of the future, while retaining the technological sophistication of the second stage. With the spotlight moving toward society, the cast of characters grew more markedly bisexual. Science fiction of the first and second stages had been notoriously masculine, with women entering in secondary roles if at all. In the third stage, however, they began to bear a more nearly equal share of the burden, and sex itself became noticeable.

With the reminder that the cleavage between these stages was never clear nor clean, I can say, in summary:

Stage One (1926–1938)—Adventure dominant
Stage Two (1938–1950)—Technology dominant
Stage Three (1950– ?)—Sociology dominant

Against this background, what can we say about Soviet science fiction as presented in this book?

Before we say anything, we had better remember that we are

dealing with only half a dozen stories deliberately selected with an English-speaking audience in mind. They may therefore not be at all representative of the field as a whole.

For instance, they do contain passages that are pro-Soviet and anti-Western. These, however, are quite subdued and scarcely deserve the name of propaganda. One can pick up any American science fiction magazine at random and find much more self-extollation and many more anti-Soviet comments. Presumably, the particular stories in this book were selected in part for their relative inoffensiveness, and it might be risky to assume that all Soviet science fiction was nonchauvinistic to such an extent.

Even allowing for the effects of selectivity, however, we can draw some conclusions. Thus, the first story, "Hoity-Toity" (clearly the oldest in the book), is a rather typical Stage One story. The remaining stories are Stage Two.

The latter are marked by painstaking efforts at technological correctness that go so far as to produce in the story "A Visitor from Outer Space," for instance, a running footnote longer than the story itself. (The footnote is intended to shore up a rather outlandish theory of the Soviet astronomer Tikhov, concerning the Siberian meteorite strike of 1908; it is completely unnecessary, however, and tedious besides, and has been mercifully omitted from the present edition.)

The question is: Is it merely chance that omits Stage Three stories or have the Soviets not yet reached that stage? It is my guess that the latter alternative is actually the case and that there is no Soviet Stage Three. The Soviet people are told, and presumably believe, that they are building a new society which is bound, by the sheer attractiveness of its superior workability, to become the dominant society all over the world. (America had much the same feeling in the nineteenth century.) It would amount, then, almost to a lack of patriotism for a Soviet writer to suggest that other societies were possible in the future, or even to look too closely at the present one.

What else can we deduce from the stories in this book? There is an absence of any suggestion of the "mad scientist" who plans to take over the world by means of evil intentions. We had them in plenty in our Stage One and Stage Two. If the stories in this book are representative in this respect, they may be evidence of less anti-intellectualism in the Soviet Union than here in the United States. (It is only fair to say that the mad scientist has all but disappeared from American Stage Three science fiction.)

The stories in this collection are marked by humane feeling. Obviously, if the Soviets are deep, dark villains (as many Americans believe), they aren't aware of it themselves, but picture themselves as rather nice fellows.

And, interestingly enough, all the stories deal with the present or with the relatively near future. I suspect this is not mere coincidence. To go into the far future (as American science fiction often does) tempts the writer to portray a radically different society. It is safer to stay closer to home.

Only in one spot, for one brief scene, is the far future glancingly depicted and that is at the very end of "Professor Bern's Awakening." The date of that future is given as September 12, 18,879 of the Era of Liberated Man. However, it is not stated when the Era began, nor what it was that Man was Liberated from.

An organization called the "World Academy" is mentioned in that same passage. If, indeed, the future holds a true world organization and if man is truly liberated, then perhaps the future depicted even so briefly is one toward which Americans and Soviet citizens alike, as well as all others, can look forward to with hope and satisfaction.

25. MORE SCIENCE FICTION FROM THE SOVIET UNION*

In the previous essay, I divided the development of American science fiction into three stages.

> Stage One: Adventure dominant
> Stage Two: Technology dominant
> Stage Three: Sociology dominant

I pointed out that the best of contemporary American science fiction was in Stage Three, dealing with the possible societies of the future that might or might not develop in response to new gadgets, rather than with the gadgets themselves. Soviet science fiction, as represented by the six stories in the earlier book, was in Stage Two, dealing with the gadgets themselves.

I even hazarded the guess that Soviet science fiction might have difficulty reaching Stage Three since social criticism is less acceptable in the Soviet Union than it is here. In making this guess, however, I (of all people!) did not take into account the infinite flexibility of the science fiction form. For here in this book are examples of Stage Three tales—though of a particular specialized form of Stage Three.

To explain what I mean, let me go into the possibilities of Stage Three science fiction in some detail.

Suppose it were your intention to construct (fictionally) a new type of society and to investigate the behavior of human beings living within that society. How would you go about it?

To my way of thinking, you can begin by making one of three possible gambits:

a) What if—
b) If only—
c) If this goes on—

The first gambit, call it Stage Three-A, produces the problem story with no necessary application to the modern day. Thus, you might begin by saying:

"What if a human colony on Mars lacks water and cannot get it from Earth?"

You would then find yourself describing a society in which water conservation is all-important; in which visitors bring their own filled water flasks; in which people out of water stop at a water-filling station and have their flasks filled out of a meter-equipped water pump. Standards of personal hygiene might change.

The actual plot of the story, the suspense, the conflict, ought to arise—if this were a first-class story—out of the particular needs and frustrations of people in such a society. The author, while attending to the plot, may well find his chief amusement, however, in designing the little details (the filigree work, if you like) of the society, even where they do not have any direct connection with the plot.

As you see, though, such a story has no lesson to teach with respect to the advanced societies of the here and now. Oh, we are approaching a fresh-water shortage, but it seems quite likely we will learn how to make do by desalting seawater. And, in any case, we have other shortages that will intervene to make life miserable long before we run out of water.

Stage Three-A is strictly contemporary. I don't know of any science fiction story possessing this detached "What if—" gambit, written prior to the 1920s.

The other two gambits, Stage Three-B and Stage Three-C, are quite old, however, and in fact antedate modern science fiction.

Stage Three-B with its "If only—" gambit would involve stories based upon thoughts such as these: "If only advancement were dictated by ability rather than birth" or "If only men were truly religious" or "If only philosophers were kings" or even "If only I could fly."

The result of such thoughts is likely to be a description of what the author would consider an ideal society. Isaiah depicted one when he said, ". . . and they shall beat their swords into plowshares, and their spears into pruning-hooks: nation shall not lift up sword against nation, neither shall they learn war any more."

That was in answer to the thought, "If only the last days were here and all men turned their hearts to God."

Plato depicted an ideal society in *The Republic* in answer to the thought: "If only a society built on justice could be designed."

Sir Thomas More, in 1516, wrote of an ideal society on an island he called Utopia. (He wrote it in Latin and it was not translated into English until 1551.) The word "Utopia" comes from a Greek root meaning "nowhere," so it is a bitter enough name.

The book proved so popular that "Utopia" has come to mean any ideal society. In fact, the Stage Three-B story has come to be known as a "Utopia story," and the Germans frequently use this expression to signify science fiction in general.

A Stage Three-B "Utopia story" requires two things: a feeling of bitterness against society as it exists, and a feeling of hope that there is some definite scheme or device which could bring about an ideal society, if only applied.

Samuel Butler, for instance, in his book *Erewhon* (which is "nowhere" spelled backward if you count "wh" as a single letter, and is thus the literal English equivalent of Utopia) found this idealizing scheme in socialism and atheism.

Modern American science fiction makes virtually no use of the Stage Three-B story, however. Part of the reason is that the bitterness against society is lacking. The American social and economic system may not be flawless, but there is serious doubt among our science fiction writers that any of the alternatives will represent an improvement. In fact, there is a prevalent doubt that *any* conceivable scheme will automatically lead to a Utopia.

Rather there is the fear of the reverse. Even to remain as well off as we are now, let alone make progress in the direction of the ideal (whatever that may be), means a constant battle against certain deteriorations that will inevitably take place if we don't watch out.

Therefore, the third gambit, "If this goes on—" has taken the place of the Utopia.

It is not, heaven knows, the invention of the American science fiction writer. One of the best-known examples of Stage Three-C is to be found in Jonathan Swift's *Gulliver's Travels*, published in 1726. This book is divided into four parts, of which the fourth is a Stage Three-B Utopia based on the gambit, "If only horses were as smart as human beings." The first and best-known portion, however, is Gulliver's involvement with the Lilliputians and that is a Stage Three-C, "If this goes on—" story.

The Lilliputians are a savage caricature of the British court and government. British society is reduced to the six-inch level and its faults and flaws and foibles are carried to the extreme, made more petty, more ridiculous, more mean and foolish. "If this goes on," in other words, "it is to this you will descend."

Modern examples of the Stage Three-C story in the "mainstream" are George Orwell's *1984* in which the gambit is: "If the tendency toward statism goes on—" and Aldous Huxley's *Brave New World* in which the gambit is: "If the advance of a soul-less technology goes on—"

American science fiction writers have taken to Stage Three-C with avidity. An excellent example, for instance, is "Gravy Planet" by Frederik Pohl and Cyril Kornbluth (which appeared, in book form, under the title of *Space Merchants*). It deals with a dreadfully overpopulated world in which advertising techniques have been made the only acceptable guide to human behavior. Its gambits are: "If the population explosion goes on—" and "If the theory that anything that is good for business is morally correct goes on—"

Stage Three-C stories have, with excellent logic, been termed "Anti-Utopia stories."

Now where, according to this analysis, can Soviet science fiction find a haven in Stage Three?

The Stage Three-A "What if—" story might prove embarrassing

if it were considered a sign of dissatisfaction with existing institutions. The Stage Three-B "If only—" would be even worse, and the warning anti-Utopianism of "If this goes on—" is worst of all.

It was by this reasoning that I eliminated the possibility of Stage Three science fiction within the Soviet Union.

However, I overlooked a possible hybrid form, which I might call "Stage Three-C/B." It is the "If this goes on—" beginning with the "If only—" ending.

The Soviet science fiction writer need only say: "If this goes on, we will achieve the ideal society" and he can proceed to write socially approved Utopia stories. It is exactly this that you will find in the present volume.

The clearest example is the lead story, "The Heart of the Serpent," by Ivan Yefremov. Here the gambit is: "If this (the Communist society) goes on, man's goodness and nobility will be free to develop and people will live under the reign of love."

On the other hand, Yefremov points out that this happy eventuality is impossible under capitalism.

In fact, the story is set in deliberate opposition to a well-known American science fiction story called "First Contact." This was written by Murray Leinster and appeared in the May 1945 issue of *Astounding Science Fiction.*

Yefremov gives the plot of the American story in some detail; in essentials, it deals with the first meeting of human beings (in a spaceship) with alien intelligences (in another spaceship). A stalemate arises out of mutual distrust and a solution is found in the psychology of shrewd business practice.

The people in Yefremov's story denounce an attitude that seems to find a relationship between different intelligences based only on either trade or war, and deplore the traces of American nationalism. The story goes on to deal with Yefremov's own version of a "First Contact" based on friendship and love.

The other stories, to a greater or lesser extent, similarly deal with the universal reign of love, a reign confined not only to the human species.

"Siema" is a robot story, one in which the old Frankenstein motif is to be found—the creature that turns upon its creator. This has been done and done and done in American science fiction, and always with the same moral: There are some things it is not fit for man to meddle with, and the creation of life, or pseudolife, is one of them.

This Frankenstein motif is terribly old hat among us now, but here it is among the Soviets—yet without the moral! The designer must simply improve the design. And the narrator ends the story by saying, "So we would soon be hearing about a new Siema. Splendid!"

One does not fear the products of science. One loves them!

The Strugatsky brothers, in "Six Matches," deal with a society in which scientists are so lovingly eager to advance science that they perform dangerous experiments upon themselves against the loving orders of the government, as represented by the "Labor Protection Inspector," who pleads with them to use animals instead. The final kicker to that story, by the way, strikes me as the most nearly American touch in the whole book.

In "The Trial of Tantalus" by Victor Saparin, the doctrine of love is carried to its extreme. In an article I myself wrote in 1958, I pointed out that it was too much to expect man to protect inimical forms of life. I said, "I don't suppose anyone would raise a finger to prevent the extinction of the tubercle bacillus."

Well, here is a story in which even pathogenic microorganisms are defended and cared for and kept from extinction.

How can we interpret this "reign of love" in view of what we are told about Soviet behavior and motives? Is it all a fake?

I suppose, if one were sufficiently skeptical, one might suppose these stories were written strictly for American consumption and are published only in order to confuse us and weaken our will; that the Soviet citizen is not allowed to see them, but is fed on pure hate.

I do not believe this, however.

A more reasonable supposition is that the stories are indeed among those written for Soviet consumption but are carefully selected and are, therefore, not representative. To check on that, one would have to obtain Soviet science fiction magazines or the equivalent and see what the general run of unselected material is like.

On the whole, though, what I would like to believe is that the Soviet citizen would really like to see the coming of a reign of love when "nation shall not lift up sword against nation, neither shall they learn war any more."

Why, after all, should he not?

If only we could believe it is what they really want, and if only they could believe it is what we really want, then perhaps things would yet end well.

V

SCIENCE FICTION WRITERS

(The First Science Fiction Novel)

Now and then, I am given a chance to discuss the history of science fiction not in a general way but in connection with a single writer of historic importance, or even a single book or story by that writer.

Such opportunities were, for instance, granted me by Caedmon Records, which put out excellent readings of various science fiction classics and then sometimes came to me for an essay related to the reading.

The following essay accompanied the recording of Mary Shelley's Frankenstein, *for instance. I am putting it first in this section because Shelley is the earliest writer I am considering and I intend to work my way forward more or less chronologically.*

26. THE FIRST SCIENCE FICTION NOVEL*

The day came, once, when the first science fiction novel was written and published.

To be sure, stories had been written, centuries before, that, in hindsight, *seemed* to be science fiction. We might even consider Homer's tales of one-eyed giants, and of witches, to have been science fiction of a sort.

Those early tales, however, had nothing to do with societies changed by technological advance, and it is that which is the hallmark of true science fiction.

Even stories about flights to the Moon, some of which were written eighteen centuries ago, made no use of scientific advance. People reached the Moon by means of waterspouts, or spirits, or

* Copyright © 1977 by Caedmon

birds, all of which were established parts of the world the writers knew. In 1657, Cyrano de Bergerac had suggested rockets as a way for reaching the Moon, but his hero didn't use them.

Right into the beginning of the nineteenth century, no one thought of scientific advance as a basic ingredient in a story. That's not surprising since, until the beginning of the nineteenth century, science advanced very slowly and its relationship to ordinary life was never obvious to the general population. But then came those applications of science and technology that led to the Industrial Revolution, and people began to sit up and take notice.

In 1771, an Italian anatomist, Luigi Galvani, noticed that the muscles of dissected frog legs twitched wildly when a spark from a static electric machine happened to strike them, or when a metal scalpel touched them while such a machine was in operation, even if the sparks made no direct contact.

Eventually, he discovered that frog-leg muscles would twitch in the complete absence of electric sparks anywhere if they made contact with two different metals, such as iron and brass, at the same time. Then, in 1800, another Italian scientist, Count Alessandro Volta, showed that two different metals could serve as the source of an electric current.

What it all came to was that electricity, the study of which had entered high gear only in the previous half century, had some mysterious but apparently intimate connection with life. People even began to speculate on the possibility of the scientific creation of life.

In 1816, Lord Byron was relaxing on the shores of Lake Geneva, having fled England and a horrible marriage. With him was another great poet, Percy Bysshe Shelley, who had fled England with his eighteen-year-old mistress, Mary Wollstonecraft Godwin. (They married at the end of the year after the first Mrs. Shelley committed suicide.) Others came, too, in order to share the delights of witty conversation.

Byron was interested, in a dilettantish way, in science and knew of the work of Galvani and Volta. It seemed to the company, as they conversed, that it would be an excellent idea to write scientific romances and, in their enthusiasm, all agreed to try their hand at it.

None of them actually produced anything except Mary. During a sleepless night, she thought of the creation of life—of a huge manlike object showing the first signs of life.

She sat down to write, and in 1818, her book *Frankenstein, or the Modern Prometheus,* was published. The hero was Victor Frankenstein who, like Galvani, was an anatomist, but who advanced beyond Galvani by infusing life into a whole body rather than into an isolated muscle, and doing so permanently rather than transiently.

There had been tales of dead objects endowed with life in the past, even manlike objects. Always, however, the life source had been magic or the supernatural. The tale of the sorcerer's apprentice infusing life into a broomstick is an example. Jewish folklore tells of the golem, created by the sixteenth-century Rabbi Löw of Prague, and that was done by the use of the ineffable name of God.

Mary Shelley was the first to make use of a new finding of science which she advanced further to a logical extreme, and it is that which makes *Frankenstein* the first true science fiction novel.

What's more, it caught the popular fancy and started Mrs. Shelley on her literary career. The popularity of the tale has never died. The tragedy of the unnamed Monster which Frankenstein had created, a Monster which found that its hideous mien brought it only misery, and the revenge it took on the man who gave it existence but not happiness, has remained in our minds for nearly two centuries. We still call any person destroyed by his own acts "a Frankenstein," and those acts, "a Frankenstein monster."

(The First Science Fiction Writer)
(The Hole in the Middle)

Naturally, Caedmon Records produced readings of a number of the writings of Jules Verne. I was asked to do an essay for three of them, and of these I am including two in this collection; the first for Twenty Thousand Leagues Under the Sea *and the second for* A Journey to the Center of the Earth.

27. THE FIRST SCIENCE FICTION WRITER*

Jules Verne, born in Nantes, France, on February 8, 1828, was the world's first science fiction writer. He was not the first person to write science fiction, of course. He was preceded by Edgar Allan Poe, who was preceded by Mary Wollstonecraft Shelley, who was preceded by a long line of earlier writers who spoke of strange lands and fearsome monsters.

Verne, however, was the first writer to *specialize* in science fiction and to make a living at it, too. He didn't call it science fiction, of course, and neither did anyone else. The very term wasn't invented till a quarter of a century after Verne died in Amiens on March 24, 1905.

Verne studied law to begin with, but was too interested in writing to be able to keep away from it. He became a stockbroker in order to make a living, and wrote plays, librettos, stories, anything he could turn his hand to, without very much success.

Then, in 1863, already in early middle age, he wrote a book called *Five Weeks in a Balloon*. In this book, Verne's balloon was more advanced than the balloons available in reality and could

* Copyright © 1978 by Caedmon

stay aloft much longer, but it was all perfectly credible, just the same. Verne told the story of an "extraordinary voyage" and it proved an instant and surprising success.

Verne realized that the public was hungry for adventures told from the new viewpoints that were made possible by science in an age when optimism concerning the coming scientific advances was at its height. Verne promptly proceeded to write other "extraordinary voyages" and ended by writing eighty novels, many of them what we would now term science fiction, and gained world renown in the process.

In a few years, in fact, he was rich enough to buy an eight-ton shrimp boat and convert it into a vessel for pleasure cruising. Sailing along on top of the vast ocean gave him an idea. He had, in his books, carried adventurers not only through the air but also to the Moon and to the center of the Earth. Why not a sea story from a new vantage point—from beneath!

The result was *Twenty Thousand Leagues Under the Sea*, published in 1870, and translated into English in 1873—the tale of the submarine, *Nautilus*, and its mysterious and misanthropic hero, Captain Nemo ("nemo" in Latin for "no one"). What resulted was a fascinating adventure of sea-bottom exploration which contained a little bit of everything—mysterious ruins of Atlantis, lost ships, embattled sea monsters, and an inconclusive ending hinting at a sequel which duly appeared in 1874 as *The Mysterious Island*.

Verne was a cautious science fiction writer, to be sure, and one who rarely ventured far from reality. That was one of his virtues, for his books carried absolute conviction in their careful attention to detail. Even when he was wrong (for he was no scientist and sometimes misunderstood), he made matters so plausible that few readers could be captious enough to criticize.

In *Twenty Thousand Leagues Under the Sea*, Verne made use of a submarine no one could possibly have built in 1870 (nor, in terms of ornate spaciousness, would one like that be built now), but he did not invent the idea or even the practice of submarining.

The first submarine was built in 1620 by a Dutchman named

Cornelis Brebbel, who submerged it repeatedly in the Thames River.

The first submarine that served as a war vessel was (you'll never guess it) built in 1776 by a Yale student, David Bushnell. It was a one-man craft, called *Turtle*, and was intended for use in planting an explosive charge below the waterline of a British warship in New York Harbor. The attempt was made. The explosive charge didn't hurt the copper-sheathed hull of the warship, but that wasn't the submarine's fault.

In 1800, Robert Fulton, who later went on to build the first commercially successful steamship, tried to build a larger and better "Turtle" for the French who were then at war with Great Britain. He called his submarine for another sea creature, *Nautilus*, and actually sank an old warship in a demonstration, but the French were not interested. Fulton shifted to the British and sank a warship for them, too, but they weren't interested, either. He returned to the United States and was building a steam-powered submarine large enough to carry a hundred men but died before he could finish the job.

By the time Verne imagined his luxurious submarine (deliberately named for Fulton's vessel) which could remain underwater indefinitely, many submarines had been built, but none could remain underwater for more than a short time.

Such was the success of Verne's book, however, that when electric motors finally made submarines practical, the first all-electric submarine, built in 1886 by two Englishmen, was named *Nautilus* in honor of Verne's vessel. And in 1955, when the United States launched the first nuclear-powered submarine, it was named *Nautilus*, too.

28. THE HOLE IN THE MIDDLE*

Jules Verne was a very careful science fiction writer who made every effort not to go beyond the credible. What made him think, then, that there might be caverns within the Earth that stretched all the way to the very center? He described this in his book *A Journey to the Center of the Earth*, published in 1864, even though Isaac Newton's law of gravity, advanced in 1687, and Henry Cavendish's determination of the mass and density of the Earth, in 1798, made it quite certain that the Earth was perfectly solid throughout.

And yet—the hollow Earth is a venerable idea, hard to abandon. There *are* caves and underground streams. When the Earth quakes, *something* must be going on below. Huge monsters might be writhing there, thought primitive men. A rushing of wind in deep, buried caverns, thought the Greek philosophers.

Then there are volcanoes. Giants must be imprisoned under the volcanoes; or else superhuman smiths kept their forges under the craters; or else there was a horrible world of fire and brimstone beneath the ground, where sinners were punished after death.

Many early peoples had legends of underground worlds where the shades of the dead dwelled in varying degrees of misery. Even today, people who believe in Hell think of it as somewhere deep underground.

The ancient Greeks were the first to realize the Earth must be spherical. This belief was never quite lost and the medieval Hell became a hollow in the center of the spherical Earth. This was described most elaborately and (for the time) most scientifically by Dante in his *Divine Comedy* which he began writing in 1307. In that work, Hell is conceived as a conical hollow, gaping wide under the inhabited portion of the Earth and narrowing to a point at the center of the Earth, where Satan himself is imprisoned.

By 1800, though, the average density of the Earth was known to be 5.5 grams per cubic centimeters. Explaining such a high density if the Earth were hollow was impossible. Explaining the existence of a hollow despite the inward pull of gravity was also impossible.

Yet belief in a hollow Earth continued. It was supported by religious fundamentalists who insisted on believing every word of the Bible as "inspired" and who disregarded the scientific theories of mere human beings. It was also supported by pseudoscientific enthusiasts.

In 1818, for instance, an American army officer and minor hero of the war of 1812, John Cleves Symmes, published a theory that the Earth was made up of five hollow spheres, nested one inside the other. The openings to all of them were at the poles.

To do Symmes justice, Cavendish's determination of Earth's density twenty years before were based on very delicate experiments that could easily be considered unreliable. What's more, both the North Pole and the South Pole were beyond the reach of human beings at that time, and there could indeed be holes there for all anyone could tell.

Symmes's theories gained considerable popularity, as such peculiar suggestions always seem to do, and he was the Velikovsky of his times. By 1864, when Verne wrote his book, Symmes's theories were still popular and the poles were still out of human reach. (In fact, fifty years later, in 1913, after both poles had been reached and were found to be solid, Edgar Rice Burroughs was still able to write the first of his very popular hollow-earth tales concerning Pellucidar.)

Accepting the hollow Earth, Verne proceeded to be as plausible as possible. He placed the entrance to the hollow in the polar regions—in Iceland, where volcanoes and hot springs indicate underground activity. (The hot spring is so typical of Iceland that the Icelandic word for it, "geyser," is the main contribution of that language to English.)

Of course, there are odd effects that should be allowed for. The intensity of gravitation would slowly decrease as one descended into the structure of the Earth, and in a central hollow it would be zero. Verne doesn't mention this, perhaps because he didn't know. (He was no scientist, after all.)

Then, air pressure would go up as one descended and would become insupportably high, long before the center of the Earth was reached. Verne does worry about that but dismisses it (unjustifiably) by saying that the increase would be so gradual that human beings would acclimate themselves to it.

Again, temperature would also quickly climb to unbearable levels as even the knowledge of 1864 indicated. Verne found refuge here in the fallacious theories (half a century old at the time) of Humphry Davy.

But what's the difference? Verne at least made the attempt to account for difficulties, as no other writer, up to and including Burroughs, did. What's more, the story Verne tells in such careful detail, is sufficiently interesting to allow us to forget the scientific shortcomings.

(The Science Fiction Breakthrough)

I did an essay on H. G. Wells for Caedmon Records, but I also did one as an introduction for Three Novels of the Future *(Doubleday, 1979), an H. G. Wells omnibus containing* The Time Machine, The Invisible Man, *and* The War of the Worlds.

Marjorie Goldstein at Doubleday asked me to do the introduction. It doesn't take much to persuade me to do an essay, and even if it did, Marjorie's twinkling eyes would have supplied the necessary. —And I'm glad, because I like this one better than the brief one I did for Caedmon and I'm including it here.

29. THE SCIENCE FICTION BREAKTHROUGH*

It is very difficult to tell when science fiction began, partly because certain strands of it arose out of what went before and did it so gently and gradually that, even with the closest attention, one can't quite point out the dividing line.

For instance, the travel tale, the recounting of marvels beyond the mountains or on the other side of the sea, is surely older than history. When a society inhabits a small patch of land that is set in an apparently endless Earth, what arcane wonders might not exist elsewhere. One could invent freely (see chapter 2).

Then there are the tales of the supernatural, designed to terrify. These are also as old as history, but they took on a modern cast with Horace Walpole's *Castle of Otranto*, the first of the Gothic novels. This eventually gave rise to Mary Shelley's *Frankenstein*

* Copyright © 1979 by Isaac Asimov

and to the works of Edgar Allan Poe, which are quite close to science fiction but are Gothic writings just the same.

And there are the satires, in which foibles of imaginary societies are used to expose human weaknesses to human audiences. These, too, are ancient and go back at least as far as Aesop's Fables, working their way forward to such borderline science fiction as Swift's *Gulliver's Travels*.

When was it, though, that we can say that science fiction began in its own right, with something that was *so* science fictional that it was no longer something else with merely science fictional overtones. When did it become no longer a travel tale masked by a veneer of science; a Gothic using a scientific advance to frighten; a satire using a scientifically advanced society as an object lesson?

What we want is something that may be a travel tale, a Gothic romance, or a social satire, or all three, for that matter; but which so catches up our mind with the strange-science aspect of the story that we see nothing else—at least not while we are reading it.

That beginning comes in the final decade of the nineteenth century and the creator was Herbert George Wells, who, by the time he was in his late twenties, found himself with a makeshift education, an unhappy marriage, a sickly body, and virtually no prospects.

He decided to make his way by writing and he succeeded beyond his hopes, primarily because he thought of a new kind of story that captured the fancy of the public.

It was science fiction. Superficially, he seemed to be following in the footsteps of Jules Verne, who over the past three decades had done enormously well—but Wells's pathway diverged and he became even more successful (rather to the disgruntlement of the aged Verne).

Verne's vision of a scientific future was both limited and narrow. He kept one foot on shore while the other was cautiously inserting one big toe into the ocean; and he involved himself quite closely with the scientific advance and the scientists involved in it. He rarely, if ever, stepped back to focus on the larger picture.

Wells, however, cut free, and took joy in his own imagination. To him, what is more, it was not merely the scientific advance that interested him but the consequences of that advance and the light that it shed on humanity.

Consider, for instance, Wells's first science fiction novel *The Time Machine*, which was published in 1895 and gained huge popularity at once.

There had been imaginary trips in time before, but they were all fantasies brought about by inadvertent slips that carried the hero of the tale forward into time against his will. They were the Rip Van Winkles who thought they had slept one night and found that twenty years had passed when they woke.

The first tale of travel into the past was Mark Twain's *A Connecticut Yankee at King Arthur's Court*, which had been published in 1889. The hero of that novel, however, found himself first in King Arthur's Court and eventually back in his own time, without having any control over either movement.

Jules Verne himself never dared tamper with time travel. It was too fantastic for his tastes.

Not so with Wells. For the first time in history, a writer envisaged the ability to travel through time at will, as one might travel through space—futureward and pastward at the turn of a lever.

It *was* fantastic, still is, and, in all likelihood, ever will be, for there are many reasons to suppose that time travel, as Wells described it, is impossible even in theory. Wells, however, had the trick (which all later science fiction writers learned from him) of explaining the impossible with just the right amount of gravity, emphasizing what sounded plausible and slurring over the implausibilities and impossibilities, so as to induce the reader to follow along joyously, even though he would know better when he was in his right mind.

Nor was Wells telling the story for entertainment only. He was too much the social critic for that. He had a point to make and it was a powerful one. In 1845, Benjamin Disraeli, who was a writer as well as a politician, had written a book entitled *The Two Nations* in which he pointed out that Great Britain's upper and lower classes were so different in all respects that they were two nations occupying the same land.

And that was Wells's point, too, made with maximum power,

for in the far future he visualized an upper class that lives in the sun and is all leisure—aristocrats who have finally reached the maximum of effeteness. There is also a lower class, literally lower, for they live underground and have reached the ultimate of degradation.

Wells then unpityingly portrays the extremes to which the division into two nations will lead.

But, mind you, one does not read the novel with the constant awareness of satire. Wells makes so interesting and detailed a story of it that you read it for the story's sake alone, and only afterward—perhaps—consider the lesson. How much deeper the shaft sinks because of the delayed reaction and how much less likely you are to forget it.

Science fiction *first*; satire, or anything else, second. That was Wells's breakthrough; the beginning of modern science fiction; the lesson we all learned of him, all we later science fiction writers.

Nor did Wells rest with his story of time travel. One by one, he developed all the fundamental plots of science fiction and, in every case, showed how it ought to be done.

Consider the tales of dangerous inventions. It is an old theme. We find it in the Greek legend of King Midas of Phrygia, who craved the ability to turn everything he touched into gold. He got his wish, thanks to the god Dionysus, and found it to be no blessing. We might go farther back and say that the fruit of the tree of knowledge of good and evil in the Garden of Eden was, in a way, a dangerous invention that turned on those who sought advantage from it.

Frankenstein with its Gothic trappings is also a tale of a dangerous invention. The artificial life that Frankenstein created turned on him.

But invisibility?

What danger is there in that? The tales and legends of heroes who had the gift of making themselves invisible are legion, and always it helped them to win. Perseus gained the helmet of invisibility as one of the gifts granted him for his pursuit of Medusa so that he could approach the dread Gorgons unseen. And as recently as Tolkien's *The Hobbit*, it is the gift of invisibility by way of the mysterious Ring that allows Bilbo Baggins to win out.

Then, in 1897, Wells wrote *The Invisible Man*.

Had Verne written it, he would undoubtedly have detailed from the start the manner in which Griffin worked out his invisibility, and once that was done, he would have introduced some interesting and humorous tales of its complications.

Wells was interested in more. From the very start, one sees the difficulties of the mysterious swathed man. What seems like such a gorgeous gift turns out to be nothing of the sort. The difficulties of smoking, of eating, of cold weather, of rain or snow—

The story becomes a tragedy.

But somehow the tale of the dangerous invention does not teach the same lesson in Wells's hands that it does in others'. All the earlier stories of this sort seemed to say "It is better not to know." They seem to be hymns to ignorance.

Wells, to me, seems to offer the cooler advice of caution. Know, but be careful how you apply. And that, after all, is an important word of advice to us today.

But again, story first, moral afterward.

The third, and most powerful, of the three novels is *The War of the Worlds* published in 1898. To understand it properly, we must know the background.

The last few decades of the nineteenth century saw what is called the "Partition of Africa." The European nations, in what was a fury of exploitation, carved up a continent three times the size of their own with utter disregard for the wishes of its population. There didn't seem to be any feeling that the "natives" were human. They were black and they didn't count except insofar as their labor could contribute to the profits of the occupying nations.

In those same decades, there was a furore over "canals" on Mars. Some astronomers reported seeing straight lines crisscrossing the Martian globe. It was known that Mars had less air and water than we had, and by the then-current theories of the origin of the Solar system, Mars was considered an older planet than Earth was. It seemed that an old and perhaps decadent Martian civilization was desperately trying to stave off final death, through an all-encroaching desert, by bringing the last bit of planetary water, the reserves in the polar ice caps, to the thirsty midlatitudes.

So Wells wrote *The War of the Worlds*. He had the Martians give up on their world and take the drastic step of moving by rocket ships to Earth in order to transplant their civilization to a larger, younger, lusher world.

To them, *we* were the "natives" and they regarded us with as little concern as Europeans regarded Africans. They simply took over.

It was the first tale of interplanetary warfare ever written. Until then, all fictional invaders from outer space had come to observe us and to laugh at our follies. Wells, however, was not interested in having them laugh at our follies; he showed us, with cool savagery, what our follies would look like if *we* were on the receiving end.

The novel did more to popularize the conception of Mars as a home of an advanced civilization than did any of the astronomical findings of the day. What's more, they inflicted a deadly fear of extraterrestrials on the world, one that has never vanished. George Pal's *The War of the Worlds* was one of the best and most effective science fiction movies of recent decades, and Orson Welles's updated version of *The War of the Worlds* on a radio show in 1938 spread panic. Even today, there are those who are not certain we ought to search too hard for extraterrestrial intelligences—lest they find us.

But read the novels.

The three novels in this book have, more than any others, set the tone for science fiction ever since. They were the first novels that were science fiction first and everything else second. They were the first novels that dealt with 1) true time travel, 2) the unforeseen side effects of scientific advance dealt with in a nonsuperstitious way, and 3) interplanetary warfare.

And they are rattling good yarns when everything else is stripped away.

(*Big, Big, Big*)

Back in 1975, I was asked to do an introduction for a collection of stories by John Campbell which, as it happened, was never published.

I was glad to do it, for Campbell was perhaps the most towering figure in the development of modern science fiction. (He also was extremely important to the development of my own career as a science fiction writer—as I explain in considerable detail in my autobiographical volume In Memory Yet Green, *published by Doubleday in 1979.)*

30. BIG, BIG, BIG*

The thing about John Campbell is that he liked things big. He liked big men with big ideas working out big applications of their big theories. And he liked it fast. His big men built big weapons in days; weapons that were, moreover, without serious shortcomings or, at least, with no shortcomings that could not be corrected as follows: "Hmm, something's wrong—oh, I see—of course." Then, in two hours, something would be jerry-built to fix the jerry-built device.

The big applications were, usually, in the form of big weapons to fight big wars on tremendous scales. Part of it was, of course, Campbell's conscious attempt to imitate and surpass Edward E. ("Doc") Smith. The world-shaking, escalating conflicts in Campbell's stories are a reflection of the escalating conflict, on the printed page, between John and Doc.

A great deal of Campbell's science is sheer gobbledygook that you must not take seriously. You have to read it as a foreign language that the characters understand and for which the action and the astronomical background serve as a translation.

* (Not previously published)

In some places, Campbell is deliberately and bullheadedly *wrong* and one can never be sure whether he actually believes the nonsense, or whether he is doing it just to irritate and provoke his readers into thinking hard.

In the December 1934 *Astounding Stories*, John Campbell, writing under the pseudonym, Karl van Campen, published "The Irrelevant," in which the heroes were rescued from a deadly interplanetary dilemma by working out a method for creating energy out of nothing. In this way, they defied the law of conservation of energy which, it can be argued, is the most fundamental of all the fundamental laws of the universe.

Campbell did this by arguing that the quantity of energy produced by a change in velocity was different according to the frame of reference you chose for it, and that by switching from one frame to another, you could create more energy than you consumed.

This is dead wrong. I won't argue the reasons here because I don't want to start a controversy. The argument that began with "The Irrelevant" continued in the letter columns of *Astounding* for an incredible length of time, with Campbell (always writing letters under the name of Karl van Campen) maintaining his views against all attacks—as in later years, he would maintain, with equal unswerving vigor, all attacks against his equally indefensible views in favor of dianetics, the Hieronymus machine, the Dean drive, and so on. He might stop arguing points and allow them to drop into oblivion, but he would never openly admit he was wrong.

Yet, on the other hand, John's incredibly vivid imagination would sometimes strike gold and would inspire other writers into striking gold also. The great writers of the Golden Age in *Astounding* were more Campbell than themselves. I admit, freely and frequently, that this was so in my case. Other writers are perhaps more reluctant to do so.

One example of Campbell's golden prescience that struck me most forcibly was in his story "The Space Beyond." There, Campbell mentions that lithium bombarded with protons gives off alpha particles and that beryllium bombarded with alpha particles gives off protons and that the two mixed together can keep each other going in a "self-maintaining atomic explosion."

Actually, this won't work. It takes a high-energy proton to initiate the lithium reaction and beryllium releases low-energy protons; at any rate, protons with too low an energy to break down the lithium. And the same is true in reverse for the alpha particles.

Nevertheless, the suggestion is remarkable. It was made in the mid-thirties and surely not many people were then thinking of the possibility of a nuclear chain reaction, which is what Campbell was suggesting. Eventually, not many years after "The Space Beyond" was written, a practical nuclear chain reaction *was* discovered, that of uranium fission. It was practical precisely because it worked under the impetus of *low*-energy neutrons.

Campbell's brightness in seeing the importance of the nuclear chain reaction may well explain the most remarkable of his predictive visions. During World War II, he kept insisting that nuclear power would be developed before the war's end. Once he heard of the discovery of uranium fission, his understanding of nuclear chain reactions made the atomic bomb seem to him a natural consequence. This was also true for the physicist, Leo Szilard, but for practically no one else.

Campbell went on to inspire a series of stories by other authors on the subject of power through uranium fission, the most notable being "Blowups Happen" by Robert A. Heinlein, "Nerves" by Lester del Rey, and "Deadline" by Cleve Cartmill. (These all appeared in *Astounding*, in the September 1940, September 1942, and March 1944 issues respectively.)

Campbell was eventually investigated by a suspicious American government for knowing too much, but it was easy for him to demonstrate that he didn't know too much. —It was the world that knew too little.

With characteristic cosmic optimism, Campbell carried nuclear power forward to its extremes without ever considering its danger. To control nuclear power meant, to him, in one of his stories, the ability to cure disease miraculously, although, alas, the reality has shown us that radiation is the most deadly potential *producer* of disease the world has ever known.

In fact, there is a peculiar blind spot in prediction that affects us all, even Campbell. One sees the extrapolations of the present in a straight-line way. One misses the surprises.

In his story, "All," Campbell lists the few chemical specifics humanity had developed by the early thirties and moves directly forward to nuclear panaceas—without ever foreseeing the antibiotics. And yet I distinctly remember sitting with him in his office once, before antibiotics had been discovered, and listening to him tell me that since almost all pathogenic bacteria were destroyed in the soil, there must be substances in soil bacteria that would destroy harmful germs and cure disease.

In a way, Campbell's vision of nuclear power was self-defeating. Lured by his success there, he went on to attempt to lead the way into a morass of semimystical pathways, through psi and related subjects, from which he never entirely emerged.

Campbell's love of bigness showed itself at its most glamorous and remarkable in his tendency to describe astronomical bodies of the largest variety in dramatic but utterly realistic prose.

But there Campbell was, at times, betrayed. In the forty years since his stories were written, astronomy has made strides (thanks to radio telescopes and planetary probes) that not even Campbell could have foreseen, and the result has been to dwarf even the most liberal imaginations of the earlier generations.

Campbell describes the supergiant stars vividly and beautifully in a novelette "The Space Beyond." He makes them Cepheids, which adds to the supernal glory (even though Campbell has the notion, it seems, that the more massive a Cepheid, the shorter its period when it is the reverse that is true).

However, no such superstar could exist by modern notions or, indeed, by the astronomical notions of the time at which the story was written. In the 1920s, Arthur S. Eddington advanced the mass-luminosity law, which made it quite clear that stars very much more massive than our Sun could not exist. The radiation pressure from within would cause them to explode at once. In the case of a star as large as those Campbell describes, the result would be an immediate supernova.

Furthermore, even if a star as massive as Campbell's supergiants could be imagined to hang together, the rate of consumption of hydrogen fuel that would be required to keep it glowing at its incredible level would probably drag it through its entire stay in the main sequence in a hundred thousand years. It would only be during that stay that planets could form and evolve in a fashion that would produce life as we know it, and if they had formed when the star itself had (at the appropriately colossal distance), there would simply have been no time for the planet to evolve any life at all, to say nothing of advanced intelligences.

Imagine what Campbell could have done had he been able to write the story a generation later. In place of such supergiant stars, even groups of them, he could have had a quasar—an entire galactic center of millions of stars interacting in some fashion to form something as far beyond a star as a star is beyond a planet.

Or he could have imagined his stars collapsing (as they would surely have done) into black holes. Given an area in space where there were black holes by the dozens, what problems would have arisen and, as sure as Campbell was Campbell, been solved.

Or perhaps he would have had his environment filled with a white hole—that area in space where, some speculate, the matter endlessly pushing into a black hole somewhere else is emerging in great gouts of radiating energy. Perhaps a quasar is a white hole and he could have combined concepts and driven through space and time by using the cosmic ferry of a black hole.

And if, since these stories were written, our knowledge of the Universe has increased a thousandfold, our knowledge of our own Solar system has been refined ten-thousandfold. We have mapped, in detail, the hidden side of the Moon, and men have stood upon our satellite's surface. Unmanned probes have landed on Mars and Venus, and the surfaces of Mars and Mercury have been mapped in detail, as well as those of the tiny Martian satellites, Phobos and Deimos. Jupiter has been seen at short distances, and a probe is gliding its way to Saturn even as I write.

Campbell's story "Marooned" deals with Jupiter and its satellites and how the march of science has outmoded it.

He makes use of "synthium" as an example of one mainstay of early science fiction—the wonder metal. Campbell gives it an atomic number of 101, but element 101 has been discovered since

Campbell wrote the story. It is named mendelevium and it is unstable, as are all elements beyond atomic number 83. Even if it were stable, we know what its properties would be like, and they would be nothing like those of synthium. In fact, the properties of no conceivable metal in the real world would be like those of synthium.

Next there is another old standby—the difficulty of getting past the asteroid belt. I used that one myself in my very first published story "Marooned Off Vesta." The asteroid belt, however, is a paper tiger. The material in it is strewn so widely over so vast a volume that any spaceship going through it is not at all likely to see anything of visible size. The Jupiter probes, Pioneer 10 and Pioneer 11, went through without trouble and detected *less* dust than had been expected.

Still a third commonplace of science fiction was its tendency toward water-oxygen chauvinism. Almost every world encountered in s.f. stories had its water ocean and its oxygen atmosphere.

Campbell needed an atmosphere for Ganymede, so he gave it one, but I think he knew better. Any gases in the vicinity of that satellite exist only in traces. However, Campbell was correct in placing quantities of ice on its surface.

And what about Jupiter? Campbell suggests that this could only be explored with something like synthium since, without it, ships could not pass the asteroid belt and could not even penetrate to the deeps of Earth's own ocean. Not so, for within a quarter century after the story had been written, not only had the asteroid belt been shorn of its terrors, but human beings had made it down to the deepest abyss of the ocean in bathyscaphes—and without synthium.

But Jupiter itself is a harder nut, and Campbell portrays its giant intractable nature gloriously well. He is wrong in details, inevitably. He describes its atmosphere as mostly nitrogen and water with helium and "some hydrogen." Later on he describes the hydrogen content as "a minute trace" and places a rather larger quantity of free oxygen there.

Undoubtedly there is water in the Jovian atmosphere; it has been detected. So has helium been detected, but not nitrogen and certainly not oxygen. Ammonia and methane, which Campbell doesn't mention, are present, but the major component is *hydrogen*. In fact, all of Jupiter is at least 90 percent hydrogen, mostly in the liquid form.

Campbell correctly assumes there is a greenhouse effect in Jupiter's atmosphere; that Solar radiation is trapped and that the temperature is higher than it might otherwise be. But he has his heroes in the Arctic Zone where he describes it as fiercely cold.

Thanks to Jupiter-probe data, gathered in 1974, however, we believe that the temperature of Jupiter rises steadily as one penetrates the atmosphere. Six hundred miles below the cloud layer, the temperature is already 3600 C. It seems quite likely that by the time the ship had penetrated to a depth in which the atmosphere had become dense enough to resist further penetration, the problem would be heat and not cold.

But what's the difference? Whenever a story is placed at the edge of science as it is known at the time, and whenever the author allows his imagination to steer him forward as best it can, making intelligent or dramatic extrapolations—the advance of real science is bound to outmode him in spots. This must be accepted, and to be wise after the event, as I have been here, or to shine in hindsight, as I do, is of no significance.

The question is this: Were Campbell's extrapolations, whether right or wrong, nevertheless intelligent and dramatic? And the answer is: A thousand times, yes!

Campbell might be outwritten by many others, in and out of science fiction, in terms of characterization, plot, and dialogue, but no one ever outdid him in visualizing the grandeur of the Universe.

(*The Campbell Touch*)

In time, an award for promising new writers was set up and it was called, appropriately, "the Campbell Award." George R. R. Martin, one of the brightest of our younger s.f. writers, was doing an anthology of stories by Campbell Award nominees and asked me to write the introduction—about Campbell, of course. I was glad to do it, and here it is.

31. THE CAMPBELL TOUCH*

My beginnings as a professional writer are utterly intertwined with the now-legendary John W. Campbell, Jr., whom I first met on June 21, 1938. That was not very long after he had assumed the editorship of what was at the time called *Astounding Stories*, but which he quickly renamed *Astounding Science Fiction*.

I have never tired of telling stories about Campbell and I never will. The luckiest thing that ever happened to me was meeting Campbell at the very beginning of his editorial career, for if ever there was a patron saint of "new voices" in science fiction, it was he. And somehow I knew it from the start. He was a blazing sun and when you were near him, you either shriveled or you were melted and re-formed. God knows I felt the heat, but I held on tightly and I didn't shrivel.

I hadn't been writing long before I realized that I would rather write than do anything else. I also well knew that Campbell had been one of the top science fiction writers of the 1930s, perhaps *the* top writer. Only E. E. Smith had rivaled him. Yet once he had become the editor of *Astounding*, he virtually stopped writing.

* Copyright © 1980 by Isaac Asimov

I thought about that and couldn't understand how he could bear to do it. How can a writer stop writing?

I didn't want to sound presumptuous but curiosity finally got the better of me and I said, nervously, "Mr. Campbell, how can you bear not to write?"

"I discovered something better, Asimov," he said. "I'm an editor."

I thought that over and then said, cautiously, "How is that better, Mr. Campbell?"

He said, enthusiastically, "When I was a writer, I could only write one story at a time. Now I can write fifty stories at a time. There are fifty writers out there writing stories they've talked with me about. There are fifty stories I'm working on."

That was the way he saw us all. We were extensions of himself; we were his literary clones; each of us doing, in his or her own way, things Campbell felt needed doing; things that he could do but not quite the way we could; things that got done in fifty different varieties of ways.

He made that his lifework, and he valued most those writers who would listen to him and then go home with his idea and put it through a sea change.

He said to me once, "When I give an idea to a writer and it comes back to me exactly the way I gave it to him, I don't give that writer any more ideas. I don't want it my way; I can do that myself. I want my idea *his* way."

It wasn't easy to get *his* idea *your* way, and he didn't accept near-misses. He had no hesitation ever in sending a writer back to his typewriter.

In recent years, a writer of my own generation told me that he had once rewritten a story for Campbell several times only to have it rejected in the end. He had said, in rather woebegone fashion, "But I worked so hard at it."

And Campbell had said, sternly, "Don't ever say that to me again. I'm not going to take a story that isn't right just because someone worked hard at it."

When my friend told me this, I thought silently of an incident in my own early career.

Back in 1939, it had occurred to me to write a future-historical

—a tale of the future using the techniques of the historical novel. The story I wrote was called "Pilgrimage" and, on March 21, I took it to Campbell.

In three days, it was back in my hands with a suggestion that I rewrite, and telling me specifically what was wrong. On April 25, I took it back a second time and it was back in my hands in four days with a suggestion I rewrite again, for my revision had introduced a new error. On May 9, I took it back a third time and it was back in my hands in eight days (I was getting better) with a suggestion I rewrite again for still another reason. On August 8, I took it back a fourth time and this time Campbell held it for *thirty* days.

Why so long? He never took that long to reach a decision, but this time he did. He was waiting for a story by Robert Heinlein called "If This Goes On—." It was to have a religious theme and my story also had a religious theme and Campbell felt he could only use one religious-theme story in one particular year, and he wanted to see which one was better.

No surprise! Heinlein's story was better and so "Pilgrimage" was back in my hands on September 7, 1939. It had been rejected four times and this time the rejection was final.

I was disappointed, of course, but unlike my friend, I didn't dare say a word. I wouldn't have dreamed of objecting to a Campbell decision. —And a lucky thing I didn't, for it would have been most ungrateful of me to have done so.

Rewriting under Campbell's direction was never just laboring to meet the idiosyncrasies of a man who was charismatic but peculiar. Campbell's sort of rewriting amounted to a course in how to write.

As it happened, "Pilgrimage" was not a good story,† but rewriting it and rewriting it and rewriting it taught me a lot. The time came, in 1941, when once again, I tried to write a future-historical. I had failed with "Pilgrimage," but thanks to the education imposed on me by Campbell's suggestions for revision, I did not fail the second time. The story I now wrote was "Founda-

---

† It was finally published in *Planet Stories*, nearly three years later, under the title "Black Friar of the Flame" and you can read it in my book *The Early Asimov* and judge for yourself.

tion" and I followed it up with the remaining stories of *The Foundation Trilogy*.

Campbell was a spider sitting in his web. To him came his fifty writers. He gave each one *his* ideas and watched for the sea changes that came back, and those sparked other ideas that he gave to other writers.

He was the brain of the superorganism that produced the "Golden Age" of science fiction in the 1940s and 1950s.

He loved the role and, as far as I know, never abused it. He took no credit for himself. The three laws of robotics, the central idea of the *Foundation* stories, the plot of "Nightfall" were all his, but although I always tried to make him take the credit for those things, he never would.

He never browbeat anyone to write; nor were his rejections ever insulting or even unkind; nor did he ever fail to deal with your stories quickly and in detail.

And although he seemed to be one large mouth forever talking, one big smile forever oblivious to your desire to respond, he could be oddly sensitive. Once when he praised the writings of another writer, he must have noticed that there was an odd expression on my face.

I did not say a word, but his voice softened and he said, "Do you think, Asimov, that because I like his stories, I like yours any less?" —I brightened up at once.

There'll probably never be anyone like him again. Young writers send me letters frequently and say, in effect, "Campbell helped you when you were young; now you help me."

That accomplishes nothing but to activate my all-too-readily-activated sense of guilt. Do you think that all I have to do to be John Campbell is to decide to be John Campbell?

I can no more be Campbell than I can be William Shakespeare. Nor can anyone else.

To help as Campbell helped takes more than a decision to do so. It takes genius to know *how*, and a sense of dedication to the task, and a glowing happiness at feeling yourself mold a fresh young talent. You have to want to fiddle with the works of new writers more than with your own. You have to joy and glory in the progress of new writers so intensely that that progress is its own reward even if the writer (all too often—but never in my case) forgets how much the help meant.

He was a genius.

I asked him once, not too long before his death, what his secret was. He said, "I have a talent that can't be taught."

"What is that?" I asked.

He said, "An eighteen-year-old named Isaac Asimov came to my office once with a story. I talked to him and read his story and found it to be impossible. From that impossible story, though, I could tell that if he were willing to work at it, he would become a great writer."

And that's what takes genius—because I certainly didn't know that about myself at the time.

All I knew was that I wanted to write. *He* knew, and on the slenderest evidence, that I *could* write.

(*Reminiscences of Peg*)

This is an obituary—not the kind of writing I am fond of doing. However, I was asked to do so by a fan magazine and there was no way in which I could refuse.

32. REMINISCENCES OF PEG

Peg Campbell was John Campbell's second wife, and, things being how they were, I virtually never saw her except when I was seeing John, either at their house, in a hotel room, or at a convention. At least, that was so while John was alive.

That, you would think, would put Peg at a disadvantage, for John was an overpowering personality. When he was in a room, he dominated it, partly out of physical size, partly out of the virtually nonstop character of his monolog (it was never really a conversation), and partly out of the aura he somehow exuded. All the rest of us shrank into pairs of quivering ears bracketing nodding heads.

Yet Peg did not shrink.

For one thing, she was herself of large physical dimensions, and she had an aura, too—one of utter sweetness. She didn't often speak (how could she?) but she would sit there smiling, and watching John occasionally with a look of love and amusement in her eyes. (I could never be sure which predominated, so well mixed were they.)

Her hair was always neatly arranged so as to hug the head. I wish I had a woman's facility to notice and be able to report the details of appearance, but I don't; so I shall simply have to risk ridicule by saying that I seem to think, somehow, that it was arranged in braids that were pinned to the rest of the hair in some fashion.

She smiled with her eyes as well as her mouth and her hands were almost always busy with yarn, I seem to remember. I don't clearly recall what she was doing with it—knitting, crocheting, hooking, or something—and making large and elaborate and quite beautiful objects as a result. I remember she once took me into her workroom to show me the supply of yarns she had. She could have opened a store. It was the first time I realized how many different colors there existed.

She and John made a team. You never saw one without the other at home or when they were traveling, and they fit each other perfectly. I don't think that John ever thought of himself as an individual after he had married her; or, rather, I think he thought of himself as an individual named "Peg-and-I."

For years, I never heard him begin any conversation except as follows: "This morning, Peg-and-I were considering the proposition that—"

And indeed I have a fantasy of John waking up each morning and saying, "Peg, what would you say to the proposition that—"

Peg was a gentle soul. She saw people as people and, as nearly as I could tell, loved them all. John saw people as an audience and he needed her to supply the human touch he sometimes lacked.

Once in the course of our voluminous correspondence, I was more than ordinarily graveled by John's social views and the letters on my side became increasingly furious. John never became furious, but his letters became increasingly stubborn and, from my point of view, obtuse. And then Peg stepped in. She, of course, read his letters and mine and there came a point when she said, to both of us, "Any more and the friendship will be destroyed and this argument is not worth a friendship." So we stopped and talked about the other things.

I was on the podium at a convention once, when John and Peg were in the audience. I was introducing celebrities in the audience and it was easy to introduce John. There were a million humorous things I could say about him and, in any case, there wasn't anyone in science fiction who could possibly fail to know who he was or be awed by his presence.

But how was I to introduce Peg? To announce that she was Mrs. John Campbell and let it go at that was not only insulting, but inadequate. She was more than an appendage-by-marriage.

So I said, "And sitting next to John is his wife, Peg. —Peg, stand up. —Ladies and gentlemen, please meet the velvet glove around the iron fist."

The audience laughed and applauded as I was sure they would, but what about Mrs. Velvet Glove and Mr. Iron Fist? I cast a somewhat uncertain glance in their direction and they were laughing, too. In fact, Peg was particularly pleased with it and on a number of occasions thereafter introduced herself (in my presence) in just that way.

The only convention I ever attended at which Peg and John were not present was, ironically, the 1955 Convention at Cleveland, at which I was Guest of Honor. Just before that occasion, Peg's son by her first marriage had died in a tragic automobile accident—one which inspired an editorial by John on highway hypnosis that I thought, at the time, was the best piece of writing he had ever done.

When they were at a convention, they were never a true part of the pro-segment of the convention scene. They were generally in their room, holding court and leading rather grave discussions. They did not drink; they did not whoop it up; they were an island of decorum in what was usually a most indecorous proceeding.

I didn't drink, either, but I whooped it up, of course, and there were few indecorous gatherings at which I didn't manage to be the most indecorous item. I remember one time at the Detroit Convention in 1959, when I was up all night with a bunch of other kindred spirits. We were all telling jokes and laughing and pinching the girls and (all but me) drinking, and it was simply hilarious. Where the time went to, I don't know, but eventually I noticed it was dawn—so I left to take my morning shower.

Having done so, and realizing that I was hungry and not particularly sleepy, I decided to head for the dining room and have breakfast.

The dining room was quite empty of fellow-pros (it is always quite empty at breakfast at conventions, as all the lushes and boon drinking companions are sunk in swinish slumber until they wake at noon with a hangover) and a quick look-around showed me only John and Peg Campbell. They were having their usual breakfast at their usual time, since they had, I am certain, retired at a civilized hour.

John greeted me gladly, taking my presence for granted, but Peg, with motherly approval, said, "I'm so glad, Isaac, that you keep regular hours and don't stay up all night in dissipation."

Could I break her heart? I said, virtuously, "Thank you, Peg. I *do* try to live sensibly."

And then, eventually, John died, unexpectedly, at the unforgivably early age of sixty-two, and Peg was a widow.

I was one of those who attended the services, along with Lester and Judy del Rey, Gordon Dickson and Harry Harrison. It was all simple and informal and quite nonreligious. Indeed, the closest approach to religion was my reading (by request) the Twenty-third Psalm.

Then we went to the Campbell house and all had dinner with Peg, and Peg was as gentle and warm as ever so that under her influence the sadness and solemnity of the occasion somehow lifted—especially for me, since even at the worst of times I have trouble with solemnity.

Pretty soon, I was telling jokes and in the middle of one, I remembered, stopped very suddenly, turned red, and managed to choke out, "I'm sorry, Peg."

She said, quite calmly, "Please go on, Isaac. I don't want this to be an unhappy occasion."

We visited back and forth for a while and when, after a year or so, she moved to Alabama, I felt the same sense of loss I had experienced when John had died.

She came back once and we were together again for an evening at the del Reys', and we corresponded now and then.

Then she died, too, in 1979.

But I remember her.

(Horace)

Horace was going to edit the 30th-anniversary issue of Galaxy *and asked me to do a reminiscence of him for the occasion. Alas, financial difficulties kept the issue from being published, but here is the reminiscence.*

33. HORACE*

Back about 1955, Horace Gold was at the height of his power as editor of *Galaxy*, which had been in existence only four and a half years and which had, from its first issue, moved in to rival the apparently not-to-be-rivaled John Campbell and *Astounding*.

As for myself, though I was by then a top-notch science fiction writer, I had not yet recovered from my early imprinting by that same John Campbell. I walked softly in the presence of editors. I smiled a lot and held the door open for them.

That sets the stage.

Now imagine me in Horace's apartment, concerned (as usual) as to whether he would take a story of mine or not. Horace had other concerns. He was a writer as well as an editor and had a certain curious insecurity about himself. He wanted his stories read and commented on.

So he handed me a manuscript and said, "Read this, Isaac, and tell me what you think of it."

I demurred. I shrank back and said, "No, no, Horace. I don't want to. What if I don't like it?"

Horace said firmly, "If you don't like it, say so. I want you to tell me the truth even if it means you'll never sell me another story."

So I read it, with him glaring at me. I liked the story very much, but about halfway through the whole atmosphere of the thing changed. It was clear to me that he had put the story aside

* Published here for the first time

for several months and then went back to it when he was in an entirely different mood.

I said, "This is fine."

Horace beamed. "Good."

"There's just one little thing wrong with it."

He was holding the armrests of his chair and his knuckles whitened. "What one little thing?"

"It's better than my stuff, so it fills me with envy," I said, hastily. —And he relaxed. —And I relaxed.

Do things change? No, they don't. A quarter century later (just a few days ago, in fact), Horace called me from California and asked me to write an article for him about himself as writer.

For a minute, I felt that old familiar pang of utter terror. Then I remembered that he was no longer an editor and I was a living legend and I said, "Sure!"

In fact, the first thought that occurred to me was to write a real stinker just to see what would happen—but then I thought: Truth above all!

After all, I happen to like Horace's stories.

For one thing, Horace has always striven to stand ideas on their heads. Heaven knows he bugged his writers to the point of insanity with his insistence that they come up with new ideas (believe me, I remember!), but the fact is he bugged himself just as remorselessly. The result was that in almost every story he wrote, there was something that stayed with me forever.

In his greatest story, "None But Lucifer" (the most terrifying story I ever read in *Unknown*), I was pinned to the wall by the manner in which everything worked for the worst. Imagine wishing to have a beautiful girl love you madly and never wanting to leave you; and imagine getting that wish and ending up hating it because she literally couldn't leave you, couldn't even go into the next room, and you couldn't get rid of her.

I never forgot that. I was only nineteen when I read "None But Lucifer" (and Horace was only twenty-four when he wrote it, for heaven's sake), but I spent countless years dreading the possibility of being overloved—till it happened. I am actually in the position now. Sometimes, when Janet and I are in a department store or a bookstore, conflicting interests separate us momentarily. I look around and can't see her. At which point, I simply stand still for two minutes and wait. Invariably, she shows up with a: "Where did you go? I thought I had lost you." Then she hangs on tight.

It's the "None But Lucifer" situation, I tell myself, but there is one all-important difference. I *like* it.

Or consider, "Trouble With Water," which appeared in *Unknown*'s first issue and was the funniest story in that issue, and in all the succeeding issues of that magazine. It fixed firmly into my mind and consciousness the style in which the ethnic-Jewish story ought to be told. I didn't often use Jewish characters in my stories, but when I did, "Trouble With Water" would usually swim to the top of my mind and direct matters.

When I wrote "The Martian Way" and Horace demanded I insert a woman character—any woman character at all—I gave him a woman modeled on Esther Greenberg, the Jewish wife and mother of "Trouble With Water." (Horace muttered, "Oy, what a woman," when he saw the revision, but kept his word and took the story.)

There's "A Matter of Form" which put me off dogs for years. Every time I would see some dog which seemed to be concerned about something—especially if it so much as looked at me—I would begin to wonder if it were trying to communicate something and, if so, whether I would be able to understand it. (I never did.)

Who needs that kind of annoyance? —No one. But that's the kind of annoyance that comes from reading stories by Horace Gold, with their curious kind of inverted but compelling logic.

Imagine creating a species of aliens who live on rock and who burrow through it mole-fashion. Well, Horace imagines it in "Man of Parts" and gives us a sentence such as this one: "Gam Nex Biad had always been considered one of the most crashing bores on Dorefel, capable of taking an enormous leap on his magnificently wiry leg, landing exactly on the point of his head with a swift spin that would bury him out of sight within instants in even the hardest rock."

It makes you jealous of the creature's capacity.

But watch out for the play on words. We know what a "crashing bore" is, but that's not what Horace means. Taken literally, it is one who crashes against rock and bores into it. The phrase is one of admiration, not contempt.

That, perhaps, is Horace's most characteristic characteristic: playing with words. "A Man of Parts" means something to those of you who read Regency romances; it refers to a man of several talents. Horace chooses to be literal: a man whose crushed body has been rebuilt with alien parts.

This is not always successful, in my opinion. I have a feeling that Horace's favorite short story is "The Man with English," but it is my least favorite story of his. (Who says my article must be entirely favorable?)

Horace is fond of the title, but I don't think it is comprehensible unless you are an American who misspent his youth in a pool hall. And even when it is comprehensible, I don't think it fits the story accurately.

Nevertheless, even a Horace Gold story that falls below his own standards is still better than any ordinary story by almost anyone else. (My own feelings only; I realize that tastes differ.)

Which brings up an important question.

Why is it that Horace doesn't rate higher as an author?

When authors are listed in the order of merit, it's not just that Horace is down there with the "who's he?"s. He's not there at all.

When the authors of the Golden Age are mentioned, we can be sure we'll hear of Heinlein, Sturgeon, del Rey, Van Vogt, and all the rest (including you-know-who), but you *won't* hear of Gold.

Why not?

Well, for one thing, he was not prolific—at least in science fiction. He wrote endless reams of true confessions and fact detective but that doesn't count. In science fiction, he wrote eighteen stories, I believe, and no more, up to the point when he became editor of *Galaxy*, and five of those were hidden under the pseudonym of Clyde Crane Campbell.

Unfortunately, prolificity counts.

Secondly, once Horace became an editor, there was a tendency to forget he was a writer, too. (That happened to John Campbell and Tony Boucher, also, the two men who, with Horace, made up the big three of the 1950s.)

To be sure, Horace the Editor was great. Not only did he get authors to write marvelous stories for him, but he also wrote delightful editorials. Horace's editorials were as controversial as any that John Campbell wrote, but unlike John's, Horace's were sprightly, light, and right-headed as well.

Thirdly, Horace had an abrasive personality. (Pardon me, Horace, but if you don't know you have one, let me be the first to tell you.) In order to get stories out of writers, he would routinely kick them in the pants and call them opprobrious names. Unfortunately, writers don't respond to that kind of treatment for long. They tend to sulk, and go off in a corner biting their lips and saying harsh things about editors.

I think that many s.f. writers, who are important opinion makers in the field, ended up thinking of Horace only as a hardhearted editor they didn't want to work for and just wiped him out of their consciousness. And because he wasn't mentioned, he was forgotten.

Which is unfair.

He was almost as remarkable a science fiction writer as he was a science fiction editor, and he should be remembered with admiration in both roles.

(*The Second Nova*)

Fame can be fleeting—in science fiction as in every-
thing else. There's no danger of forgetting Verne and
Wells, and it seems to me that science fiction greats
such as Heinlein, Bradbury, Clarke (and even myself)
will be remembered a long time.

Yet when Judy-Lynn del Rey of Ballantine Books
was preparing to do a volume of the collected short
stories of Stanley G. Weinbaum, she told me that a
common reaction she got was "Who?"

I promptly offered to do an introductory essay that
would answer that question and here it is.

34. THE
SECOND NOVA*

Three times in the half-century history of magazine science
fiction a new writer has burst into the field like a nova, capturing
the imagination of the readers at once, altering the nature of science fiction and converting every other writer into an imitator.
(Nor may there ever be a fourth time, for since 1939, when the
third nova appeared, the field has surely grown too large and too
diverse to be turned in its path by any single story by any new
writer.)

Let me tell you about the first and third novas, then, so that
you can see the similarities between them and will have a better
appreciation of the truly remarkable nature of the second and
greatest of the three.

In the August 1928 issue of *Amazing Stories*, at a time when
magazine science fiction was only a little over two years old, there
appeared the first installment of *The Skylark of Space*, by Edward

* Copyright © 1974 by Isaac Asimov

Elmer Smith and Lee Hawkins. It was E. E. Smith's first published science fiction story.

For the first time in a science fiction magazine, man was whirled off into the depths of interstellar space, with all the Universe open before him. For the first time, the reader had the chance to visualize man as a creature of infinite capacity—man as God, almost.

The readers loved it. *The Skylark of Space* became a classic at once, and other writers did their best to imitate it. The field was never the same again, and E. E. Smith was a demigod of science fiction for the remainder of his life.

E. E. Smith was the first nova.

In the August 1939 issue of *Astounding Science Fiction*, there appeared the short story "Life-Line," by a new author, Robert A. Heinlein. It attracted attention at once for its low-keyed, naturalistic style, for the utter absence of histrionics or the cardboard attitudes common in most science fiction.

The story did not, perhaps, instantly grab the readers and shake the field into a new form, for it was a little obscured by the nearly simultaneous appearance of the more spectacular and longer "Black Destroyer," by A. E. van Vogt, another new writer, in the July 1939 *Astounding*. But Heinlein continued to write stories rapidly and *Astounding* continued to publish them. Within the year it became quite obvious that Robert A. Heinlein was the best living science fiction writer.

Again readers demanded more, and again almost every writer in the field (including myself) began, more or less consciously and more or less thoroughly, to imitate Heinlein.

Robert A. Heinlein was the third nova.

In many ways, Smith and Heinlein were alike. Both, for instance, published their initial, attention-capturing pieces in what was at the time the foremost magazine in the field. *Amazing* published Smith's story, *Astounding* published Heinlein's. (At the time of *The Skylark of Space*, *Amazing* was indeed, the only science fiction magazine being published.)

In both cases an important and seminal editor had created an exciting magazine within which the nova could show its luster to the full. It was Hugo Gernsback in Smith's case, John W. Campbell, Jr., in Heinlein's.

In neither case was the writer a born writer in the sense that he had been fiddling with pen and paper since he could toddle, had been submitting from the age of twelve and publishing from the age of sixteen. Both Smith and Heinlein had engineering backgrounds, and neither had any intention of becoming a professional writer until, more by accident than anything else, each discovered how "easy" writing was. Both were past thirty when their first stories were published.

In both cases, their fame was enduring. Each continued to produce for many years, so that there were always new stories to add to the canon and to their reputation in the hearts of new generations of readers.

The February 1948 issue of *Astounding* carried the fourth and last installment of *Children of the Lens*, Smith's last important work. Twenty years after *The Skylark of Space*, he was still read avidly.

As for Heinlein, he is writing and publishing today, thirty-five years after the publication of his first story, and he has lost none of his reputation. In a recent fan poll, he *still* finished in first place as all-time favorite science fiction writer.

The second nova appeared in 1934, just six years after Smith and just five years before Heinlein. In the July 1934 issue of *Wonder Stories*, a short story entitled "A Martian Odyssey" appeared by a never-before-published writer, Stanley G. Weinbaum.

Observe the differences. At the time the story appeared, *Wonder* was *not* the foremost science fiction magazine. It was, in my opinion, third in a field of three. Its publisher was indeed Hugo Gernsback, but Gernsback was no longer in the forefront of creative thinking in the field. The editor was Charles D. Hornig, who, in the history of science fiction editing, is undistinguished and whose sole claim to fame, indeed, may be the recognition of the worth of this particular story.

Yet, hidden in this obscure magazine, "A Martian Odyssey" had the effect on the field of an exploding grenade. With this single story, Weinbaum was instantly recognized as the world's best

living science fiction writer, and at once almost every writer in the
field tried to imitate him.

The second nova differed in another important quality from the
first and third.

Although E. E. Smith was a wonderful human being, beloved
by all who knew him (including myself), the sad truth is that he
was an indifferent writer, who developed only moderately with the
years. Heinlein was a much better writer than Smith, but his first
story, "Life-Line," is minor Heinlein and on no one's list of all-
time great tales.

How different the case with "A Martian Odyssey." This story
showed at once a writing skill as easy-flowing and as natural, not
merely as Heinlein's, but as Heinlein's at its best. "A Martian
Odyssey" is *major* Weinbaum.

In 1970, the Science Fiction Writers of America voted on the
best science fiction short stories of all time, and among those that
proved the favorites "A Martian Odyssey" was the oldest. It was
the first science fiction story ever published in the magazines to
withstand the critical scrutiny of professionals a generation later.
And it did more than merely withstand the test. It ended up in
second place.

Like Smith and Heinlein, Weinbaum was not a born writer.
Like Smith and Heinlein, he had an engineering background (he
was a chemical engineer, like Smith). Like Smith and Heinlein,
his first story was published when he was over thirty.

And there the resemblance ends, for the tragic truth is that
Weinbaum, even as he entered the field and became at once its
leader, was a dying man.

On December 14, 1935, at the age of thirty-three, and only one
and a half years after the publication of his first story, Weinbaum
died of cancer and his career was over. By the time of his death,
he had published twelve stories; eleven more appeared posthumously.

Yet even without the advantage of decades of accomplishment
and development, he remains alive in the memories of fans. Any
new collection of his stories remains, and must remain, a major
event in science fiction.

Now what was most characteristic of Weinbaum's stories? What was it that most fascinated the readers? The answer is easy —his extraterrestrial creatures.

There were, to be sure, extraterrestrial creatures in science fiction long before Weinbaum. Even if we restrict ourselves to magazine science fiction, they were a commonplace. Yet before Weinbaum's time, they were cardboard, they were shadows, they were mockeries of life.

The pre-Weinbaum extraterrestrial, whether humanoid or monstrous, served only to impinge upon the hero, to serve as a menace or as a means of rescue, to be evil or good in strictly human terms —*never* to be something in itself, independent of mankind.

Weinbaum was the first, as far as I know, to create extraterrestrials that had their *own* reasons for existing.

He did more than that, too; he created whole sense-making ecologies.

Weinbaum had a consistent picture of the solar system (his stories never went beyond Pluto) that was astronomically correct in terms of the knowledge of the mid-1930s. He could not be wiser than his time, however, so he gave Venus a dayside and a nightside, and Mars an only moderately thin atmosphere and canals. He also took the chance (though the theory was already pretty well knocked-out at the time) of making the outer planets hot rather than cold so that the satellites of Jupiter and Saturn could be habitable.

On each of the worlds he deals with, then, he allows for the astronomic difference and creates a world of life adapted to the circumstances of that world. The super-jungle of the dayside of Venus as pictured in "Parasite Planet" is, in my opinion, the most perfect example of an alien ecology ever constructed.

In Weinbaum's stories, the plots, though tightly and well-constructed, exist in the reader's mind largely for the opportunity they present for a voyage of discovery of strange worlds and of ever-fascinating life-forms.

Of all his life-forms, the most fascinating perhaps are Tweel, the pseudo-ostrich in "A Martian Odyssey," and Oscar, the intelligent plant in "The Lotus Eaters." In both cases, Weinbaum met the challenge of a demand John Campbell was to make of his writers in later years: "Write me a story about an organism that thinks as well as a man, but not *like* a man." I don't think anyone has done it as well as Weinbaum in all the years since Weinbaum.

And what would have happened if Weinbaum had lived? It is likely, sad to say, that he would have left magazine science fiction for brighter, greener, and more lucrative fields.

Yet what if he had not? What if he had stayed in magazine science fiction over the years as some other major talents have, talents such as Arthur C. Clarke, Poul Anderson, and even Robert A. Heinlein?

In that case, there would never have been a "Campbell revolution," I think.

In 1938, when John Campbell took over complete control of *Astounding,* he turned the field toward greater realism and, at the same time, toward greater humanism—a double direction he had himself marked out with his story "Twilight," which had appeared in the November 1934 *Astounding.* In so doing, he developed a stable of authors, including Heinlein, Van Vogt, and many others—myself for one.

But Weinbaum was a Campbell author before Campbell. "A Martian Odyssey" appeared half a year before "Twilight," so Weinbaum is clearly one author who owed nothing to Campbell. Had Weinbaum continued producing there would have been no Campbell revolution. All that Campbell could have done would have been to reinforce what would undoubtedly have come to be called the "Weinbaum revolution."

And in Weinbaum's giant shadow, all the Campbell authors would have found themselves less remarkable niches. Weinbaum, who would be in his early seventies now had he lived, would surely be in first place in the list of all-time-favorite science fiction writers.

(Ray Bradbury)
(Arthur C. Clarke)

Of the still living science fiction writers, two of the most important (aside from myself, of course) are Ray Bradbury and Arthur C. Clarke.

TV Guide *asked me to do an essay on Ray in connection with the TV production of his* The Martian Chronicles. *That essay was published in the January 12, 1980, issue of the magazine.*

As for Arthur, I did an essay for the Caedmon recording of Childhood's End.

35. RAY BRADBURY*

Ray Douglas Bradbury was a science fiction anomaly from the start.

That start was in the early 1940s, a time at which the science fiction world was far different from what it is today. There was no television of any kind in the early 1940s. The only science fiction on the radio or in the movies were children's shows prepared by people who knew little or nothing of the field (with a few honorable exceptions). The world of paperbacks were just dawning and no reputable hard-cover publisher even knew that s.f. stood for anything but San Francisco.

There was some primitive science fiction in the comic magazines and everything else was squeezed into a handful of science fiction magazines with circulations, for the most part, of 50,000 or less and payment rates of one cent a word or less.

In all the s.f. world—comics, movies, magazines—the only *good* science fiction appeared in *Astounding Science Fiction* which, in 1937, came under the editorship of a twenty-seven-year-old, charismatic editor, John Wood Campbell, Jr. What Campbell pub-

lished was science fiction, and everything else was apple dump-
lings.

And what Campbell wanted was "hard" science fiction—s.f.
that dealt with scientists, engineers, inventors, as written by authors who were familiar with such matters. He collected about
himself a stable of authors who dazzled the world of s.f. with their
brilliance, the survivors of whom *still* dominate the field now,
nearly forty years later, even if only as elder statesmen.

Among the stars of the 1940s, Ray Bradbury was the *only* one
who was *not* a Campbell author. He had not gone to college; he
knew no science and was, indeed, antagonistic to science; he had
an odd and choppy style; his characters tended to be fey, his
mood nostalgic, his plots veering toward the weird and fantastic.

Campbell could make nothing of him and, with one or two
very minor exceptions, he did not buy anything of him. Bradbury's first published story appeared in *Super Science Stories* in
1941, and thereafter he published in other minor science fiction
magazines. To publish only in the minors was the kiss of death as
far as serious s.f. fans were concerned.

Except that Bradbury somehow didn't die. The *Astounding* devotees, those who scorned reading anything but The Magazine
might never have heard of Ray Bradbury, but a groundswell, a distant murmur, arose at the conventions and in the fan magazines.

With more and more of the fans, Ray Bradbury became an ob-
session. He was different. He was accessible.

Campbell authors were sometimes opaque, heavy, given to
coldly reasoning their way from point to point and rarely allowing
emotions to overtake their thin-lipped, narrow-eyed, lofty-browed
space pilots, engineers, or scientists.

Bradbury's writings, on the other hand, created moods with few
words. He wasn't ashamed to tug at the heartstrings and there was
a semipoetic nostalgia to most of those tugs. He created his own
version of Mars straight out of the nineteenth century, totally ig-
noring the findings of the twentieth century.

In fact, one gets the idea that Bradbury *lives* in the nineteenth
century and in the small-town Midwest in which he grew up—
though he and his family moved to Los Angeles when he was
fourteen. Bradbury won't fly and, though he has lived in Los An-

geles for forty-five years now, he can't drive a car. He still views science with intense suspicion, but supports the space effort enthusiastically, largely because (I think) he finds it poetic.

In 1949, came a turning point. Doubleday & Company, Inc., decided to establish a line of hard-cover science fiction books under the editorship of Walter I. Bradbury (no relation to Ray). It was the first major publisher to recognize s.f. in this fashion, and the line is still alive and flourishing today.

The first book published under the "Doubleday science fiction" imprint was *The Big Eye* by Max Ehrlich, a writer not known to s.f. fandom. The second book was *Pebble in the Sky* by Isaac Asimov.

For the third, they put together some of Bradbury's evocative stories of Mars, of the attempts of Earth to colonize the planet, of the haunting traces of the native Martians and their civilization. It is a celebration of small-town innocence and nostalgia in a futuristic setting. The title of the book was *The Martian Chronicles*.

Again, a strange thing happened. Short story collections are supposed to be poison at the literary box office, but the Bradbury collection was the most successful of the three, even though the other two were novels. And, indeed, it has never lost its popularity in the decades since.

Ray Bradbury became the apostle to the Gentiles, so to speak; science fiction's ambassador to the outside world. People who didn't read science fiction, and who were taken aback by its unfamiliar conventions and its rather specialized vocabulary, found that they could read and understand Bradbury.

He became famous, rather to the surprise of the s.f. world. To those not actually part of the s.f. world, it seemed that the only science fiction writer they knew, and the only name they could recognize, was Ray Bradbury.

That meant that science fiction lost him. He moved up and away. Once the 1940s were done, Bradbury no longer appeared in the minor science fiction magazines. Hurdling right over *Astounding*, he began to appear in general fiction magazines, with much larger circulations and much higher word-rate—which meant even greater and more widespread fame.

He moved into the Hollywood orbit and wrote screenplays such as that for *Moby Dick*. He wrote nostalgic "straight" novels such as *Dandelion Wine*. He wrote poetry and plays. —But, throughout, it was his early science fiction that was Bradbury at his best— and particularly *The Martian Chronicles*. If everything else he produced were to disappear, that one collection would be enough to make him important in the history of science fiction.

The science fiction world is completely different now. There are many Campbell authors who are now international celebrities. Heinlein's *Stranger in a Strange Land*, Clarke's *Childhood's End*, Asimov's *Foundation Trilogy* are perennial classics going through endless reprintings. Each of these "Big Three" is now honored with a biographical sketch in the Encyclopedia Brittanica; and there is just one other so honored—Ray Bradbury, the non-Campbell author who made it big.

And in a science fiction world which seems now to be overshadowed by Hollywood-hype and by overpowering special effects—as in *Star Wars, Close Encounters of the Third Kind,* and *Star Trek* —and where the old comics have come into new, glossy, enlarged, but childish form as in "Superman" and "Buck Rogers"—there is still room for *The Martian Chronicles* and for the special Bradbury mood which no one else has ever successfully imitated.

36. ARTHUR C. CLARKE*

Arthur Clarke is a good friend of mine. In fact, we have a treaty that was put together in a taxi barreling down Park Avenue about fifteen years ago. This "Asimov-Clarke Treaty of Park Avenue" states that I must insist at all times that Arthur Clarke is the best science fiction writer in the world (accepting second place for myself) while Arthur must equally insist that Isaac Asimov is the best science writer in the world (accepting second place for himself).

I don't think either one of us means it, since humility is a word neither of us has ever heard of, but we are honorable men who stick to the bargain.

In many respects, Arthur is my undoubted superior. He is my superior in age, for instance, by three years, having been born in 1917 so that he is now a little over sixty, whereas I am (as everyone knows) only a little over thirty. He is also my superior in baldness and ugliness, being both balder and uglier than I am, and I confess that freely.

He entered the field of professional science fiction writing in 1946 (seven years after I did) with a short story named "Loophole" in the April 1946 *Astounding,* and it was quickly to be seen that he and I belonged to the same school of s.f. writing.

It turns out that anyone who likes my writing will bashfully confess to liking Arthur's as well, and vice versa. There is also an extraordinary tendency to confuse his writings with mine, something to which we both react with resignation.

There are two poles to s.f. writing—cool versus warm; logical versus emotional; scientific versus humanistic. Both Arthur and I are warm, emotional, and humanistic in spots, but there is no question that our favored mode of expression is cool, logical, and scientific.

Arthur is strongly technology-oriented. He has been scientifically trained and his imagination is a disciplined one. It roams the Universe but remains within the bounds of natural law. He was the first, for instance, to conceive of communications satellites, explaining their workings in an article he wrote in 1948. It sounded like science fiction, but it wasn't. We now have them and Arthur says, sadly, that if he had had the forethought to patent some of his basic notions, he would now be an incredibly rich man. (Weep not, Gentle Reader, he has managed to become an incredibly rich man anyway.)

This disciplined imagination of his characterizes his stories, which do not rely on either sex or violence, nor on purple prose— but on a mind-boggling view of the Universe that you know has a chance of being quite correct, like those communications satellites of his.

It was in 1953 that Arthur hit the big time with the publication of *Childhood's End*. This vision of man and the future, which rises spirally in vastness from the Cold War of the 1950s to an almost ungraspable climax, has been popular ever since.

The general Clarkeian notion of Overlords, of guardian life-forms in the Universe, was to make itself felt again in the classic motion picture *2001: A Space Odyssey*, and is hinted at in his recent award-winning *Rendezvous with Rama*.

The grand original, though, and the key to Arthur's thinking of the benign influence of technology, the unending horizons of human advance, the victory of life in a friendly Universe, is present right here in *Childhood's End*.

Arthur claims he has retired now, and, to be sure, there are few people with the excuse for retiring that he has. He is respected alike by scientists and by science fiction enthusiasts; he has won every appropriate award in existence; he has gained fame and wealth.

He has no family and lives in splendor in a servant-laden mansion on the shores of Sri Lanka (once called Ceylon, and earlier, Serendib), where he has indulged in the sport of scuba-diving and where he has the privilege of watching the only TV set in the entire nation. He is Sri Lanka's natural wonder, and tourists come to gaze at him from afar.

For the last twenty years, in poll after poll intended to determine the favorite science fiction writers, the top three winners (in alphabetical order) have *invariably* been Isaac Asimov, Arthur C. Clarke, and Robert A. Heinlein. —Which raises only one question. How did Robert get into the act?

(The Dean of Science Fiction)

In the following essay, I discuss some of the more ancient members of our craft. The ones I discuss are roughly my contemporaries but by a peculiar twist of Fate, they have grown elderly, while I am, and remain, intensely youthful.

This essay appeared as an editorial in the November 1979 issue of my magazine, and just to show you the power of the press, I must tell you that at the 1980 Nebula Awards Banquet there was no Grand Master award. You'll see the significance of this once you finish the essay.

37. THE DEAN OF SCIENCE FICTION*

This morning I was interviewed (by phone) on a radio talk show. I submit to it every once in a while since I don't travel, and in that way I get to talk to people I wouldn't otherwise reach.

I must tell you, however, that I don't enjoy it. The endless interruptions for advertisements and service announcements are in the highest degree annoying and the repetitions of the interviewer are wearisome.

The interviewer this morning had to introduce me to his audience some fifteen times (once after each interruption) and always managed to mispronounce my last name in the same way, even though every caller who phoned pronounced my name clearly and correctly. He also, in each one of the fifteen introductions, identified me as "the dean of science fiction."

Which I'm not.

The word "dean" is the English version of the Latin *"decanus"* used in the Roman army for a leader of ten men (from the Latin "*decem*" meaning "ten"). The term can be used in military organizations, in clerical organizations, or in scholastic organizations, always to mean some particular person in authority, though he needn't be set over ten men exactly.

That more or less literal meaning of the word does not come into play in the phrase "dean of science fiction," however. There it has an honorary meaning.

The honorary use of the term signifies a senior member of some group, and it began, I think, in connection with the diplomatic corps. At any capital, there are gathered numerous diplomatic representatives of various other nations and one of them is bound to be the senior man or (these days) woman, and is then referred to as the dean of the diplomatic corps. Since the language of diplomacy (at least until recently—and perhaps still, for all I know) is French, the term sometimes used is "*doyen*."

I don't know that the dean of the diplomatic corps had any special reward for being the dean. Perhaps there was some sort of social prestige to it, or precedence. Perhaps the dean of the diplomatic corps had the honor of leading the cotillion, or of getting to perform the first bow when the king entered.

In any case, by extension, every other group with pretensions to prestige or intellect began to speak of one of themselves as the dean.

The next question is: What does one mean by the "senior member."

The obvious suggestion that the senior member be the oldest in years makes no sense to me. As a matter of courtesy, one must defer to age, but surely an old man just appointed to a diplomatic post for the first time cannot take precedence over a somewhat younger man who has held his place for twenty years. The senior member has to be the one who is senior in service.

So the dean of science fiction is a man who has been writing science fiction longer than anyone else in the field—regardless of his age (although of course one can't have been writing science fiction for a long time without having grayed a little).

I must admit that, at first blush, I might be considered a candidate for the post, since my first science fiction story appeared in the March 1939 *Amazing*, over forty years ago.

*

Believe it or not, however, there are some members of my profession who are long-lived scoundrels and persistent rascals and who manage to be senior to myself both in age and in point of service.

Naturally, though, it should not be quite enough to be senior in both age and service and nothing more. We should make it difficult to qualify for the post of dean since we want to make sure that whoever holds it is a credit to the profession and is sufficiently glorious to allow us all to bask in his radiance.

Someone like my good friend, Dr. John D. Clark, for instance, should not qualify. He published two very good stories in *Astounding* in 1937 and then, for one reason or another, never published another story in all the time since. John is a sterling fellow, but we can't make him the dean. We need someone who has not only been published a long time ago, but has continued to be published over a long period, rather frequently, and who has been continually identified with the field.

Then again, we can't have someone as dean who has published a considerable number of stories over a considerable period of time, but who has never really been recognized as a leading figure in the field.

That makes things a little rough, to be sure, because who is going to draw the invidious distinction between "a leading figure" and "not a leading figure." Certainly not I. And yet I think we can have a feeling that some writers have won awards and have written stories and books that have been continually popular.

In that case, weighing length of service, quality of service, and continuity of service, who would I suggest as the dean of science fiction? Easy. I am not only ready to name the dean. I am ready to name three other writers, in order, as runners-up. Here they are:

1) *Jack Williamson* is, to my way of thinking, the dean of science fiction at present. His first published story was "The Metal Man" in the December 1928 *Amazing*, more than ten years before my first story was published. He has already celebrated his Golden Anniversary as a writer and is currently the president of the Science Fiction Writers of America. He was the second person chosen by the Science Fiction Writers of America as Grand Master

of Science Fiction for the lifetime body of his work. Can there possibly be any argument about this, then?

2) *Clifford D. Simak* had his first published story, "The World of the Red Sun," in the December 1931 *Wonder*, more than seven years before my first. He is still actively writing and he was the third person chosen by the Science Fiction Writers of America as Grand Master.

3) *L. Sprague de Camp* had his first published story, "The Isolinguals" in the September 1937 *Astounding*, a year and a half before my first. He is still working away busily, and some of his stories have appeared recently in this magazine and received considerable reader acclaim. He was the fourth person chosen by the Science Fiction Writers of America as Grand Master.

4) *Lester del Rey* had his first published story, "The Faithful," in the April 1938 *Astounding* nearly a year before my first. He is now (along with his wife, Judy-Lynn) the guiding spirit behind Del Rey Books, one of the important outlets for paperback science fiction and fantasy. He is the youngest of the four, having been born in 1915, and he is the only one of them who is still on the sunny side of seventy.

The one person who is not on the list and whose absence might startle people is Robert A. Heinlein.

If any science fiction writer may be considered to be the *best* science fiction writer by general consensus, it would have to be Heinlein. Every time a vote is taken of fans, readers, or teachers, the same "Big Three" writers show up as most popular, and in first place is *always* Heinlein. As a matter of fact, this was recognized when he was the *first* person chosen by the Science Fiction Writers of America as Grand Master.

So why isn't *he* the dean of science fiction? Well, the only reason I didn't select him is that matter of length of service. Heinlein's first story was "Life-Line," which appeared in the August 1939 *Astounding*. In that respect he is behind even me by almost half a year.

Which brings up one last point—

I don't know how the Science Fiction Writers of America choose their Grand Masters. It certainly isn't by vote, since I've never been asked to vote. I presume that someone, perhaps the

234 ASIMOV ON SCIENCE FICTION

officers, select the Grand Masters according to their royal whim.

So far they have made absolutely magnificent choices and I congratulate them. Yet I wonder if it would be considered decent to make a suggestion as to the next Grand Master. In view of the points I've made in this editorial, it seems to me that the fifth Grand Master should be Lester del Rey.

(The Brotherhood of Science Fiction)

I should not write about science fiction writers without stressing something very important about the field —the warmth and friendship among them.

I imagine this may exist to some extent in other subsections of the arts, but somehow I cannot bring myself to believe it can possibly be as intense as among science fiction writers, especially among those of us who remember it when it was an unbelievably small and unimportant part of the vast world.

In any case, the following essay is my homage to that phenomenon.

38. THE BROTHERHOOD OF SCIENCE FICTION*

There has always been a brotherhood of science fiction that has transcended the petty feuds and bad-mouthing that have occasionally disfigured the fanzines and even the meetings of the august Science Fiction Writers of America.

We may fight among ourselves over inconsequential matters, but how we join forces in adversity! And, most of all, how our sense of union rises above any feeling of "competition!"

Perhaps it dates back to the days when science fiction was the most disregarded portion of the pulp magazine field, the corner with the fewest opportunities and the smallest pay—the least of the least, so to speak. It followed, then, that those who were its devotees had a feeling of isolation and pariahhood and clung together in self-defense. And it followed that those who actually strove to write for the medium *had* to know that they did it for

* Copyright © 1977 by Davis Publications, Inc.

love and not for money, and they *had* to feel themselves to be a band of brothers. How could there be competition when there was neither money nor renown to compete for?

It may be that those who enter the field now—when science fiction has survived the death of the pulps; when it has entered into a time of almost exaggerated respect, both in the public eye and among the academics; when it has invaded the visual media in triumph—no longer feel themselves to be members of quite so tight a fraternity, as we old-timers† did. If so, I regret it on their behalf.

I came to be aware of this once again when a misadventure occurred to me that was rather humiliating for one of my well-known vigorous youth. What happened was that, on 18 May 1977, I suffered a mild myocardial infarct, a coronary to use another term—or, if you want to be utterly plebeian, a heart attack. (Fear not, O Gentle Reader, I survived and the prognosis is good, provided I lose weight, exercise a little, and ease up a bit in my inhuman pursuit of the deadline.)

The first question my doctor (a superb internist; the best in the world, actually) asked me was whether I wanted to go public on the matter?

"Sure," I said. "I will undoubtedly write articles about it." (See?)

So we did, and at once and from all over the country expressions of concern began arriving from my extended family of science fictioneers. Harlan Ellison, with an emotion that totally belied the persona of "hard-boiledness" he cultivates as sedulously as I cultivate my persona of self-satisfaction, twice called from California to offer to fly east and help out in any way he could. Naturally, we screamed at him to stick to his typewriter and stop worrying.

I was forced to cancel all engagements for a period of six weeks, including the commencement address I was to make at Johns Hopkins University only two days later. Actually, it had been eight days since my coronary, since my symptoms had been very misleading and had first suggested gallstones so that it took time

† If I may use the term for someone like myself who am ever youthful.

to make the correct diagnosis. I therefore pointed out to my doctor that two more days wouldn't hurt and I should give the address. My doctor, however, very annoyed with me for daring to have had atypical symptoms that delayed my treatment, had me in a cardiac-care unit within the hour.

For as many engagements as possible, my science fiction family rallied round as replacements. George Scithers went to Brown University in my place. And *who* took over three of my other talks, even forcing himself into the indignity of a rented tuxedo for one of them? Why, none other than my prime competitor, Ben Bova, editor of *Analog*.

Analog and its ancestor *Astounding* have led the field in circulation and prestige for over a third of a century and this magazine intends to catch it and overtake it, and, of course, *Analog* intends it to do no such thing.

But that does not affect Ben and me. Buddies we were before and buddies we are now and buddies we will be in the future, win or lose, because the "competition," however it turns out, can only help science fiction and it is science fiction that is our life and brotherhood.

He came to visit me in the hospital and I said to him, "Ben, how did the talks go? Did you remember to be not quite as good as I am?"

"I was rotten," he said.

"You were not, Ben," I said, accusingly. "The reports from one and all are that you were great and that no one is ever going to want me as a speaker again—so I've put out a contract on you. I'm going to give you the kiss of death."

"Hah!" said Ben, scornfully. "What does a Jew know about the kiss of death? Only Italians can give the kiss of death."

Foiled, I said, "Well, then, I'm very greatly indebted to you for pitching in. How can I ever repay you?"

"What are you talking about?" said Ben. "I've been in debt to you for years and I'm still looking for a way to repay *you*. This has been nothing."

"Even the rented tuxedo?" I said, disbelievingly.

That shook him. But then he said, in a low, suffering voice, "Even the rented tuxedo."

"Well, you're crazy. I'm the one who's in debt to you."

There followed such an unseemly wrangle over who was in debt to whom that a nurse, looking at us reproachfully, closed the door because we were disturbing the entire floor.

"How can you sit there, Ben," I said, hotly, "in your Italian innocence and refuse to take credit, thus activating my Jewish guilt, when you *know* my heart won't stand the strain?"

"What Italian innocence?" he said, just as hotly. "It's Italian superstition. Surely you've heard of Italian superstition?"

"Which one?"

"The one that says it is bad luck to take credit and thus profit through the misery of a friend."

"What are you talking about? The Mafia profits by huge sums—"

"Oh, well," said Ben, "it's different if you *cause* the misery."

And that broke me up and ended the discussion.

But thank you, Ben, and thank you, all my science fiction family of publishers, editors, writers, and fans, who filled my hospital stay so tightly with flowers and gifts and cards and visits that the hospital kicked me out a day early by general request of the staff.

VI
SCIENCE FICTION FANS

(Our Conventions)

Many years ago, someone said "Fandom is a way of life" and many fans believe that implicitly. The phrase abbreviated to an acronym, "fiawol," is the rallying cry of the fan movement.

I suppose that there are many specialized interests that devour their practitioners, but I find it difficult to believe that anything can be quite like science fiction and its fans. No one who has ever been part of it ever entirely recovers.

I was not in fandom to the extent that many of my contemporaries were, but I was in it sufficiently to be marked, and the following essay commemorates my high point as a fan.

39. OUR CONVENTIONS*

Over a six-week period in early 1975, the city of New York was the site of not one, but three, Star Trek conventions. Each was attended by thousands of fans—a large number of whom attended all three, in whole or in part.

I myself attended all three, and I could not help but think of the very first science fiction convention that was more than a gathering of local club members.

It took place in 1939 and was the brainchild of a big-name fan, Sam Moskowitz. Fans from all over the nation were in correspondence, but surely that was not enough, thought Sam. Why not a *world* gathering at which all the fans could get together and view each other with wide-eyed wonder? With grit and determination Sam, barely twenty, turned that brainstorm into actuality.

On July 2, 1939, I was one of those who actually attended the

---

First World Science Fiction Convention at a hall on Fifty-ninth
Street between Park and Madison avenues.

Nor was I merely a fan. I had published two stories in *Amazing
Stories*, and my third published story, *Trends*, appeared in the
July 1939 *Astounding Science Fiction*, which was actually on the
stands at the time of the convention. I attended as a *pro*.

The fact that I was a pro, however, lent me no feeling of self-
possession whatever, any more than did my attainment of the status of college graduate three weeks before. The fact was that I was
still in my teens and was incredibly unsophisticated.

But if it was unsophistication to be excited and deliriously
happy, then worldly wisdom would have been folly. My diary for
July 2 (a Sunday, by the way) details the lengths to which I went
to appear civilized. I was "all dressed up in new suit, tie, stiff shirt,
etc.—and it was hot." Not only that, but I had gone to the utter
extreme: "I shaved just before going, too."

I didn't go directly to the convention, however, but met with a
number of cronies at an automat across the street. It seems that
Sam Moskowitz, who was running the convention, of course, was
(together with his friends) locked in a Homeric struggle with six
rebels—three of whom have since become giants in the field.
These were Cyril Kornbluth (who died, alas, in 1958), Donald A.
Wollheim, and Frederik Pohl.

I didn't know what the roots of the struggle had been, but I
had met Pohl and the others not long before and I didn't know
Sam (who has since become a dear friend), so naturally I sided
with the known against the unknown.

Fred Pohl was the only one not present since he had had a doctor's appointment which had delayed him, and the group finally
made its move without him. Up the steps we went and there
stood Sam and his cronies barring the way. I was expecting a
mighty battle and was convinced that the dead and wounded
would soon be clogging Fifty-ninth Street, so I hung back a little
in order to play the part of strategic reserve.

There was no battle, however. The rebels simply stopped and
turned back. As for me, Sam didn't know me, didn't recognize me
as an enemy, and ignored me. Rather confused, I found myself inside the hall.

I ought to have placed principle above desire. I ought to have said, "If you refuse entrance to my friends, you refuse entrance to me," and I should then have stalked out. I should have—but I didn't. I wanted to attend the conference.

Once inside, along with a hundred others, I was goggle-eyed with happiness.

I met fans, giants in the field, whose letters had littered the magazines—Forrest J Ackerman, Jack Darrow, Milton A. Rothman.

I met godlike writers, with whom I could now hobnob on terms of only slightly tongue-tied familiarity. Some I had already met: John Campbell, Jack Williamson, L. Sprague de Camp. Some I met for the first time and kept forever after as a friend, John D. Clark, for instance. Some I met for the first and, alas, only time: Nelson Bond, Harl Vincent, Manly Wade Wellman.

After a while, the world called and I had to leave High Olympus for a while. I went out and had lunch with my friends in exile. They didn't hold my treason against me. They knew I was not really part of the Great Fan War and that I wanted to be at the convention. My diary records that for lunch I bought "sliced chicken sandwiches and hot coffee" and that "it cost me 30¢." (It would cost more like 300¢ now.)

In the afternoon, we saw the motion picture *Metropolis*, a silent movie that had been produced in Germany thirteen years previously. It struck me as having been produced during the Dark Ages and I hooted all through it. I never saw it again until about half a year ago. By then it was fifty years old and it seemed to have matured considerably in the interval. (Well, either it or I.)

Frank Paul, the illustrator and guest of honor, delivered his speech, and various editors rose to say a few words. Mort Weisinger, of *Thrilling Wonder Stories*, said to the audience of fans, "I didn't know you were so darned sincere" and was quoted in the next issue of *Time*.

Then notables were introduced from the audience, and I clapped madly as literary giant after literary giant rose to accept homage. Finally, John D. Clark, who was sitting next to me, shouted, "How about Asimov?" and I was called up to the platform.

It was the first time in my whole life that I had been a notable and I went up the aisle very shakily. I passed John Campbell (good heavens, he had only just turned twenty-nine) and he helped me good-naturedly along with a push that nearly sent me sprawling. I made it to the microphone, announced myself as "the worst science fiction writer unlynched," and sat down, with my face a charming vermilion. It was my first time facing an audience, and my last time embarrassed about it.

I spent a total of nine hours at the convention, 10 A.M. to 7 P.M., and they were pretty nearly the most delirious nine hours of my life up till then.

There have been about three dozen world science fiction conventions since then (the World War II years were skipped) and numerous regional conventions. Thousands now attend given conventions. The delirium continues and, if anything, is intensified—even for me, though I have been out of my teens for a few years.

(The Hugo)

All purely spontaneous expressions of joyous fore-gathering become (as they are continued) more calcu-lated in nature.

These days, one of the great purposes of the meet-ings of members of a subculture is the handing out of incestuous awards to members, from members, by members.

We can regard this phenomenon with mild con-tempt and a smile of superior amusement until such time as we ourselves get an award. Then it becomes very important.

40. THE HUGO*

Awards of one sort or another are the breath of life to people. A ribbon, a statuette, a medal, a plaque, a scroll—all these things can mean more than money.

The contestants at the Olympic Games in ancient Greece strove for the honor of a wreath of leaves—ideally, the only material gain. The Roman general who was granted a triumph also had his laurel wreath.

Various medieval monarchs established orders of knighthood, and whatever gewgaw symbolized that order was dearer than blood to the candidates.

Napoleon Bonaparte handed out the ribbons of the Legion of Honor freely, knowing that the hope of winning one and the satis-faction of having earned one would keep men fighting and dying for him.

The Nobel Prizes instituted in 1901 have gained unexampled prestige perhaps because, in addition to the usual medal, they offered a sizable sum of money.

The awards, however, that first caught the public's fancy were the golden statuettes handed out by the U. S. Academy of Motion Picture Arts and Sciences every year—statuettes commonly called "Oscars."

The Oscars, which have been handed out since 1927, were given to people who were familiar to all Americans, for work that was also familiar to all Americans. Eventually, the whole ceremony was placed on television so that it could be watched by all Americans.

After that, all sorts of other associations of specialized groups began handing out similar awards, usually endowed with pet names—Tonys, Grammys, Edgars, and so on.

And should science fiction be any different? Ever since 1939 (except for three of the World War II years) there has been an annual World Science Fiction Convention. Ought not such a convention seize the opportunity of a large gathering of science fiction pros and fans and use the convention banquet as a setting against which to hand out Achievement Awards?

Sure this is what should happen, except that for fourteen years it just didn't occur to anyone. And then in 1953, a Philadelphia fan named Hal Lynch was watching the Academy Awards on television and got an idea! It came to fruition. The 11th World Science Fiction Convention was held in Philadelphia in 1953 and the first Achievement Awards for excellence in science fiction were handed out. They were stainless-steel rocket ships on a wooden base, and they were called "Hugos" in honor of Hugo Gernsback who, twenty-seven years earlier, had published the first magazine in history to be devoted entirely to science fiction.

There was some vague notion in Philadelphia that the Hugos were to be an annual affair, but there is no continuity of supervision in the annual conventions. The 12th Convention in San Francisco in 1954 was run by an entirely different group of fans and no Hugos were given out.

Then, at the 13th Convention in Cleveland in 1955, the Hugo Awards were reinstated and with such success that they *did* become an annual affair thereafter. Not a year has been missed since.

And in that same year of 1955, my own peculiar involvement with the Hugos began. Consider—

1) At the 1955 convention, the one in which the Hugos first became an annual feature, I was the Guest of Honor.

2) When the idea arose of issuing anthologies of Hugo Winners in the novella, novelette, and short-story categories, I was chosen by Doubleday as the editor. In 1962, I edited *The Hugo Winners*; in 1971, *The Hugo Winners, Volume Two*; in 1977, *The Hugo Winners, Volume Three*. Undoubtedly, I will continue editing periodic volumes of Hugo winners while they and I both last.

3) I eventually began winning Hugos myself. Unfortunately, the days in which I wrote science fiction almost exclusively were over by the time the Hugos became well-established so that I rarely had anything available for nomination. Nevertheless, I managed to win a Hugo for my science fact articles in 1963; a retrospective Hugo for my novel series *The Foundation Trilogy* in 1966; a Hugo for my novel *The Gods Themselves* in 1973; and a Hugo for my novelette, *The Bicentennial Man* in 1977.

You wouldn't think that anything would be left that would give me greater pleasure still, would you? Well, let's move on to current events.

Over the Labor Day weekend of 1978, the 36th World Science Fiction Convention was held in Phoenix, Arizona. I didn't attend because I do not fly, but George Scithers, the editor of my magazine, was there, of course.

I had nothing in nomination; nothing I had personally written, that is. On the other hand, my magazine *might* have been in contention, for until 1972, it was common to hand out an award in the category of "Best Professional Magazine."

By then, however, it was realized that magazines were no longer the major source of science fiction. There were editors of original anthologies, editors at paperback houses, editors at hardback houses, all of which contributed importantly to the science fiction world. The category was therefore shifted to "Best Professional Editor."

And, of course, George was nominated, along with a number of others.

George labored under handicaps. He had been a professional science fiction editor for only a short time and at the time the votes were being counted, only nine issues of my magazine had appeared. He was not a major name in professional science fiction prior to his agreeing to work with me. What's more, he labored under the tremendous disadvantage of having to do his chores under the umbrella of my name. Given the name of the magazine, how many fans might think of me as the editor, rather than of George.

So I was not very sanguine.

On the morning of Labor Day, September 4, I received a call from Phoenix, from George. He sounded very calm. "I have some bad news for you and some good news," he said.

My heart sank. "Give me the bad news first," I said.

"I spent $200 on a loser's party," he said.

"Well, then, what possible good news could there be?"

"I didn't have to go," he said.

I didn't dare jump to any fancy conclusions. "Tell me who won, George," I said, urgently.

Still calm, George said, "I did! That's why I didn't have to go." Then, maybe just a little less calm, he said, "I'm overwhelmed."

It was simply a *tour de force*, considering everything. I called Joel Davis, the publisher, at his Connecticut home at once, and he shared in the jubilation.

There's no money involved; it's just a stainless-steel model of a spaceship on a wooden base. I doubt that it will raise our circulation, or put money in anyone's pocket, but it's a tribute to what we've done.

And, of course, to George in particular. As far as responsibility for the magazine is concerned, as far as thought and care over ways and means, over its principles and general direction, Joel, George, and I are a triumvirate.

Where day-to-day work is involved, however, it is *George* who does it. He is the editor in the fullest sense of the word. I may be the editorial director and Joel may be the publisher, but it is the *editor* who withstands the heat of the kitchen. It is the *editor* who deserves the credit. And it is the *editor*, George Scithers, who got the Hugo.

(*Anniversaries*)

The golden age of science fiction fandom was also the golden age of science fiction magazines when fans could read every word of science fiction that was printed, and know it all. Things have gotten away from us since—at least from those of us who are contemporaries of mine and who have managed (except for me) to grow superannuated.

One of the signs of the superannuation is the incredibly large numbers involved in the anniversaries we celebrate.

41. ANNIVERSARIES*

Think of this— In all of history, right through the first quarter of this century, there was no such thing as a science fiction magazine.

There was science fiction, of course. If you want to be broad in your definition of science fiction, then it is as old as the *Odyssey* or even as old as the *Epic of Gilgamesh*. Perhaps it is even as old as the first tale of imaginary adventure grunted out over a paleolithic campfire.

Coming farther toward the present, there were also science fiction stories in magazines. *Argosy* published some as did *Science and Invention, Blue Book, Radio Experimenter, Weird Tales,* and so on.

There was never a magazine, however, that was devoted entirely and exclusively to science fiction until Hugo Gernsback published *Amazing Stories*. The first issue of that magazine was dated April 1926, and it has been publishing ever since.

In 1976, therefore, *Amazing Stories* (and magazine science fiction generally) celebrated its Golden Anniversary.

That meant something to me personally, for *Amazing Stories* was the first science fiction magazine, indeed the first commercial enterprise of any sort, to buy something I had written. That was "Marooned Off Vesta" which appeared in the March 1939 issue of *Amazing Stories*, when the magazine was not quite thirteen years old.

Isaac Asimov's Science Fiction Magazine had not yet been born when magazine science fiction passed its half-century mark, or we would have hailed *Amazing Stories* on that occasion and wished it a healthy continuation for another half century and, indeed, for all eternity.

It may seem strange for this magazine thus to take note of our "competitors," but we do not believe them to be competitors in the sense that their success is our failure and vice versa. We are all of us engaged in one task: we are all trying to encourage the production and dissemination of good science fiction. If we are successful, the whole field profits and all the magazines have a chance to do better.

In fact, if but *one* of the magazines is notably successful in heightening the quality of the product and the quantity of the readership, it will, of necessity, encourage more writers to enter the field and to work harder to produce a still better product. Then *all* the magazines profit.

So we take joy over the successes of our "competitors" and we know they take equal joy over ours.

Nor is *Amazing Stories* the only magazine to enjoy a significant anniversary in the 1970s. With its October 1979 issue, *The Magazine of Fantasy and Science Fiction* celebrated its thirtieth anniversary.

Like *IASFM*, *F & SF* began life as a quarterly, progressed to bimonthly in its second year, and to monthly in its third year. It has remained monthly ever since.

Like *Amazing Stories*, *F & SF* has had important personal meaning to me. In its November 1958 issue, its ninetieth, when it was just passed its ninth birthday, it published an article of mine entitled "The Dust of Ages."

The blurb by Robert P. Mills read, in part, as follows: "*F & SF* announces delightedly that it has managed to retain . . . the good

Dr. Asimov, and that the intriguing results of his restless curiosity about physical phenomena and related matters will appear regularly in this new column."

That was the first use of the phrase "the Good Doctor" as applied to myself. Bob Mills used it regularly and genial old-timers still use it today—and I have never objected.

Bob probably did not guess how "regularly" that column would appear. In the thirtieth anniversary issue of *F & SF*, its 341st issue, my 252nd essay appeared. In the twenty-one years that had passed since the first, neither the magazine nor myself had missed a month.

It's been a wonderful association and I hope it continues unfalteringly as long as we both live.

Again, the October 1980 issue of *Galaxy* will mark its thirtieth birthday.† Those of us whose memories go back thirty years to the first few issues of *Galaxy* under the editorship of Horace L. Gold will remember the excitement they brought to the field.

They seemed to mark a rejuvenation, a new freshness to science fiction that was the beginning of a great rocketing expansion in the field. For a few years, there were more different magazines than had ever been seen before—or since.

I was part of it, too. Of the first thirteen issues of *Galaxy*, no less than seven contained fiction by myself.

But all of this is just by way of introduction. The most significant of the anniversaries of magazine science fiction comes this very month.

Not long after the great market crash of 1929 (a most unpropitious time for new business ventures) there appeared the first issue —January 1930—of a new science fiction magazine, *Astounding Stories*. It was the first pulp-size science fiction magazine; and it cost only 20¢ an issue as compared with 25¢ for the other (large size) magazines then in existence.

It was published by Clayton Publishers and they put out thirty-four issues before the pressures of the Great Depression forced

† Alas, the viscissitudes of fate prevented *Galaxy* from reaching its birthday.

them to close down both the magazine (with its March 1933 issue) and the publishing house itself.

The magazine was not dead, however; it was but sleeping. Street & Smith Publications, Inc., bought it and the October 1933 issue appeared with no break in its volume-issue numbering. It was still *Astounding Stories*.

Within a few issues, under the editorship of F. Orlin Tremaine, it came to be generally considered the leading magazine in the field, a position it has retained ever since (although *Galaxy* challenged it in the early 1950s, and *IASFM* is challenging it in the late 1970s).

At the close of 1937, John W. Campbell, Jr., took over the editorship of the magazine and the March 1938 issue was renamed *Astounding Science Fiction*. With that, the magazine and the whole field took a mighty leap forward. It was the Campbell Revolution, if I may coin a phrase, and by the July 1939 issue the "Golden Age" had begun.

Campbell discovered, and trained (or in a few cases, retrained), and encouraged, and supported a group of science fiction writers the like of which had never before been seen and (with all apologies to you rotten kids who are crowding the portals this last couple of decades) have never been seen again.

There are now four Grand Masters of Science Fiction, as chosen by the Science Fiction Writers of America. These are: Robert A. Heinlein, Jack Williamson, Clifford D. Simak, and L. Sprague de Camp. The first of these was a Campbell discovery and creation; the last three had published material before Campbell but were given a new birth by the man. I suspect it will be quite a while before a Grand Master will be chosen who was not, in one way or another, involved with Campbell.

And of course, as everyone knows, there wasn't anyone as close to Campbell, as hovered over by Campbell, as molded by Campbell, as I myself was in the late 1930s and throughout the 1940s.

Campbell remained editor of *Astounding* (the name of which he changed to *Analog* in 1960) for thirty-three years and finally left his job in the only way it was possible for him to do so—by dying in 1971 at the too-early age of sixty-one.

Ben Bova succeeded as editor of *Analog* and, after seven

years, he stepped aside (voluntarily) for Stanley Schmidt, who now rules the domain. The spirit of John Campbell still hovers over the magazine, however, and over science fiction. It will continue to do so as long as any of those he developed remain alive.

And now, this month, with the January 1980 issue, its 590th, *Astounding/Analog* celebrates its Fiftieth Anniversary.

All of us at *IASFM*, Joel, George, Shawna, myself, and everyone, raise a glass to it, to all its years, to all its issues, to all its editors, to all its writers, to all its stories.

Live long and prosper, competitor and friend!

(The Letter Column) (The Articles of Science Fiction)
(Rejection Slips)

Since science fiction fandom and science fiction magazines are so intimately connected (at least in my heart), it is not surprising that I do my best to see to it that my magazine is aimed at the fan and that he is brought into a kind of partnership with us.

Several of my editorials have dealt quite frankly with various aspects of the science fiction magazine business in general, and with my magazine in particular. The three essays that follow are all examples of what I mean. They appeared respectively in the May 1980, the April 1979, and the December 1979 issues.

42. THE LETTER COLUMN*

One of the problems that faces a science fiction magazine is the letter column. Should there be one? Should there not be one? If there is one, what kind should it be?

Those are not easy questions to answer, and I was the one who had to supply those answers. It's George, with the able assistance of the beauteous red-haired Shawna, who edits the magazine, but it's I who am supposed to set the tone, and the letter column is part of the tone.

The letter column became part of the science fiction phenomenon in the very first science fiction magazine, *Amazing Stories*, and it sprang to life at the behest of the very first science fiction editor, Hugo Gernsback.

He had some arcane financial reason for starting a letter column, but it got away from him almost at once. It turned out that science fiction fans were garrulous, articulate, and incredibly hungry both for exposure and for communication with each other. The department grew enormously popular and nobody ever dreamed of saying, "If you cut out the letters, you'll have room to give us more stories."

People *wanted* to read the letters. The constant letter writers became friends with each other and out of that burgeoned the fan movement—fan clubs, fan magazines, and fan conventions. And, of course, some of the constant letter writers rose to become constant story writers; I among them.

But everything changes, even letter columns. If one isn't careful, a letter column tends to gain a juvenile touch. There is nothing like the intensity with which a young teenager can love science fiction; and if he is a bright and articulate young teenager (and what other kind would love science fiction), he will turn out novelettes of golly-gee-whiz enthusiasm filling quires of paper—and often get printed.

Some editors could not resist playing up to this segment and in *Thrilling Wonder Stories* there was, for a while, "Sergeant Saturn" answering the letters with a kind of phony subjuvenile joviality.

On the other hand, to those who wanted, above all else, for science fiction to be adult and respectable, such juvenility was anathema. To the more sensitive, any fan letter that discussed the stories or the magazine was juvenile by that very fact. *Astounding Science Fiction* therefore decided to turn the letter column into total edification. Readers were to concentrate only on the scientific points within the stories. The title of the letter column was changed from "Brass Tacks" to "Science Discussions."

Both changes, of course, represented (in my opinion) an unacceptable extreme. Sergeant Saturn's silly clowning embarrassed everyone over the mental age of eight. On the other hand, the dull pontifications of "Science Discussions" were thoroughly opaque.

It was not surprising, then, that when *Fantasy and Science Fiction* began publication in 1949, and aimed at neither children nor engineers, they simply omitted a letter column.

The next year when Horace Gold was founding *Galaxy*, he sent out queries to groups of science fiction readers as to what they would or would not like to see in his magazine. He was utterly astonished to discover that, by a healthy majority, they wanted no letter column at all.

You can see the reason. If one must choose among childishness, boredom, and nothing—it will be nothing that will be chosen.

The two extremes, however, are not the only choices. Have we forgotten the middle ground?

So I decided on a letter column in the middle ground and, thank goodness, George agreed with me. It was going to be my kind of letter column and I was to choose the letters to be published.

Here's the way it's done. George, Shawna, and Joel look through the letters as much as their curiosity drives them to, but then they send the whole thing to me, leaving out nothing. I am bombarded by endless masses of manila envelopes crammed with letters. (Yes, it does make a dent in my tight schedule and no, I am not overjoyed—but it must be done.)

I read every one of them and I pick out just about twice as many letters for publication as we can possibly have room to print. I then append to each a one-liner which I try to make light, fluffy, and (I earnestly hope) witty. George then makes the final selection on the basis of the exact amount of space available in a given issue.

Now the question arises (I can hear you out there): Which letters do I choose for publication?

First, they have to be reasonably easy to read. I don't want to seem ungracious, but I can't possibly spend time poring over a letter in order to make out dim pencil marks or chicken-track handwriting. Even typing isn't a dream of happiness if it is with an old ribbon, or clogged keys, or is heavily x'd. Aside from its being difficult for me to read, I wouldn't dare send it to the printer, who is a hard-working fellow with troubles of his own. So, please, if you would like to make the letter column, neat typing would help.

Second, they have to make some interesting point or other. I know it's annoying to have the address sticker obscure the cover, and we grovel with embarrassment over it, but it would be dull to publish the fifth letter on the same subject, let alone the twenty-eighth. For that matter, if a hundred of you write to praise a particularly praiseworthy story, we can no longer print any more once we have inserted two or three. Even too much praise sickens (everyone but the author, that is).

Third, we are not any more anxious to publish a badly written letter than a badly written story. And we do love a clever letter as long as it isn't too clever by half. Where's the dividing line? You don't have to worry about that. We'll decide.

Fourth, it's obvious we can't print long letters. Two or three paragraphs are plenty. If your letter is longer, but contains good material, we're liable to print excerpts rather than the whole thing.

Fifth, I like a letter that gives me a chance to say something lightly humorous in return. The editorial reply, in fact, is an important part of the letter. They lend the tone, and "lightly humorous" is the tone I want and strive for.

Now, then, are we accomplishing what we have set out to do? I think so, but how can I be sure? As everyone knows, I'm full of cheerful self-appreciation and like everything I do. That doesn't mean other people are pleased.

For instance, some of our correspondents complain that the letter column is self-serving; that we print too many letters that praise us and apparently dump those that call us bad names.

Actually, that's not so. Candor forces me to admit that we like praise better than blame (who doesn't?) but we make a definite effort to include carpings and criticisms. This is not because we are masochists or superhumanly full of integrity—but because it lends variety to the column and makes it interesting to the reader, and interest is the name of the game.

The trouble is, in all honesty, that we *do* get far more letters praising us than blaming us. And if that's the way it must be, let it be so. I don't want any of you writing letters of blame that you're not really sincere about just because you want to redress the balance.

Then, too, there are occasional remarks to the effect that my replies are too flip and, on at least one occasion, that they were insulting. Naturally, I don't intend to be insulting and George (who has a marvlous sense of equanimity) rides herd on me to make sure I don't get overenthusiastic. But—humor is tricky.

One last thing—every once in a while someone writes a letter to

IASFM that is clearly addressed to me as an individual—that talks about me as a writer, or discusses stories of mine that appeared in other magazines, or asks personal questions. Such letters cannot, of course, appear in the letter column but, when I can, I answer them personally.

I say "when I can" because times have changed. For many years, I took pride in answering every single fan letter I received, even if only with a brief postcard. But, alas, my mail seems to get ever heavier and my writing and lecturing schedule ever tighter. It is no longer possible to answer every letter and for that I apologize to all of you.

43. THE ARTICLES
OF SCIENCE FICTION*

The word "magazine" comes, oddly enough, from the Arabic, and its original meaning was that of a storehouse containing a miscellaneous supply of things needed for trading purposes.

What we *now* most frequently call magazines are periodicals that contain a supply of miscellaneous reading material. Or, at least, some do. There has always been a tendency for specializing in order to more nearly meet the needs of a particular subaudience. One specialization has been in the direction of an exclusively fiction periodical.

Indeed, in the heyday of the pulp magazines of the 1920s and 1930s, the content was not merely fiction, but a precise variety of fiction, and the first science fiction magazines were in that tradition.

The early science fiction magazines might contain a short message from the editor, a letter column, an occasional book review, and perhaps a "science quiz" (and advertisements, of course), but with those minor and nonsignificant exceptions, fiction—and science fiction at that—filled every page.

I'm not sure when and how the notion of having a nonfiction article in the s.f. magazines first arose. However, the first nonfiction articles of which I was personally aware and which ground themselves into my memory came in 1934.

Charles Fort had written a book called *Lo!* and *Astounding Stories* ran it in eight installments beginning with the April 1934 issue.

Why? —Because the book had a science fictional aura.

Charles Fort was the Immanuel Velikovsky of his time. He believed in all sorts of unorthodox notions that were frowned on by conventional scientists. Whereas Velikovsky supports his notions by quoting myths and legends that he carefully selects for the purpose, Fort supported his notions, in even less reliable fashion, by collecting newspaper articles reporting bizarre events.

Though *Lo!* drove me mad with its silliness, it proved extraordinarily popular with the readers; and the editor of *Astounding*, F. Orlin Tremaine, searched for other nonfiction that readers of science fiction would welcome.

Beginning with the June 1936 issue of *Astounding Stories*, for instance, Tremaine ran John W. Campbell's *A Study of the Solar System*, which ran for eighteen consecutive issues, and which was eaten up alive by the readers. I myself found it wonderful.

Since most science fiction stories in those days were adventure tales placed on various worlds of the Solar system, it was delightful (and, for the writers, useful) to read the then-latest knowledge of those worlds written in Campbell's dramatic style.

It was not long after the conclusion of Campbell's series that he became editor of the magazine, replacing Tremaine. Campbell naturally believed in the nonfiction article as owning a place in science fiction magazines, and he cultivated new and better nonfiction as assiduously as he cultivated new and better fiction.

There was, for instance, Willy Ley. Ley was German-born but had left Germany as soon as Hitler came to power (out of conviction and not out of fear, for he was not Jewish). He was interested in the full breadth of science, but his specialty was rocketry and an article of his, "The Dawn of the Conquest of Space," appeared in the March 1937 *Astounding*, while it was still under Tremaine.

Campbell published many of Ley's articles and Ley, in his turn, published many articles in the other science fiction magazines. In fact, it is quite fair to say that Willy Ley was the father of the nonfiction article as it exists today in science fiction magazines. He dealt with subjects on the frontiers of science, subjects that shaded off into science fiction, but did so always with firm rationalism and with thorough scientific knowledge.

Other writers followed his lead. L. Sprague de Camp (my personal favorite in the field) wrote several top-notch articles for *Astounding*, including "Language for Time Travelers" in the July 1938 issue, "Design for Life" in the May and June 1939 issues, and "The Sea-King's Armored Division" in the September and

October 1941 issues. Robert S. Richardson, the astronomer, wrote several dozen astronomical articles for *Astounding* through the 1940s.

Willy Ley had an article in the first issue (October 1950) of *Galaxy Science Fiction* and, eventually, became its monthly science columnist, a post he held till his death in 1969. It was a very popular feature in the magazine, and was always the item I turned to first.

I myself felt the lure of the science article. The first ones I wrote were for Campbell, of course, and my very first was "Hemoglobin and the Universe" which appeared in the February 1955 issue of *Astounding*. (Unless you want to count my gag piece "The Endochronic Properties of Resublimated Thiotimoline," which appeared in the March 1948 issue.)

It was in response to these articles, and to the success of Ley's column, that Robert P. Mills, editor of *Venture Science Fiction*, asked me to do a similar science column for that magazine. I accepted and my article "Fecundity Limited!" appeared in the January 1958 issue of that magazine.

Alas, I only had time to publish four articles before the magazine folded, but by then, Mills was convinced that I was the only person who could match Ley in erudition. I *didn't* feel that, but you can bet I had no intention of disillusioning him.

Consequently, he asked me to shift my column to *Venture*'s sister publication, *The Magazine of Fantasy and Science Fiction*. This I did, and my first article there, "The Dust of Ages," appeared in the November 1958 issue. It continues to this day without missing an issue.

Several questions now arise:

First, since *Isaac Asimov's Science Fiction Magazine* is now a monthly, since it has a higher circulation than *F & SF*, and since its pay rate is higher, too, am I going to switch my column from the latter to the former?

I'm sorry. The answer is "No." There's such a thing as loyalty and both George and Joel understand thoroughly that I have old-fashioned ideas about such things.

Well then, are we going to have someone else as a monthly science columnist?

We have nothing against this notion in theory, but probably not.

The trouble is that there are some difficult criteria to meet before we can have one. The monthly science columnist has to be a polymath, acquainted with a wide breadth of subjects, or he or she will not be able to have sufficient variety in the subject matter.

He or she must have an endless fund of ideas, for it isn't enough merely to repeat the material out of the sources; one should be able to add some original thoughts, conjectures, inferences.

He or she must be able to write both authoritatively and entertainingly, and the combination isn't very easy to find.

Finally, and *most important of all*, he or she must be compulsive enough to meet a monthly deadline.

We're keeping our eyes open for someone who'll meet all the criteria, but we're steeling ourselves against disappointment.

Well, then, are we going to have science articles?

Of course! We've had them in the past and we'll have them in the future. Thanks to Campbell and Ley, science fiction readers have been educated into the virtue of science articles.

We may not have one every issue, however. We would rather not be forced to run a dull or trivial article just because that happens to be the only thing we have on hand and because we feel bound to have one in every issue.

And to some extent, you readers have your responsibility, too. Thousands of you must have special knowledge of some science-related subject that our eclectically minded readers would love to hear about.

Query George on the subject matter, if you wish. If he gives you the work, then go ahead and write it up. He may still reject it, of course, but even so you won't be a complete loser. As one who has tried both in copious measure, I assure you there's even more fun in writing a science article than in writing a science fiction story.

44. REJECTION SLIPS*

Virtually all writers get rejection slips; some only occasionally and some frequently. A number of writers, alas, get nothing but rejection slips even after they have been at it for years.

Usually, writers receive such slips with emotions that range from sorrow through disappointment to frustration. I can't blame them, and I don't. I experience the same emotions myself on such occasions.

Sometimes, though, these emotions explode into anger and bitterness and are expressed as such in the furious letters we receive.

It occurs to me therefore that I ought to write on the subject. It is not a particularly pleasant one, but we cultivate a very informal atmosphere in this magazine and I feel that I can talk to you about anything at all.

Let's try some questions and answers, therefore:

1) *Why must there be rejections?*

Suppose we have room for ten stories each month, and suppose we get a hundred submissions each month. Clearly, ninety of these submissions must be returned to the submitter. We get no pleasure out of that, but we can't help it. It is with the sure knowledge of this ineluctable fact of publishing life that we ask that all unsolicited manuscripts be accompanied by a stamped self-addressed envelope large enough to hold that manuscript comfortably. The cruel situation is that the odds on rejection are uncomfortably great.

2) *Which stories get rejected?*

If we can only print a small percentage of what we get, then we must accept the small percentage that is highest in quality and reject everything else. Again, we have no choice.

3) *Ah, but the level of quality is a subjective matter and no two people would agree on which stories are the best. So who decides?*

The answer is easy. The editor decides, and in the case of this magazine, the editor is George Scithers. Where the question of acceptance or rejection is concerned, the editor (George Scithers, still) is an absolute monarch. He is the law and from his ukase there is no appeal.

There are others who work with George, notably Shawna. Their opinions are requested and are valued and may sway George, but in the end George makes the decision. When George is more than usually doubtful, he may send me the manuscript for my opinion and I will then express my feelings with varying degrees of vehemence, either for or against, and again George may be swayed, but again he makes the final decision. Joel, our esteemed publisher, reads as many manuscripts as he can find time to, and he, too, is free to express an opinion (and does so) and George will listen—and then make his own decision.

4) *Why this absolutism? Why George?*

Because George bears the responsibility as well. If the magazine does well and meets the approval of the readers, it is George who wins the Hugo; not I, not Joel, not Shawna. If the magazine does poorly and if the readers should begin to depart, heaven forbid, it is George who is likely to be replaced.

Under these circumstances, George must have a free hand. To attempt to subvert his decisions by fiat (as opposed to discussion, argument, and reasoning) would destroy his usefulness at once.

5) *But why are some stories held so long before a decision is made? Is George lazy, by any chance?*

A more conscientious, harder-working man simply doesn't exist. George is not lazy. He makes every attempt to reach a decision as quickly as possible either way, and, on the whole, he succeeds. After all, some stories are so good, or fall so far short of requirements, that virtually on the instant of reading a decision to accept or reject can be made.

Some stories, however, are (inevitably) borderline. There may be virtues and shortcomings in such balance that no clear certainty can be reached as to which overrides. It may seem, too, that a revision might save a story, or make a fairly good story into a very good one, but there may be some question as to the nature or extent of revision that ought to be requested. For these, and for other reasons, too, there can be an extended period of agonized soul-searching, as unpleasant for the editor as for the writer.

6) *Why should there be a soulless rejection slip—a curt printed form—a list of items of which one or two are casually checked off? Granted that rejections are necessary, is this a way to treat a writer, even a beginner? And of what use is such a slip in educating and developing that beginner?*

Quite right. Rejection slips, or form letters, however tactfully phrased, are lacerations of the soul, if not quite inventions of the devil—but there is no way around them.

It would be best for everyone, including George, if somehow every rejection could be accompanied by a thorough analysis of the story, pointing out defects and ways of correcting them. If, in this way, a hundred beginners could be force-fed into expertise each year—what a magazine we would have!

Unfortunately, there is no way of doing this. There are not years enough in the day and George could not survive two weeks of it, even though he is a jovial and rugged soul. In order to leave time for all the manifold editorial duties, and even for such trivia as eating and sleeping, George must dispose of some manuscripts briefly—and naturally does so in the case of the least satisfactory.

In all borderline cases, and reasonably near misses, however, George does make the effort to talk about the story as thoroughly as he can reasonably be expected to, and many burgeoning writers have testified to that with gratitude.

7) *Sometimes George encloses directions on "How to Write." Isn't that insulting, especially if the writer is not exactly a beginner?*

Well, there are times when its inclusion would not be appropriate. If a topflight professional were sent such directions, George might very well get a letter in return that might frizzle him about the edges a bit.

Except in obvious cases, however, such directions are useful even to writers who have already made sales. Remember that different editors have different tastes and different needs. George is not so much interested in teaching you How to Write on some vast objective scale as in teaching you How to Write in such a way as to meet his tastes and needs.

8) *How should you react to a rejection?*

I personally kick and scream and there isn't any reason why you shouldn't either, if it makes you feel better. However, once you are quite done with the kicking and screaming, sit down and reread the story in the light of anything George may have told you, and see if you can find out what's wrong, how to correct that wrong, and how to avoid that wrong in the future. If the rejection teaches you something, you may in the long run have gained more from it than from a too-easy acceptance of a flawed story.

9) *How should you not react to a rejection?*

a) Don't stay mad and decide you are the victim of incompetence and stupidity. If you do, you'll learn nothing and you'll never become a writer.

b) Don't try appealing, say, over George's head to me. I will under no circumstances read a manuscript George has rejected.

c) Don't get huffy because you have already made sales and therefore feel that no editor dare reject you. That's just not so. He *can* reject you and he need not even offer any reason. I've made nearly two thousand sales of all kinds, and I still get rejections now and then, and some pretty offhanded ones at times, too. Indeed, George himself has rejected two of my stories. (He says only one but it was *two*.)

d) Don't make the opposite mistake and decide the story is worthless. Editors differ and so do tastes and so do magazines' needs. Try the story somewhere else. Some of the stories we publish have been rejected by other magazines and some of our rejects are published elsewhere. Why not? What doesn't fit one magazine might easily fit another.

Finally, please remember George Scithers' Golden Rule of Rejection: "We don't reject writers; we reject pieces of paper with typing on them."

So just sit down and produce other pieces of paper with typing on them, and we'll be glad to see them from all you nonrejected writers.

VII
SCIENCE FICTION
REVIEWS

(What Makes Good Science Fiction?)

> I'm not a critic (it's no secret that I am not overly fond of critics and reviewers), and I never willingly take up the role of criticism, of weighing virtues and shortcomings, and of making lordly pronouncements.
>
> At times, however, I am asked for my opinion and sometimes I just can't resist trying to correct what seem to me to be obvious flaws. I try not to discuss literary values, concerning which I know very little, but I do have some opinions on the merits and demerits of science fiction that involve other aspects of the art.

45. WHAT MAKES GOOD SCIENCE FICTION?*

The phenomenal success of *Star Wars* could not help but initiate a new wave of science fiction in the movies and in TV, and the first drenchings have already washed over our television screens. It is inevitable that along with the good comes the bad, and in the case of science fiction, at least, the bad is horrible.

Why is that? What makes some science fiction bad?

In considering a piece of science fiction writing, the first rule is that if it is bad fiction, it is bad science fiction. There is no magic that can convert something bad into something good just because it is science fiction.

The reverse is not true, however. A piece of science fiction writing may be good fiction and yet bad science fiction.

There is an extra ingredient required by science fiction that makes literary and dramatic virtue not entirely sufficient. There

* Copyright © 1977 by Triangle Publications, Inc.

must, in addition, be some indication that the writer knows science.

This does not mean that the science has to be detailed and stultifying; there need only be casual references—but the references must be correct. Nor does it mean that the writer cannot take liberties—but he must know what liberties he can take and how he can justify them without sounding like an ignoramus.

It may be that most of the audience knows so little science that they wouldn't recognize ignorance if they saw or heard it, or care either. That doesn't matter. I am not trying to define what makes a science fiction show popular or successful, but what makes it good. It is perfectly possible for a dreadful science fiction show (or a dreadful *anything* show) to make a lot of money, but that doesn't make it one whit less dreadful; it simply tells us something about the audience.

Let's take some examples.

I enjoyed *Star Wars*. It is deliberately campy and it is utterly brainless, but the special effects are fun and it is restful sometimes to park one's brain outside. One can even forgive the kind of slip that makes "parsec" a unit of speed rather than of distance, and consider it the equivalent of a typographical error.

But— The most popular scene in the picture involves numerous extraterrestrials gathered round a bar, drinking. It is the interplanetary equivalent of the ask-no-questions-and-no-holds-barred saloon in many Westerns. As a deliberate satire on these Western bars, it is funny, and we must admire the imagination of the makeup artists in creating the different beings.

However, are all these strange beings perfectly at home in a single atmosphere, at a single temperature and pressure? Should some not find an environment insufferable that others find comfortable?

It might spoil the fun if such a complication had to be introduced and it could, after all, be supposed that all these creatures just happened to find an Earth-type atmosphere endurable. That would violate no scientific law, only the rules of probability.

Yet one of these creatures might have had to wear a space suit, or might have had to keep sniffing at a gas cylinder or ducking its head into a bowl of water. It would have meant very little trouble and would have made the scene much better science fiction.

Consider, in contrast, the television science fiction show "Logan's Run." Some of the people working for it worked for "Star Trek," so it's not surprising that its attitude toward science shows promise.

In one episode, for instance, an extraterrestrial spaceship is picking up samples of the dominant species from different worlds. They have just picked up our hero and heroine, and on the ship are also several pairs of extraterrestrials who have been picked up on their own planets. One pair is in a cage that is filled with an atmosphere that they can breathe but which is poisonous to human beings. This is good science fiction, and it is satisfactory to have it made pertinent to the plot.

Consider another point from the same show. In recent years, there has arisen the illiterate fancy that the word "galaxy" refers to anything that is not in our own Solar system. Everyone and everything "comes from a different galaxy." (This is like supposing that everything that does not come from our own town comes from a different continent.)

In "Logan's Run," however, one of the characters refers to extraterrestrials as being "from another Solar system" and a great peace descended on me. At least the writer knows what a galaxy is and is not.

There is no such effort made in "The Man From Atlantis." The core of the plot involves a creature (manlike, but a nonhuman species) who can live under water and who has webbed hands and feet. We can accept that as given.

In one episode, Victor Buono, as the unctuously comic villain, is melting the Earth's ice caps by a microwave device in order to raise the sea level and "attract attention."

The energy required to melt the ice caps as rapidly as he is described as doing it would be utterly prohibitive. It would take centuries to melt the ice caps under any rational human-made urgings and, once partial melting had taken place, it would take centuries to persuade the water to refreeze.

There is almost an understanding of this. The villain gets the hero to cooperate by saying he has ceased the melting process and

shows faked movies to indicate the sea level is receding. After a
long time, the hero suddenly realizes that the sea level wouldn't
recede once the process is stopped. The excess water must evapo-
rate first, he says. (That's right, and it must refreeze in the polar
regions, which would take a long, long time.) He therefore knows
that Buono has faked the pictures and in his anger he does what
he should have done at the very start—he destroys the microwave
equipment with his mental powers.

And, of course, the instant the equipment is destroyed, the sea
level *does* recede. —Unbearably bad science fiction!

Even children's programs must not show scientific ignorance—
they least of all, in fact. On Saturday mornings, there is "Space
Academy" and in one particular half-hour segment, two ships pass
through a black hole, and later return.

There isn't a single sign, however, that anyone connected with
the show knows one single thing about black holes, what they are
or what they do.

It would seem that the hard-working, but uneducated, people
behind the show think that a black hole is a gap among the stars,
or perhaps a space whirlpool, through which one can scoot and return.

Actually, a black hole is a quantity of mass so great and so com-
pressed as to produce a gravitational field that will let nothing escape, not even light. Anything moving too close to a black hole
will fall in and be forever unable to emerge.

There are, indeed, some theories (not universally accepted)
that, if a black hole rotates, matter falling in may emerge in a far
different part of the Universe. Even then, however, any organized
bit of matter such as a ship or a human being, or even an atom, is
destroyed and will emerge as energy only.

A black hole can give rise to a number of highly dramatic situations—but you must understand it first.

And although children's shows need not necessarily be educational, it is surely not too much to ask that they not be miseduca-
tional.

To the general public, science fiction may seem to include the
"superman" story and, in fact, this can almost be justified.

"The Bionic Woman," for instance, traces the superpowers of
its protagonist to the use of powered prostheses and of bionic or-

gans with greater ranges of abilities than the living organs they replace.

One can imagine, without too much embarrassment, an artificial eye sensitive to a broader range of light-waves and to dimmer illumination than a natural eye is; to nuclear-powered limbs of supernormal strength and capable of great bursts of speed or thrust. Given that, one needs only imaginative plots and good acting (a big "only," of course) to have decent science fiction.

"Wonder Woman," on the other hand, is hopeless, since the conversion of an ordinary woman to a superkangaroo in red, white, and blue is achieved merely by spinning in place. (Superman at least stepped into a phone booth.)

"Wonder Woman" is mere fantasy, therefore, and can in no way be considered science fiction. —To be sure, lest anyone think I failed to notice, Wonder Woman herself is a supernormal resting place for the eye, but that doesn't make it science fiction, just terrific biology.

"Wonder Woman" might be saved if it took the attitude that the old "Batman" show did. In "Batman" the science was laughable, but it was used for that very purpose. "Batman" was deliberate farce, which made effective fun of many of the trappings of popular literature and of science fiction, too. And it becomes good science fiction to make fun of science fiction *knowledgeably*.

A very faint echo of that laughter is still to be found in the cartoon version of "Batman" which is on, for children, Saturday morning. A little mouselike creature "Bat Mite" is added, and, true to the tradition (from Samson and Hercules onward) that supermuscles mean microbrains, Bat Mite is the only character in the cartoon that shows any spark of intelligence—and that must be on purpose.

AFTERWORD 45

(*What Makes Good Science Fiction?*)

I was apparently wrong in my remark on Star Wars.
I had only seen the motion picture once (not a dozen

*times, like some enthusiasts) and I had failed to no-
tice, in the bar scene, that some of the characters did
require alien conditions.*

*Well, I could wish that the producers and directors
had emphasized that a bit more; but then I suppose
they could legitimately express the wish that people
like myself be a little more observant. No matter what
my rationalization, I'm afraid I lose on that one.*

(1984)

I've been writing a four-part article for Field News-paper Syndicate at the beginning of each year for several years now and in 1980, mindful of the approach of the year 1984, FNS asked me to write a thorough critique of George Orwell's novel 1984.

I was reluctant. I remembered almost nothing of the book and said so—but Denison Demac, the lovely young woman who is my contact at FNS, simply sent me a copy of it and said, "Read it."

So I read it and found myself absolutely astonished at what I read. I wondered how many people who talked about the novel so glibly had ever read it; or if they had, whether they remembered it at all.

I felt I would have to write the critique if only to set people straight. (I'm sorry; I love setting people straight.)

46. *1984**

A. *The Writing of* 1984

In 1949, a book entitled 1984 was published. It was written by Eric Arthur Blair under the pseudonym of George Orwell.

The book attempted to show what life would be like in a world of total evil, in which those controlling the government kept themselves in power by brute force, by distorting the truth, by continually rewriting history, by mesmerizing the people generally.

This evil world was placed only thirty-five years in the future so that even men who were already in their early middle age at the time the book was published might live to see it if they lived out a normal lifetime.

I, for instance, was already a married man when the book appeared and yet here we are less than four years away from that apocalyptic year (for "1984" has become a year that is associated with dread because of Orwell's book), and I am very likely to live to see it.

In this chapter, I will discuss the book, but first: Who was Blair/Orwell and why was the book written?

Blair was born in 1903 into the status of a British gentleman. His father was in the Indian civil service and Blair himself lived the life of a British Imperial official. He went to Eton, served in Burma, and so on.

However, he lacked the money to be an English gentleman to the full. Then, too, he didn't want to spend his time at dull desk jobs; he wanted to be a writer. Thirdly, he felt guilty about his status in the upper class.

So he did in the late 1920s what so many well-to-do American young people in the 1960s did. In short, he became what we would have called a "hippie" at a later time. He lived under slum conditions in London and Paris, consorted with and identified with slum dwellers and vagrants, managed to ease his conscience and, at the same time, to gather material for his earliest books.

He also turned left wing and became a socialist, fighting with the loyalists in Spain in the 1930s. There he found himself caught up in the sectarian struggles between the various left-wing factions, and since he believed in a gentlemanly English form of socialism, he was inevitably on the losing side. Opposed to him were passionate Spanish anarchists, syndicalists, and communists, who bitterly resented the fact that the necessities of fighting the Franco fascists got in the way of their fighting each other. The communists, who were the best organized, won out and Orwell had to leave Spain, for he was convinced that if he did not, he would be killed.

From then on, to the end of his life, he carried on a private literary war with the communists, determined to win in words the battle he had lost in action.

During World War II, in which he was rejected for military service, he was associated with the left wing of the British Labour party, but didn't much sympathize with their views, for even their feckless version of socialism seemed too well organized for him.

He wasn't much affected, apparently, by the Nazi brand of totalitarianism, for there was no room within him except for his private war with Stalinist communism. Consequently, when Great Britain was fighting for its life against Nazism, and the Soviet Union fought as an ally in the struggle and contributed rather more than its share in lives lost and in resolute courage, Orwell wrote *Animal Farm* which was a satire of the Russian Revolution and what followed, picturing it in terms of a revolt of barnyard animals against human masters.

He completed *Animal Farm* in 1944 and had trouble finding a publisher since it wasn't a particularly good time for upsetting the Soviets. As soon as the war came to an end, however, the Soviet Union was fair game and *Animal Farm* was published. It was greeted with much acclaim and Orwell became sufficiently prosperous to retire and devote himself to his masterpiece, 1984.

That book described society as a vast worldwide extension of Stalinist Russia in the 1930s, pictured with the venom of a rival left-wing sectary. Other forms of totalitarianism play a small role. There are one or two mentions of the Nazis and of the Inquisition. At the very start, there is a reference or two to Jews, almost as though they were going to prove the objects of persecution, but that vanishes almost at once, as though Orwell didn't want readers to mistake the villains for Nazis.

The picture is of Stalinism, and Stalinism only.

By the time the book came out in 1949, the Cold War was at its height. The book therefore proved popular. It was almost a matter of patriotism in the West to buy it and talk about it, and perhaps even to read parts of it, although it is my opinion that more people bought it and talked about it than read it, for it is a dreadfully dull book—didactic, repetitious, and all but motionless.

It was most popular at first with people who leaned toward the conservative side of the political spectrum, for it was clearly an anti-Soviet polemic, and the picture of life it projected in the London of 1984 was very much as conservatives imagined life in the Moscow of 1949 to be.

During the McCarthy era in the United States, 1984 became increasingly popular with those who leaned toward the liberal side of the political spectrum, for it seemed to them that the United States of the early 1950s was beginning to move in the direction of thought-control and that all the viciousness Orwell had depicted was on its way toward us.

Thus, in an afterword to an edition published in paperback by New American Library in 1961, the liberal psychoanalyst and philosopher Erich Fromm concluded as follows:

"Books like Orwell's are powerful warnings, and it would be most unfortunate if the reader smugly interpreted *1984* as another description of Stalinist barbarism, and if he does not see that it means us, too."

Even if Stalinism and McCarthyism are disregarded, however, more and more Americans were becoming aware of just how "big" the government was getting; how high taxes were; how increasingly rules and regulations permeated business and even ordinary life; how information concerning every facet of private life was entering the files not only of government bureaus but of private credit systems.

1984, therefore, came to stand not for Stalinism, or even for dictatorship in general—but merely for government. Even governmental paternalism seemed "1984ish" and the catch phrase "Big Brother is watching you" came to mean everything that was too big for the individual to control. It was not only big government and big business that was a symptom of *1984* but big science, big labor, big anything.

In fact, so thoroughly has 1984-ophobia penetrated the consciousness of many who have not read the book and have no notion of what it contains, that one wonders what will happen to us after December 31, 1984. When New Year's Day of 1985 arrives and the United States is still in existence and facing very much the problems it faces today, how will we express our fears of whatever aspect of life fills us with apprehension? What new date can we invent to take the place of 1984?

Orwell himself did not live to see his book become the success it did. He did not witness the way in which he made 1984 into a year that would haunt a whole generation of Americans. Orwell died of tuberculosis in a London hospital in January 1950, just a few months after the book was published, at the age of forty-six. His awareness of imminent death may have added to the bitterness of the book.

B. The Science Fiction of 1984

Many people think of 1984 as a science fiction novel, but almost the only item about 1984 that would lead one to suppose this is the fact that it is purportedly laid in the future.

Not so! Orwell had no feel for the future, and the displacement of the story is much more geographical than temporal. The London in which the story is placed is not so much moved thirty-five years forward in time, from 1949 to 1984, as it is moved a thousand miles east in space to Moscow.

Orwell imagines Great Britain to have gone through a revolution similar to the Russian Revolution and to have gone through all the stages that Soviet development did. He can think of almost no variations on the theme. The Soviets had a series of purges in the 1930s, so the Ingsoc (English Socialism) had a series of purges in the 1950s.

The Soviets converted one of their revolutionaries, Leon Trotsky, into a villain, leaving his opponent, Joseph Stalin, as a hero. The Ingsoc, therefore, convert one of their revolutionaries, Emmanuel Goldstein, into a villain, leaving his opponent, with a moustache like Stalin, as a hero. There is no ability to make minor changes, even. Goldstein, like Trotsky, has "a lean Jewish face, with a great fuzzy aureole of white hair and a small goatee beard." Orwell apparently does not want to confuse the issue by giving Stalin a different name so he calls him merely "Big Brother."

At the very beginning of the story, it is made clear that television (which was coming into existence at the time the book was written) served as a continuous means of indoctrination of the people, for sets cannot be turned off. (And, apparently, in a deteriorating London in which nothing works, these sets never fail.)

The great Orwellian contribution to future technology is that the television set is two-way, and that the people who are forced to hear and see the television screen can themselves be heard and seen at all times and are under constant supervision even while sleeping or in the bathroom. Hence, the meaning of the phrase "Big Brother is watching you."

This is an extraordinarily inefficient system of keeping everyone under control. To have a person being watched at all times means that some other person must be doing the watching at all times (at least in the Orwellian society) and must be doing so very narrowly, for there is a great development of the art of interpreting gesture and facial expression.

One person cannot watch more than one person in full concentration, and can only do so for a comparatively short time before attention begins to wander. I should guess, in short, that there may have to be five watchers for every person watched. And then, of course, the watchers must themselves be watched since no one in the Orwellian world is suspicion-free. Consequently, the system of oppression by two-way television simply will not work.

Orwell himself realized this by limiting its workings to the Party members. The "proles" (proletariat), for whom Orwell cannot hide his British-upper-class contempt, are left largely to themselves as subhuman. (At one point in the book, he says that any prole that shows ability is killed—a leaf taken out of the Spartan treatment of their helots twenty-five hundred years ago.)

Furthermore, he has a system of volunteer spies in which children report on their parents, and neighbors on each other. This cannot possibly work well since eventually everyone reports everyone else and it all has to be abandoned.

Orwell was unable to conceive of computers or robots, or he would have placed everyone under nonhuman surveillance. Our own computers to some extent do this in the IRS, in credit files, and so on, but that does not take us toward 1984, except in fevered imaginations. Computers and tyranny do not necessarily go hand in hand. Tyrannies have worked very well without computers (consider the Nazis) and the most computerized nations in today's world are also the least tyrannical.

Orwell lacks the capacity to see (or invent) small changes. His hero finds it difficult in his world of 1984 to get shoelaces or razor blades. So would I in the real world of the 1980s, for so many people use slip-on shoes and electric razors.

Then, too, Orwell had the technophobic fixation that every technological advance is a slide downhill. Thus, when his hero writes, he "fitted a nib into the penholder and sucked it to get the grease off." He does so "because of a feeling that the beautiful creamy paper deserved to be written on with a real nib instead of being scratched with an ink-pencil."

Presumably, the "ink-pencil" is the ball-point pen that was coming into use at the time that 1984 was being written. This means that Orwell describes something as being "written" with a real nib but being "scratched" with a ball-point. This is, however, *precisely* the reverse of the truth. If you are old enough to remember steel pens, you will remember that they scratched fearsomely, and you know ball-points don't.

This is not science fiction, but a distorted nostalgia for a past that never was. I am surprised that Orwell stopped with the steel pen and that he didn't have Winston writing with a neat goose quill.

Nor was Orwell particularly prescient in the strictly social aspects of the future he was presenting, with the result that the Orwellian world of 1984 is incredibly old-fashioned when compared with the real world of the 1980s.

Orwell imagines no new vices, for instance. His characters are all gin hounds and tobacco addicts, and part of the horror of his picture of 1984 is his eloquent description of the *low quality* of the gin and tobacco.

He foresees no new drugs, no marijuana, no synthetic hallucinogens. No one expects an s.f. writer to be precise and exact in his forecasts, but surely one would expect him to invent *some* differences.

In his despair (or anger), Orwell forgets the virtues human beings have. All his characters are, in one way or another, weak, or sadistic, or sleazy, or stupid, or repellent. This may be how most people are, or how Orwell wants to indicate they will *all* be under tyranny, but it seems to me that under even the worst tyrannies, so far, there have been brave men and women who have withstood the tyrants to the death and whose personal histories are luminous flames in the surrounding darkness. If only because there is no hint of this in 1984, it does not resemble the real world of the 1980s.

Nor did he foresee any difference in the role of women or any weakening of the feminine stereotype of 1949. There are only two female characters of importance. One is a strong, brainless "prole" woman who is an endless washerwoman, endlessly singing a popular song with words of the type familiar in the 1930s and 1940s (at which Orwell shudders fastidiously as "trashy," in blissful non-anticipation of hard rock).

The other is the heroine, Julia, who is sexually promiscuous (but is at least driven to courage by her interest in sex) and is otherwise brainless. When the hero, Winston, reads to her the book within a book that explains the nature of the Orwellian world, she responds by falling asleep—but then since the treatise Winston reads is stupefyingly soporific, this may be an indication of Julia's good sense rather than the reverse.

In short, if 1984 *must* be considered science fiction, then it is very bad science fiction.

C. The Government of 1984

Orwell's 1984 is a picture of all-powerful government, and it has helped make the notion of "big government" a very frightening one.

We have to remember, though, that the world of the late 1940s, during which Orwell was writing his book, was one in which there had been, and still were, big governments with true tyrants —individuals whose every wish, however unjust, cruel or vicious, was law. What's more, it seemed as though such tyrants were irremovable except by the chance of outside force.

Benito Mussolini of Italy, after twenty-one years of absolute rule, was overthrown, but that was only because his country was suffering defeat in war.

Adolf Hitler of Germany, a far stronger and more brutal tyrant, ruled with a steel hand for twelve years, yet even defeat did not, in itself, bring about his overthrow. Though the area over which he ruled shrank and shrank and shrank, and even though overwhelming armies of his adversaries closed in from the east and west, he remained absolute tyrant over whatever area he controlled—even when it was only over the bunker in which he committed suicide. Until he removed himself, no one dared remove him. (There were plots against him, to be sure, but they never worked, sometimes through quirks of fate that seemed explainable only by supposing that someone down there liked him.)

Orwell, however, had no time for either Mussolini or Hitler. His enemy was Stalin, and at the time that 1984 was published, Stalin had ruled the Soviet Union in a rib-breaking bear hug for twenty-five years, had survived a terrible war in which his nation suffered enormous losses and yet was now stronger than ever. To Orwell, it must have seemed that neither time nor fortune could budge Stalin, but that he would live on forever with ever increasing strength. —And that was how Orwell pictured Big Brother.

Of course, that was not the way it really was. Orwell didn't live long enough to see it but Stalin died only three years after 1984 was published, and it was not long after that that his regime was denounced as a tyranny by—guess who—the Soviet leadership.

The Soviet Union is still the Soviet Union, but it is not Stalinist, and the enemies of the state are no longer liquidated (Orwell uses "vaporized" instead, such small changes being all he can manage) with quite such abandon.

Again, Mao Tse-tung died in China, and while he himself has not been openly denounced, his close associates, as "the Gang of Four" were promptly demoted from Divinity, and while China is still China, it is not Maoist any longer.

Franco of Spain died in his bed and while, to his very last breath, he remained the unquestioned leader he had been for nearly forty years, immediately after that last breath, Fascism abruptly dwindled in Spain, as it had in Portugal after Salazar's death.

In short, Big Brothers do die, or at least they have so far, and when they die, the government changes, always for the milder.

This is not to say that new tyrants may not make themselves felt, but they will die, too. At least in the real 1980s we have every confidence they will and the undying Big Brother is not yet a real threat.

If anything, in fact, governments of the 1980s seem dangerously weak. The advance of technology has put powerful weapons— explosives, machine guns, fast cars—into the hands of urban terrorists who can and do kidnap, hijack, gun down, and take hostages with impunity while governments stand by more or less helplessly.

In addition to the immortality of Big Brother, Orwell presents two other ways of maintaining an eternal tyranny.

First—present someone or something to hate. In the Orwellian world it was Emmanuel Goldstein for whom hate was built up and orchestrated in a robotized mass function.

This is nothing new, of course. Every nation in the world has used various neighbors for the purpose of hate. This sort of thing is so easily handled and comes as such second nature to humanity that one wonders why there have to be the organized hate drives in the Orwellian world.

It needs scarcely any clever psychological mass movements to make Arabs hate Israelis and Greeks hate Turks and Catholic Irish hate Protestant Irish—and vice versa in each case. To be sure, the Nazis organized mass meetings of delirium that every participant seemed to enjoy, but it had no permanent effect. Once the war moved onto German soil, the Germans surrendered as meekly as though they had never Sieg-Heiled in their lives.

Second—rewrite history. Almost every one of the few individuals we meet in 1984 has, as his job, the rapid rewriting of the past, the readjustment of statistics, the overhauling of newspapers —as though anyone is going to take the trouble to pay attention to the past anyway.

This Orwellian preoccupation with the minutiae of "historical proof" is typical of the political sectarian who is always quoting what has been said and done in the past to prove a point to someone on the other side who is always quoting something to the opposite effect that has been said and done.

As any politician knows, no evidence of any kind is ever required. It is only necessary to make a statement—any statement— forcefully enough to have an audience believe it. No one will check the lie against the facts, and, if they do, they will disbelieve the facts. Do you think the German people in 1939 *pretended* that the Poles had attacked them and started World War II? No! Since they were told that was so, they believed it as seriously as you and I believe that they attacked the Poles.

To be sure, the Soviets put out new editions of their Encyclopedia in which politicians rating a long biography in earlier editions are suddenly omitted entirely, and this is no doubt the germ of the Orwellian notion, but the chances of carrying it as far as is described in 1984 seems to me to be nil—not because it is beyond human wickedness, but because it is totally unnecessary.

Orwell makes much of "Newspeak" as an organ of repression—the conversion of the English language into so limited and abbreviated an instrument that the very vocabulary of dissent vanishes. Partly he got the notion from the undoubted habit of abbreviation. He gives examples of "Communist International" becoming "Comintern" and "Geheime Staatspolizei" becoming "Gestapo," but that is not a modern totalitarian invention. "Vulgus mobile" became "mob"; "taxi cabriolet" became "cab"; "quasi-stellar radio source" became "quasar"; "light amplification by stimulated emission of radiation" became "laser" and so on. There is no sign that such compressions of the language have ever weakened it as a mode of expression.

As a matter of fact, political obfuscation has tended to use many words rather than few, long words rather than short, to extend rather than to reduce. Every leader of inadequate education or limited intelligence hides behind exuberant inebriation of loquacity.

Thus, when Winston Churchill suggested the development of "Basic English" as an international language (something which undoubtedly also contributed to "Newspeak"), the suggestion was stillborn.

We are therefore in no way approaching Newspeak in its condensed form, though we have always had Newspeak in its extended form and always will have.

We also have a group of young people among us who say things like "Right on, man, you know. It's like he's got it all together, you know, man. I mean, like you know—" and so on for five minutes when the word that the young people are groping for is "Huh?"

That, however, is not Newspeak, and it has always been with us, too. It is something which in Oldspeak is called "inarticulacy" and it is not what Orwell had in mind.

D. The International Situation of 1984

Although Orwell seemed, by and large, to be helplessly stuck in the world of 1949, in one respect at least he showed himself to be remarkably prescient, and that was in foreseeing the tripartite split of the world of the 1980s.

The international world of 1984 is a world of three super-powers: Oceania, Eurasia, and Eastasia—and that fits in, very roughly, with the three actual superpowers of the 1980s: the United States, the Soviet Union, and China.

Oceania is a combination of the United States and the British Empire. Orwell, who was an old Imperial civil servant, did not seem to notice that the British Empire was in its last throes in the late 1940s and was about to dissolve. He seems to suppose, in fact, that the British Empire is the dominant member of the British-American combination.

At least, the entire action takes place in London and phrases such as "the United States" and "Americans" are rarely, if ever, mentioned. But then, this is very much in the fashion of the British spy novel in which, ever since World War II, Great Britain (currently about the eighteenth strongest military and economic power in the world) is set up as the great adversary of the Soviet Union, or of China, or of some invented international conspiracy, with the United States either never mentioned or reduced to the small courtesy appearance of an occasional CIA agent.

Eurasia is, of course, the Soviet Union, which Orwell assumes will have absorbed the whole European continent. Eurasia, there-fore, includes all of Europe, plus Siberia, and its population is 95 percent European by any standard. Nevertheless, Orwell describes the Eurasians as "solid-looking men with expressionless Asiatic faces." Since Orwell still lives in a time when "European" and "Asiatic" are equivalent to "hero" and "villain," it is impossible to inveigh against the Soviet Union with the proper emotion if it is not thought of as "Asiatic." This comes under the heading of what Orwellian Newspeak calls "double-think," something that Orwell, like any human being, is good at.

It may be, of course, that Orwell is thinking not of Eurasia, or the Soviet Union, but of his great *bête noir*, Stalin. Stalin is a

Georgian, and Georgia, lying south of the Caucasus mountains, is, by strict geographic considerations, part of Asia.

Eastasia is, of course, China and various dependent nations.

Here is prescience. At the time Orwell was writing 1984, the Chinese communists had not yet won control of the country and many (in the United States, in particular) were doing their best to see that the anticommunist, Chiang Kai-shek, retained control. Once the communists won, it became part of the accepted credo of the West that the Chinese would be under thorough Soviet control and that China and the Soviet Union would form a monolithic communist power.

Orwell not only foresaw the communist victory (he saw that victory everywhere, in fact) but also foresaw that Russia and China would *not* form a monolithic bloc but would be deadly enemies.

There, his own experience as a Leftist sectary may have helped him. He had no Rightist superstitions concerning Leftists as unified and undistinguishable villains. He knew they would fight each other as fiercely over the most trifling points of doctrine as would the most pious of Christians.

He also foresaw a permanent state of war among the three; a condition of permanent stalemate with the alliances ever-shifting, but always two against the strongest. This was the old-fashioned "balance of power" system which was used in ancient Greece, in medieval Italy, and in early modern Europe.

Orwell's mistake lay in thinking there had to be actual war to keep the merry-go-round of the balance of power in being. In fact, in one of the more laughable parts of the book, he goes on and on concerning the necessity of permanent war as a means of consuming the world's production of resources and thus keeping the social stratification of upper, middle, and lower classes in being. (This sounds like a very Leftist explanation of war as the result of a conspiracy worked out with great difficulty.)

In actual fact, the decades since 1945 have been remarkably war-free as compared with the decades before it. There have been local wars in profusion, but no general war. But then, war is not required as a desperate device to consume the world's resources.

That can be done by such other devices as endless increase in population and in energy use, neither of which Orwell considers.

Orwell did not foresee any of the significant economic changes that have taken place since World War II. He did not foresee the role of oil or its declining availability or its increasing price, or the escalating power of those nations who control it. I don't recall his mentioning the word "oil."

But perhaps it is close enough to mark Orwellian prescience here, if we substitute "cold war" for "war." There has been, in fact, a more or less continual "cold war" that has served to keep employment high and solve some short-term economic problems (at the cost of creating long-term greater ones). And this cold war is enough to deplete resources.

Furthermore, the alliances shift as Orwell foresaw and very nearly as suddenly. When the United States seemed all-powerful, the Soviet Union and China were both vociferously anti-American and in a kind of alliance. As American power decreased, the Soviet Union and China fell apart and, for a while, each of the three powers inveighed against the other two equally. Then, when the Soviet Union came to seem particularly powerful, a kind of alliance sprang up between the United States and China, as they cooperated in vilifying the Soviet Union, and spoke softly of each other.

In 1984 every shift of alliance involved an orgy of history rewriting. In real life, no such folly is necessary. The public swings from side to side easily, accepting the change in circumstance with no concern for the past at all. For instance, the Japanese, by the 1950s, had changed from unspeakable villains to friends, while the Chinese moved in the opposite direction with no one bothering to wipe out Pearl Harbor. No one *cared*, for goodness' sake.

Orwell has his three great powers voluntarily forego the use of nuclear bombs, and to be sure such bombs have not been used in war since 1945. That, however, may be because the only powers with large nuclear arsenals, the United States and the Soviet Union, have avoided war with each other. Were there actual war, it is extremely doubtful that one side or the other would not finally feel it necessary to push the button. In that respect, Orwell perhaps falls short of reality.

London does, however, occasionally suffer a missile strike, which sounds very much like a V-1 or V-2 weapon of 1944, and the city is in a 1945-type shambles. Orwell cannot make 1984 very different from 1944 in this respect.

Orwell, in fact, makes it clear that by 1984, the universal communism of the three superpowers has choked science and reduced it to uselessness *except* in those areas where it is needed for war. There is no question but that the nations are more eager to invest in science where war applications are in clear view, but, alas there is no way of separating war from peace where applications are in question.

Science is a unit, and everything in it could conceivably be related to war and destruction. Science has therefore *not* been choked off but continues not only in the United States and Western Europe and Japan, but also in the Soviet Union and in China. The advances of science are too numerous to attempt to list, but think of lasers and computers as "war weapons" with infinite peaceful applications.

To summarize, then: George Orwell in 1984 was, in my opinion, engaging in a private feud with Stalinism, rather than attempting to forecast the future. He did not have the science fictional knack of foreseeing a plausible future and, in actual fact, in almost all cases, the world of 1984 bears no relation to the real world of the 1980s.

The world may go communist, if not by 1984, then by some not very much later date; or it may see civilization destroyed. If this happens, however, it will happen in a fashion quite different from that depicted in 1984 and if we try to prevent either eventuality by imagining that 1984 is accurate, then we will be defending ourselves against assaults from the wrong direction and we will lose.

(*The Ring of Evil*)

The occasion for the following essay was the fact that a TV version of the last part of The Lord of the Rings *trilogy was about to be shown on television. A new magazine,* Panorama, *asked me to write a commentary on the trilogy—any aspect of it I wished—so I did.*

It was written before I saw the show since it had to be published concurrently with the showing. The essay, therefore, was not a review of the show but a discussion of one aspect of its symbolism (from my point of view).

After the essay appeared, I actually saw the TV show and didn't like it—but that had nothing to do with what I had written.

47. THE RING OF EVIL*

The Lord of the Rings is a three-volume epic of the battle between Good and Evil. The first volume is *The Fellowship of the Ring*, the second, *The Two Towers*, and the third is *The Return of the King*.

The canvas is broad, the characters are many, and the action is endlessly suspenseful and exciting. And the central object of the epic, about which all revolves, is the One Ring.

There are twenty rings altogether, which give power, but Sauron, the "Dark Lord," the embodiment of Evil, the Satan figure, is the Lord of the Rings. He has made One Ring to be the master of the rest—

"One Ring to rule them all, One Ring to find them,
One Ring to bring them all and in the darkness bind them,
In the Land of Mordor where the Shadows lie."

As long as this One Ring exists, Evil cannot be defeated. Mordor is the blasted land in which Sauron rules and where everything is twisted and bent and perverted into his service. And Mordor will extend its poisoned atmosphere over all the world once the One Ring returns to Sauron.

For Sauron does not have it. In the long distant past, Sauron lost control of it, and through a series of events, part of which are described in *The Hobbit*, a kind of children's prologue to *The Lord of the Rings*, the One Ring had fallen into the hands of Bilbo Baggins, the Hobbit of the title.

There are numerous forces trying to fight for the Good and to defeat Sauron, but of them all the Hobbits are the smallest and weakest. They are about the size of children and are as unsophisticated and simple as children. Yet it falls upon another Hobbit, named Frodo, the nephew of Bilbo, to dispose of the One Ring and make sure that it will never again fall into the hands of Sauron.

At first as part of a small fellowship, struggling through a deadly and hostile world, and later with only the company of his faithful servant Sam, Frodo must find some way of avoiding Sauron's allies so that he might take the One Ring into Mordor itself. There, in Sauron's very lair, he must take it to Mount Doom, the seething volcano where the One Ring had been forged and in whose fires alone it could be melted and destroyed. With that destruction, if it can be carried through, Sauron's powers would end, and, for a time at any rate, Good would prevail.

What does this struggle represent? What contributed to its construction inside Tolkien's mind? We might wonder if Tolkien himself, if he were still alive, could tell us entirely. Such literary constructions take on a life of their own and there are never simple answers to "What does this mean?"

Tolkien was a student of the ancient Teutonic legends and one gets a feeling that the One Ring may be an echo of the Ring of the Nibelungen, and that behind Sauron is the evil and beautiful face of Loki, the traitorous Norse God of fire.

Then, too, *The Hobbit* was written in the 1930s and *The Lord of the Rings* in the 1950s. In between was World War II, and Tolkien lived through the climactic year of 1940, when Great Britain stood alone before the forces of Hitler.

After all, the Hobbits are inhabitants of "the Shire," which is a transparent representation of Great Britain at its most idyllic, and behind Sauron there might be the demonic Adolf Hitler.

But then, too, there are wider symbolisms. Tom Bombadil is a mysterious character who seems to represent Nature as a whole. The treelike Ents characterize the green forests, and the Dwarves represent the mountains and the mineral world. There are the Elves, too, powerful but passé, representatives of a time passing into limbo, who will not survive even though Sauron were destroyed.

Always, though, we come back to the One Ring. What does it represent?

In the epic, it controls unlimited power and inspires infinite desire even though it is infinitely corrupting. Those who wear it are weighed down by it and tortured, but they can't let it go, though it erodes them, body and soul. Gandalf, who is the best and strongest of the characters in the book who fight for the Good, won't touch it, for he fears it will corrupt even him.

In the end, it falls upon Frodo, small and weak, to handle it. It corrupts and damages him, too, for when he stands on Mount Doom at last, and it will take but the flick of a finger to cast the One Ring to destruction and ensure the end of Evil, he finds he cannot do it. He has become the One Ring's slave. (And in the end, it is Evil that destroys Evil, where Frodo the Good fails.)

What is the One Ring, then? What does it represent? What is it that is so desirable and so corrupting? What is it that can't be let go even though it is destroying us?

Well—

My wife, Janet, and I, on occasion, drive down the New Jersey Turnpike through a section of oil refineries where the tortured geometry of the structures stands against the sky, and where waste gases burn off in eternal flames, and where a stench reaches us that forces us to close the car windows. And as we approached it once, Janet rolled up the windows, sighed, and said, "Here comes Mordor."

She was right. The Mordor of *The Lord of the Rings* is the industrial world which is slowly developing and taking over the whole planet, consuming it, poisoning it. The Elves represent the preindustrial technology that is passing from the scene. The Dwarves, the Ents, and Tom Bombadil represent the various facets of Nature that are being destroyed. And the Hobbits of the Shire represent the simple, pastoral past of humanity.

And the One Ring?

It is the lure of technology; the seduction of things done more easily; of products in greater quantity; of gadgets in tempting variety. It is gunpowder, and the automobile, and television; all the things that people snatch for if they don't have them; all the things that people can't let go once they do have them.

Can we let go? The automobile kills fifty thousand Americans every year. Can we abandon the automobile because of that? Does anyone even seriously suggest we try?

Our American way of life demands the burning of vast quantities of coal and oil that foul our air, sicken our lungs, pollute our soil and water, but can we abandon that burning? To feed the needs of our society, we need more oil than we can supply ourselves, so that we must obtain fully half from abroad. We obtain it from lands that hold us in chains in consequence and whom we dare not offend. Can we diminish our needs in order to break those chains?

We hold the One Ring and it is destroying us and the world, and there is no Frodo to take the load of it upon himself, and there is no Mount Doom to take it to, and there are no events to insure the One Ring's destruction.

Is all this inevitable? Has Sauron won? Have the Shadows of the Land of Mordor fallen over all the world?

We might think so, if we wish to look at only the worst of the industrial world and visualize an impossible best of the preindustrial world.

But then, the happy pastoral world of the Shire never existed except in the mind of Nostalgia. There might have been a thin leaven of landowners and aristocrats who lived pleasant lives, but those lives were made pleasant only through the unremitting labors of servants, peasants, serfs, and slaves whose lives were one long brutality. Those who inherit the traditions of a ruling class (as Tolkien did) are too aware of the past pleasantness of life, and too unaware of the nightmare that filled it just beyond the borders of the manor house.

With all the miseries and terrors that industrialization has brought, it has nevertheless, *for the first time*, brought literacy and leisure to hundreds of millions; given them some share of the material goods of the world, however shoddy and five-and-ten they might be; given them a chance at appreciating the arts, even if only at the level of comic book and hard rock; given them a chance at a life that has more than doubled in average length since preindustrial days.

It is easy to talk of the fifty thousand Americans (1 out of 4,400) who are killed by automobiles each year. We forget the much larger fractions of the population who were killed each year by infectious epidemics, deficiency diseases, and hormone disorders that are today thoroughly preventable or curable.

If we cannot give up the One Ring, there's a good reason for that. If the One Ring is drawing us to our destruction that is because we are misusing it in our greed and folly. Surely, there are ways of using it wisely. Are we so willing to despair so entirely of humanity as to deny that we can be sane and wise if we must be?

No, the One Ring is not wholly Evil. It is what we make it, and we must rescue and extend those parts of it that are Good.

—But never mind.

One can read *The Lord of the Rings* without getting lost in the symbolism. It is a fascinating adventure that doesn't get consumed with the reading. I have myself read it four times and like it better each time. I think it is about time I read it a fifth time.

And in doing so, I will take care to look upon the One Ring as —a ring.

(*The Answer to* Star Wars?)

The newspaper Newsday *invited me to watch a private showing of the initial episode of the TV program "Battlestar Galactica" and review it for their Sunday TV section. Well, my brother is one of the vice-presidents on the paper so how could I refuse?*

I had liked Star Wars, *and I hoped "Battlestar Galactica" would be as good. I was anxious to see good science fiction appear on TV, even if only of the cowboys-and-Indians variety.*

Unfortunately, I was terribly disappointed and the following essay, which appeared in the September 17, 1978, Newsday, *under the title* "'Battlestar Galactica': Creativity (?) in Full Force," *explains why.*

48. THE ANSWER TO *STAR WARS*?*

I'm not sure I understand the psychology of people who produce movies and TV; I'm a book man myself. But it may work like this . . .

Some person invests millions of dollars to do something that is a relative departure from what has been done before. The expectation of his competitors is that everyone involved in the new project will lose their jobs, their reputations, their lives, and worst of all, money.

Why? Because they're doing something different; because they're not sticking firmly to the good old things that did it for D. W. Griffith.

However, surprise! The new project makes money; it makes a lot of money; it makes a whole mountain of money.

Why? Because it's a little bit different and therefore seems new and fresh. (Perhaps it doesn't seem so to the very sophisticated viewers, but sophistication has always been a minority exercise.)

Well, then, what do the other producers do? Why, when they see that something different makes money, they at once go to work and produce something different also. The same something different.

"Battlestar Galactica" is this season's science fiction blockbuster on television, and I've viewed it. I didn't quite view the three-hour pilot show that will be on television Sunday night (ABC at 8 P.M. EDT), but I saw the two-hour version that has been playing in Canada and Europe, and I'm told it's essentially the same thing.

I'm also told that it's television's answer to *Star Wars*. Having seen it, I now know what the answer is—another *Star Wars*.

The same person, I understand, was in charge of the special effects in both productions and, with admirable economy of creative effort, he produced the same special effects in both productions.

There was a lot of space battling in both *Star Wars* and "Battlestar Galactica." (Why not! In the titles, you work your way down from a war to a battle, and up from a star to a galaxy, but the implication is plain. You're there to see war. The two people who want peace in "Battlestar Galactica" are, in one case, a fool, and in the other case, a villain.)

In "Battlestar Galactica" there is, in fact, almost unbroken space-fighting for the first forty minutes or so. I was sorry afterward I had not counted the number of spaceships that had exploded, because I have a feeling that that's how you rate these epics. (I can see it now. "See our great s.f. show. One hundred fifty-four special-effect fake explosions. Count them. One hundred fifty-four.")

What's more, the space-fights seemed very familiar to me. There were spaceships with vanes in the rear; the kind of vanes that are very useful in atmospheres, for taking advantage of aerodynamic forces to turn and veer. This was odd, for they were in space, surrounded by vacuum, and maneuvering would be quite different in vacuum.

Then there's the matter of aiming at the enemy. You've got to get them on the cross hairs of your sighting mechanism and then you press a button and out go your bazooka shots, making the usual who-o-o-shing sound of bazooka shots. . . . Which is odd, for there are no sound waves, and therefore no sound, across a vacuum.

What's more, the first few shots miss, but, as the good guys adjust the aim manually, one shot finally hits and you know what happens. Spaceships in these epics are designed to withstand exactly zero shots. The slightest glancing blow and they have but one response. They explode into nothingness. (Why design such sure-fire coffins? Or fly them? And how is a crew persuaded to get on board?)

Besides, why the manual aiming? A technology capable of building all those miniature special-effect spaceships should also be able to devise miniature special-effect laser beams and computers that would locate the enemy ship, aim the bazooka automatically and unerringly, and explode every member of the enemy fleet in a microsecond—while the bad guys were doing the same to us, of course.

And then I realized what those space battles reminded me of. From first to last, they were World War I airplane duels. It was the Red Baron versus good old Eddie Rickenbacker down to the final detail.

They hadn't even gotten up to World War II.

Did you see *Star Wars*?

Remember the bad guys who were all wearing chromium suits with their faces covered up? Remember the good guys who were all wearing shirts and pants with their faces hanging out in plain view? Remember how the armored bad guys in 57,243 shots never once even knicked a good guy? Remember how the unarmored good guys killed rows and rows of the armored bad guys, without ever dinting the armor or showing any blood?

Here's the way "Battlestar Galactica" did it. The bad guys were all wearing chromium suits with their faces covered up. The good guys were all wearing shirts and pants with their faces hanging out in plain view. The armored bad guys in 57,243 shots never once even knicked a good guy. The unarmored good guys killed rows and rows of the armored bad guys, without ever dinting the armor or showing any blood.

There's creativity for you!

Remember the most popular character in *Star Wars*? That was that cute little robot, R2D2, who looked like a fire hydrant. Naturally, producers now know all about robots. They're cute. Any robot that ever appears in these pictures from now on will have to be cute.

Of course, a fire hydrant isn't cute in itself, so R2D2 had to do cute things to make up for it. In "Battlestar Galactica," it was decided to go that one better. Get a robot who looks cute and he doesn't have to do anything, thus sparing wear-and-tear on day-to-day creativity as far as the scriptwriters are concerned.

What looks cute in itself? Right. A fuzzy dog. So there's a robot fuzzy dog.

Well, you can't have a cute fuzzy dog without a cute little urchin, too, right? . . . Quick! Borrow one cute little urchin from *Close Encounters of the Third Kind*.

Wait, did I say the robot fuzzy dog does nothing? Not quite. As soon as we're in some strange scary place that looks full of hidden danger that would make any real dog hide under the bed, our robot fuzzy dog runs off. What does little urchin do? He runs after. What does pretty lady do? She runs after. What does noble hero do? He runs after.

What does audience do? They relax. They know it is against the rules of creativity to allow anything to happen to a robot fuzzy dog, or an urchin, or a pretty lady, or a noble hero.

Never mind all these frills. What's the gist of the plot??

Well, in *Star Wars*, we had a whole galaxy in which the good guys are just about destroyed by the bad guys and it all came down to just a few doughty heroes trying to turn the tide.

But in "Battlestar Galactica," we have a whole galaxy in which the good guys are just about destroyed by the bad guys and it all comes down to just a few doughty heroes trying to turn the tide. . . . Get the subtle difference.

Naturally, you want a real boffo climax. In *Star Wars*, a whole planet of bad guys is destroyed for a rousing final special-effect miniature. In "Battlestar Galactica," on the other hand, a whole planet of bad guys is destroyed for a rousing final special-effect miniature.

To be sure, *Star Wars* then ends, with a ceremony and medals and a happy-ever-after—and an eventual sequel.

"Battlestar Galactica," however, does not end. There is still the mission. The heroes must, for some reason I didn't quite get, continue to seek a certain mythical, half-forgotten planet, in a far-distant galaxy that's named—(dramatic pause)—EARTH.

What they want with Earth, which has troubles of its own, I don't know, but it's a novel twist. In "Logan's Run," the heroes kept looking for Sanctuary which was a place on Earth. In "Space: 1999," the heroes kept looking for Earth, but they had come from Earth. In "Battlestar Galactica," the heroes keep looking for Earth which is not where they come from. . . . It's these subtle differences that are the mark of Hollywood creativity.

Oh, well, what am I being so sardonic about? I'm sure that "Battlestar Galactica" will do well. People will watch the explosions, and look at the pretty women, and listen to occasional light-hearted dialogue. Why not? It beats digging ditches. And the creators will make barrels of money and rejoice that they could do so without overstraining their brains.

The trouble is that it's all trivial. Where does it go? The similarities between *Star Wars* and "Battlestar Galactica" aren't there only because of fear of brain strain if a change is made. It's because there isn't anywhere to go, as long as all you want are shoot-em-up special effects.

(Speculative Fiction)

Newsday *asked for another review of a television sci-ence fiction show a little over a year later. I agreed, and the essay that resulted appeared in the January 6, 1980, issue of the paper under the title of "Science or Speculative Fiction."*

On this occasion, it was "The Lathe of Heaven" by Ursula K. LeGuin that was being shown and I had high hopes since LeGuin is one of the most highly rated of contemporary science ꜰiction writers. I had not read the book on which the show was based, how-ever, and I was disappointed again.

49. SPECULATIVE FICTION*

I saw "The Lathe of Heaven" at a private showing at Channel 13 and to my right was a very pretty young woman from the mo-tion picture's publicity office.

I said to her gallantly (as is my wont), "It will be hard to keep my mind on a science fiction movie with you sitting next to me."

And she replied, quite firmly, "We prefer to call it speculative fiction."

"Aha," I said, quite enlightened, and knowing something about the movie at once.

You see, to write good science fiction presupposes a certain knowledge of science on the part of the writer. Without that knowledge, what comes out is *bad* science fiction. Don't get me wrong. It might be good fantasy, good horror, good occult, even good fiction in general—but it is bad science fiction.

There is a way out. Don't call what you write science fiction. Call it fantasy, horror, or occult. —Ah, but what if you want to set

* Copyright © 1980 by *Newsday*

the story in the future, use futuristic costumes and futuristic situations? That is the very stuff of science fiction, so what can you do if you don't want to get yourself involved with the bore of having to understand science?

In that case, make up a brand-new name. How about "speculative fiction"? After all, if you are just speculating, you can speculate *anything*, can't you? Although the term was, I believe, first used by Robert Heinlein, who thoroughly understands science, it has been seized on by a number of people who know very little science and who feel more comfortable speculating freely and without having to raise a sweat by learning the rules of the game.

To be sure, I don't believe the phrase will catch on. "Speculative" is a four-syllable word with the accent on the first syllable, so it sounds like a one-syllable spit and a three-syllable dribble. After a few attempts to use it in ordinary conversation, it will be abbreviated to "spec-fic," which sounds like two spits. And if you get it down to "s.f.," you will have "science fiction" again.

"The Lathe of Heaven" is speculative fiction all right. The speculation is this. What if someone had the power to control reality? What if that someone dreamed, and the dreams became real to the whole world?

This is legitimate speculation. It is a form of "solipsism," from Latin words meaning "one's self alone." This is the view that all that exists is subjective; that you cannot know anything at all but your own existence and what your senses tell you about the rest of the world; that, for all you know, nothing else in the Universe exists except as a thought in your own mind.

Exactly that viewpoint was reached as the climax of Mark Twain's final exercise in bitterness and disillusionment, *The Mysterious Stranger*, published posthumously in 1916. It is akin to the view expressed with solid logic and an even more frightening conclusion in Robert Heinlein's *They*, published in 1941.

The thing about solipsism is that it can't be either proved or disproved in any conceivable way. There is no way of demonstrating that you are a thought in my mind—or that I am a thought in yours.

If I make a building disappear because it is just a figment of my mind, you see, and let you watch it disappear—that is not solipsism, that is magic. In solipsism you change the *reality*; that building *never* existed, and no one ever remembers it because in the new reality I have created, that building never existed.

So if I point to a vacant lot and say, "There, the O'Brien Building just vanished," you will answer, "What O'Brien Building?"

In "The Lathe of Heaven," then, we have a young man, George Orr, who is a working and involuntary solipsist and whose "effective dreams" change reality for everybody.

In his first effective dream, he dreams of his young aunt—a pest who lives with the family, who bothers everybody, and who first arouses and then humiliates George. He dreams she has died in an automobile accident and wakes to find that she has.

So much is only prescience, but *reality* has changed, which makes it solipsism. It turns out the aunt never lived with the family. No one experienced her pesthood. She is simply dead, far away, and only George remembers the earlier reality, concerning which it is useless to try to convince anyone else.

In such reality changes, however, you can't have just one thing changed. If she didn't live with the family, a variety of impingements on the family didn't take place and this produces effects, which in turn produce others in a widening set of ripples that could well end in making quite noticeable but irrelevant changes that George should notice.

If she lived somewhere else, there were impingements elsewhere that similarly must have produced changes.

George himself says, later in the picture, that no one thing can be changed by itself, but this is not shown in the case of this first reality change. It is shown only sporadically and ineffectively thereafter.

With only George able to detect reality changes, the choice is between George as a solipsist and George as a victim of psychotic illusion, and any sane person will naturally choose the latter alternative.

George inevitably finds himself in the presence of William Haber, who is called an "oneirologist" ("dream specialist") as a touch of futurism. He looks like a psychiatrist, however, acts like one, and now and then is called one. Nor does the motion picture succeed in avoiding the stereotype.

In movies and television, psychiatrists (an extraordinarily hard-working group of well-meaning individuals) are routinely portrayed as either comic bumblers or diabolic villains. Well, in "The Lathe of Heaven" the psychiatrist is a megalomaniac liar and rat.

At first the psychiatrist, William Haber, is unaware of reality change, as he should be in a solipsistic event. When the picture on his wall changes as a result of one of George's dreams, Haber is unaware of the change but insists that the picture has always been there.

He begins to experiment, however, using a magic invention of his called the Augmenter (for which no shadow of scientific justification is even attempted) to direct the dreams. George is directed to dream away the eternal rains that are affecting Portland, Oregon—and Haber catches the change in the process of taking place. He sees the clouds blowing away and the sun emerging, and Portland is now in a reality of eternal sunshine. Haber seems to remember both realities now, as George does.

So do others. On a bus, George hears a woman say, "It was better when it rained all the time." This sort of thing continues. The picture never seems to make up its mind whether people remember the old reality or not; or whether some people do and some people don't. The result is confusion to any viewer who tries to follow events with some consistency.

Nor does the change to Portland exist in a wider context. How did it get to be located in Tucson? Has the Earth changed its orientation relative to the Sun? If so, is northern Europe at the North Pole? Does it turn out that Great Britain never existed and the United States speaks Arabic? No, of course not. The change is just a change.

Haber continues to direct George's dreams, and it rapidly turns out that whatever he asks George to arrange is arranged—but always in a horrible way. Overpopulation is cured by a worldwide plague. World peace is gained when the nations unite against aliens who take over the Moon. The aliens are removed from the Moon—when they leave our satellite to invade the Earth.

This business of getting what you want in a dreadful way was explored very effectively on a very personal level in W. W. Jacobs's classic *The Monkey's Paw*, published in 1902. That may be the best horror story ever written because it plays its spine-chilling grizzle against a background of a lower-middle-class family with lower-middle-class wants. Magnify the whole thing one trillion times and you don't magnify the horror one trillion times. In fact, you reduce it.

Of course, there's a moral, which is more or less explicitly stated by George. If you attempt to make things better, you only make them worse—so leave everything to God.

That's not a very inspiring moral, since I don't know if anyone can suggest with a straight face that we all sit right down where we are and do nothing at all and let God take care of it all. Nor do I particularly admire the kind of God who so petulantly resents any attempt on the part of human beings to improve things that he visits us with horrible plagues and disasters.

In the end, the psychiatrist decides to become his own dreamer, thanks to his Augmenter, and begins an attempt to change the Universe drastically. Here, apparently, he suddenly becomes the Sorcerer's Apprentice and loses control.

George, who until now, has been a completely ineffective pawn in the hands of Haber, suddenly (and without warning) graduates into a Sorcerer and comes running in to save it all.

Well, it's speculative fiction, so there's no necessity for me to comment on the science. I couldn't anyway. There isn't any.

But surely I am allowed to comment on the logic? There are holes in the logic large enough to hold Portland, Oregon; and the confusion grows steadily worse as the picture progresses until it ends in a shambles.

Does it matter? —Well, I'm old-fashioned. I have an affection for logic. I kind of like it and when things get silly and stupid, I kind of don't like it. I'm sorry.

(The Reluctant Critic)

*Finally, I would like to include, as the closing essay
in this section, my thoughts on being a critic—the role
I played in the preceding few essays.*

*It is a remarkably uncongenial role for me as I try to
explain in the following essay.*

50. THE RELUCTANT CRITIC*

Writers rarely agree on anything about their craft, but they do
tend to join forces against the critic. I am far too gentle a soul myself to say nasty things about people, but here is what I managed
to say in a book of mine called *Familiar Poems Annotated* while
talking about Robert Frost:

"His poetry seems to please the critics, and because it is plain-
spoken, rhymes and scans, it pleases human beings as well."

Here's what Lord Byron says: "As soon / Seek roses in December—ice in June; / Hope constancy in wind, or corn in chaff; /
Believe a woman or an epitaph, / Or any other thing that's false,
before / You trust in critics."

Coleridge's opinion is this: "Reviewers are usually people who
would have been poets, historians, biographers, etc., if they could;
they have tried their talents at one or at the other, and have
failed; therefore they turn critics."

And Laurence Sterne's: "Of all the cants which are canted in
this canting world,—though the cant of hypocrites may be the
worst,—the cant of criticism is the most tormenting!"

Enough! You get my point!

And yet—every once in a while—I find myself trapped—forced
to the wall—driven into the ground—and very much against my
will—

I am forced to be a critic!

Science Digest asked me to see the movie *Close Encounters of the Third Kind* and write an article for them on the science it contained. I saw the picture and was appalled. I remained appalled even after a doctor's examination had assured me that no internal organs had been shaken loose by its ridiculous sound waves. (If you can't be good, be loud, some say, and *Close Encounters* was very loud.)

To begin with there was no accurate science in it; not a trace; and I said so in the article I wrote and which *Science Digest* published. There was also no logic in it; not a trace; and I said that, too.

Mind you, I'm not one of these purists who sees nothing good in anything Hollywood does. Hollywood must deal with large audiences, most of whom are utterly unfamiliar with good science fiction. It has to bend to them, meet them at least halfway. Fully appreciating that, I could enjoy *Planet of the Apes* and *Star Wars*.

Even when my good friends, Ben Bova and Harlan Ellison, denounced the latter unstintingly, I remained firm. *Star Wars* was entertainment for the masses and did not try to be anything more. Leave your s.f. sophistication at the door, get into the spirit, and you can have a fun ride.

Close Encounters, however, took itself seriously or put on a show of doing so. It was *pretentious*, and that was fatal. What's more, it made its play for Ufolators and mystics and, in its chase for the buck, did not scruple to violate every canon of good sense and internal consistency.

I said all this in my article and then the letters came.

Some of them complained that I had ignored the virtues of the picture. "What about the special effects?" they asked. (They were referring to the flying chandelier at the end.)

Well, what about them? Seeing a rotten picture for the special effects is like eating a tough steak for the smothered onions, or reading a bad book for the dirty parts. Optical wizardry is something a movie can do that a book can't, but it is no substitute for a story, for logic, for meaning. It is ornamentation, not substance. In fact, whenever a science fiction picture is praised overeffusively for its special effects, I *know* it's a bad picture. Is that all they can find to talk about?

Some of those who wrote me were hurt and appalled that anyone as obviously good-natured as I could possibly say such nasty things. I did rather bite my lips at that; it's no fun to force one's self into the twisted semblance of a critic. Yet there comes a time when one has to put one's self firmly on the side of Good.

Some asked me angrily who I thought I was and what made *me* a judge of science fiction anyway? They had seen every science fiction movie made in the last five years and they knew a lot more about science fiction than I did. —Well, maybe they did; I didn't argue the point.

And one and all, they came down to the same plaintive cry, "Why do you criticize its lack of science, Dr. Asimov? It's *just* science fiction."

God, how that stings! I've spent a lifetime loving science fiction, and now I find that you must expect nothing of something that's *just* science fiction.

It's *just* science fiction, so it's allowed to be silly, and childish, and stupid. It's *just* science fiction, so it doesn't have to make sense. It's *just* science fiction, so you must ask nothing more of it than loud noise and flashing lights.

That's the harm of *Close Encounters*; that it convinces tens of millions that that's what *just* science fiction is.

My favorite letter, though, came from someone whose name was familiar to me. He had written me on a number of earlier occasions and I quickly learned never to answer. He has ideas on every possible scientific subject and in every single case he is wrong, calamitously wrong, mastodonically wrong. He is an unappreciated national treasure, for he is so unanimously wrong that by taking the direct opposite of his views you will be more often right than if you listened to the wisest sage.

His Erroneousness took issue with my comment that the aliens in *Close Encounters* acted with utter illogic (and I had cited a number of instances). They're *aliens*, he said, explaining it to me carefully so that I would understand. They're *supposed* to be illogical.

Well, then, I suppose all you need are illogical writers; writers who never heard of logic. Illogic would come so natural to them that they would have no trouble portraying aliens.

It was a well-rounded incomprehension totally worthy of my correspondent.

John Campbell once issued the challenge: "Show me an alien thinking as well as a man, but not *like* a man."

Easy? I've tried many a hard thing in my science fiction career, but I've never had the nerve to tackle that one (except maybe a little in the second part of *The Gods Themselves*). Stanley Weinbaum managed a bit of it in the case of Tweerl in A *Martian Odyssey*. Olaf Stapledon managed a bit of it in the case of John in *Odd John*.

Do you suppose that those fellows who put together the screenplay of *Close Encounters* could do it by just pushing in some of their own native illogic?

Let me give you an example of what I mean in the other direction.

Suppose you wanted to portray an amiable nitwit, a pleasant simp with about as much brains as you can pack into a thimble. And suppose you want him to be the first-person narrator. Do you suppose you can find yourself an amiable nitwit or a pleasant simp and have *him* write the book? After all, he *is* one; whatever he writes is what an amiable nitwit or a pleasant simp would say.

Let me point, then, to P. G. Wodehouse's books about Bertie Wooster and Jeeves. Bertie Wooster tells the story and with every line reveals himself to be an amiable nitwit, a pleasant simp. But those books are perfectly written by someone who is nothing of the sort. It takes damned clever writing to have someone betray himself as a silly ass in every line and yet do it so smoothly you never ask yourself, "How is it that that silly ass is telling the story so well?"

Or to come closer to home, consider Daniel Keyes's *Flowers for Algernon*, in which the narrator begins as a moron, becomes brighter and brighter, then duller and duller, and ends as a moron. The moron parts were clearly the hardest to write, for Keyes had to make Charly *sound* like a moron without making the story sound moronic. If it were easy, the best way to do it would be to have a moron write it.

So *Close Encounters* has its uses, too. It is a marvelous demonstration of what happens when the workings of extraterrestrial intelligence are handled without a trace of skill. It makes one feel added wonder and awe at stories in which extraterrestrial intelligence and other subtleties are handled with painstaking skill—as in those written by the best of the real science fiction writers.

VIII
SCIENCE FICTION
AND I

(There's Nothing Like a Good Foundation)

A number of the essays in this book deal with me to some extent. This is unavoidable, I suppose, in anyone as self-centered as I am.

There are, however, some essays I have written on science fiction that deal entirely with my science fiction and with me. Those I have reserved for this final section.

The following essay was written at the request of my professional organization, the Science Fiction Writers of America, Inc.

51. THERE'S NOTHING LIKE A GOOD FOUNDATION *

During the 1940s, I was avidly engaged in writing two series of stories—the Foundation Series and the Positronic Robot Series. I had no intention in either case of writing a series when I started.

The Foundation Series had its origin in 1941, in the course of a subway ride to see John W. Campbell, Jr., editor of *Astounding Science Fiction*. In those days, I visited him frequently and always brought with me the plot of a new s.f. story. We discussed it and I went home and wrote it. Then he would sometimes accept it and sometimes not.

On this subway ride, I had no story idea to present him with, so I tried a trick I still sometimes recommend. I opened a book at random, read a sentence, and concentrated on it till I had an idea. The book was a collection of the Gilbert and Sullivan plays which I just happened to have with me. I opened it to

Iolanthe and my eye fell on the picture of the fairy queen kneeling before Private Willis of the Grenadier Guards.

I let my mind wander from the Grenadiers, to soldiers in general, to a military society, to feudalism, to the breakup of the Roman Empire. By the time I reached Campbell I told him that I was planning to write a story about the breakup of the Galactic Empire.

He talked and I talked and he talked and I talked and when I left I had the Foundation Series in mind. It lasted for seven years, during which I wrote eight stories, ranging in length from a short story to a three-part serial.

The Positronic Robot Series began less oddly. I had written a robot story which I liked, but which Campbell rejected, so that I was forced to sell it elsewhere. In it, however, I had a kind of rudimentary notion of what have since become known as the Three Laws of Robotics. I had a character say in it, concerning my nursemaid robot: "He just can't help being faithful and loving and kind. He's a machine—*made* so!"

That reference to the First Law of Robotics interested Campbell even though the story did not, and we discussed it till we had the Three Laws worked out. Over the next ten years, I wrote nine short stories based on those Three Laws. (Since then I have written others, too, and two novels as well.)

There is no question but that writing those series was a Good Thing for me. The individual stories in a successful series have a cumulative effect. Readers who have liked the first story are pleased to see a second story and wait for the third story eagerly. They welcome the familiar situation and/or characters and are sold on each new story in the series even before they begin it.

The author benefits personally. The reader is grateful to him for each new installment of the series and is keenly aware of the author's power to grant or withhold the favor. The author begins to gain fans, to collect reader loyalty, and when this is evidenced in the letters he receives, he begins to think better of himself. (And never underestimate the power of a satisfied ego to minimize the dangers of that most horrible of all diseases—writer's block.)

And writing the series can be pleasant too. The writer has a familiar background to deal with so that part of his work is done for him before he as much as starts the story. He has the satisfying feeling that people are waiting for the story (and that the editor is, too, with a check all written out).

Besides, a writer can be as pleased as a reader to meet a familiar and loved character or idea. I always was. I was in love with Susan Calvin of my Positronic Robot Series, and was delighted to meet her every time she showed up in my typewriter.

Then, too, the writer, working on a series, has the opportunity to develop ideas in depth and variety. What he misses in one story, he can catch in the next.

But there are disadvantages, too. There is, for one thing, the bugaboo of self-consistency. It is annoying to be hampered, in working out a story, by the fact that some perfectly logical development is ruled out since, three stories before, you had to make such a development impossible because of the needs of the plot of *that* story.

Of course, you might take the attitude that too much self-consistency is bad, and I tried not to worry about it in my Positronic Robot Series. Yet in 1950, when I put the stories into book form, I found that I had to straighten out a few things and that my easygoing attitude had just made work for me in the long run. For instance, I had to kill off one of my continuing characters who would otherwise have been about 150 years old by the end of the book.

Matters were much worse in the Foundation Series because here the stories were told consecutively, with one story leading directly to the next, and with the plots of all very intricate and closely knit.

Before I could write a new Foundation story, I had to sit down and reread all the preceding ones, and by the time I got to the eighth story that meant rereading some 150,000 words of very complicated material. Even so, my success was limited. In April 1966, a fan approached me with a carefully made out list of inconsistencies in dates, names, and events that he had dug out of the series by dint of close reading and cross-reference.

Furthermore, in designing each new Foundation story, I found I had to work within an increasingly constricted area, with progressively fewer and fewer degrees of freedom. I was forced to seize whatever way out I could find, without worrying about how difficult I might make the next story. Then, when I came to the next story, those difficulties arose and beat me over the head.

Then again, I had to start each story with some indication of what had gone before, for those readers who had never read any of the earlier stories. When I wrote the eighth story, I was forced to begin with a long introduction which I had to disguise as an essay my adolescent girl heroine was writing for class. It was not at all easy to make such an essay interesting. I had to introduce a number of human-interest touches and interrupt it by action at the first possible opportunity.

Finally, time passes for the author, and he changes. I was twenty-one when I started the Foundation Series and twenty-eight when I wrote the eighth story. I was no longer very enthusiastic at the end about some of the ideas I had had at the start. I was also coming to be afraid that I was overspecializing myself and working myself into a situation where I could write *only* Foundation stories.

The eighth story had carried me only one third of the way through the original plan of describing one thousand years of future history. However, to write a ninth story meant rereading the first eight, starting with a longer prologue than ever, working in a narrower compass than ever, and so on. So, I quit—permanently.

The Positronic Robot Series is much looser and it is still alive. I will undoubtedly write additional stories in the future—if I live.

On the whole, the series stories have much more in their favor than against them and I recommend the notion to those writers who find it congenial.

The years I spent on the Foundation Series were the most rewarding of my writing life—professionally, if not financially. They placed my name before the public in a way that an equal number of disconnected stories would not have succeeded in doing. They gave me a sense of success (very important!)—and kept me working at an increasingly difficult task that helped develop my writing technique. And they gave me indefinite insurance into the future.

The Foundation Series were first published in book form in three volumes in the early 1950s and they have never gone out of print. As book club selections, in paperback form, in foreign editions, in hard-cover reissues and paperback reissues, they seem to have an indefinite number of lives. Even as I write, Avon Books is putting them out once again in paperback form.

No week passes without some piece of fan-mail referring to the the Foundation stories, and usually asking for more. And at the 24th World Science Fiction Convention, held in Cleveland in 1966, the Foundation Series was awarded a Hugo as the All-Time Best Series.

What more can I ask for having opened a book in the subway twenty-five years ago?

(The Wendell Urth Series)

Back in 1977, my anthologist buddy, Martin H. Greenberg, asked me to write an essay on my Wendell Urth stories for an anthology he was working on. I obliged, and here it is.

52. THE WENDELL URTH SERIES*

I suppose it is common for an early writer to long to get into some particular magazine. Even if he is a regular contributor to some magazine already, he may long to get into some other particular magazine.

In my early youth, for instance, when I was a contributor to *Astounding Science Fiction*, the best magazine in its field, I nevertheless longed to sell something to its fantasy sister magazine, *Unknown*. In a two-year period from mid-1939 to mid-1941, I submitted five stories to *Unknown*—and all were rejected. Then, in April 1943, I tried a sixth time and succeeded. But though my story was accepted, the magazine ceased publication before it could be printed.

Ten years later, by which time I had grown to be much better known, I had a similar desire to get into *Ellery Queen's Mystery Magazine*. I had, after all, written science fiction stories which were, in a way, mystery stories as well. I had even written and published *The Caves of Steel* which, although a science fiction novel, was a classic mystery in every way.

Why, then, should I not sell to *EQMM*? *EQMM* paid higher rates than the science fiction magazines did, and reached a different and larger audience. A sale to *EQMM* would afford me a visible breakthrough into a second field of fiction, and I was feel-

* Copyright © 1980 by Frederik Pohl, Joseph D. Olander, and Martin Harry Greenberg

ing, increasingly, the need to move beyond the beloved, but narrow, bounds of science fiction.

Naturally, it didn't occur to me to write a "straight" mystery. I was well known for my science fiction, and it seemed to me that *EQMM* would be interested in a science fiction mystery, if only for novelty's sake, and would recognize me as a specialist in the field.

I therefore decided to write a story about a murder on the Moon and to have it solved by some technique specifically applicable to the Moon. I would even call it "Murder on the Moon."

It struck me, too, that I might make the story symbolize my movement from science fiction to the classic mystery, by having the first half of the story pure science fiction, and the second half pure detection.

To do that meant I would have to write an inverted detective story. The crime would be described in the first half, complete with the identity of the criminal and his method of operation. In the second half, the accent would be not on who committed the crime, or how, or why—but simply on how the investigator uncovers the details and pins the criminal.

This was not the usual method of telling a mystery story, but it was by no means new. R. Austin Freeman had pioneered it in his well-thought-of Dr. Thorndyke stories, so I knew the gimmick was an acceptable one.

Next I needed a detective.

There is a long history of eccentric, humorous, or whimsical detectives in the history of mystery fiction. Sherlock Holmes himself lives on because of his many peculiar and out-of-the-way character traits. There is Sir Henry Merrivale and his egotism and raffish sense of humor; there is Nero Wolfe, among whose tissue of eccentricities, is his refusal to leave his house on business; there is Hercule Poirot and his passion for symmetry and order.

So I decided on a whimsical detective.

I myself am thought to be whimsical in some respects. I won't fly in airplanes, and already by 1953 I had encountered innumerable people who seemed to find it incredible that someone who wrote science fiction and who led his protagonists all over the Galaxy should himself refuse to fly.†

Why, then, shouldn't I capitalize on this seeming contradiction and even strengthen it?

I would have a detective who would be involved with other worlds not by way of fiction, as I was, but by way of his serious profession. He would be an extraterrologist, a specialist in the environments and properties of worlds other than Earth. *And* he would be a stay-at-home. He would not merely refuse to fly, as I did; he would refuse to enter any conveyance and would confine himself to his office and to places he could reach by walking—to his University campus, in other words.

Murders in space would be brought to him and he would solve them by means of armchair detection—another respectable ploy in mystery fiction. To symbolize this contradiction, I would name my extraterrologist Urth (Earth). The first name, Wendell, was chosen merely because it seemed to make a euphonious combination.

Appearance? Well, if I were going to have a whimsical detective, he might as well have a whimsical appearance and a whimsical behavior. At that time, I had just become acquainted with the great mathematician Norbert Wiener, and if there was anyone whimsical in appearance and behavior, it was he—so I adopted both. When Wendell Urth talked or acted, I thought Norbert Wiener.

I was now ready, and on October 27, 1953, I began "Murder on the Moon." I finished it on November 3, and sent it into *EQMM*.

Alas, my plan failed; it was rejected. In dejection, I then sent it on to science fiction outlets. It was rejected by *Astounding*, by *Galaxy*, and by *Argosy*. I submitted it to *Ballantine* for inclusion in an anthology of originals and they rejected it, too. It was not until June 31, 1954, that I finally managed to sell it to *The Magazine of Fantasy and Science Fiction (F & SF)*, under the altered name of "The Singing Bell."

I was delighted with the sale and decided not to let Wendell Urth die. I therefore wrote other space mysteries involving him.

† My usual answer is "Mystery writers don't commit murders and fantasy writers don't talk to rabbits, so why should a science fiction writer have to fly?"

And what about *EQMM*? Did my failure there endure forever?

No, a long literary lifetime has its advantages and, sixteen years later, in March 1971 (by which time I had become even better known), I wrote a "straight" mystery short story about an organization called "The Black Widowers" which was modeled on a club to which I actually belong. That story was accepted by *EQMM* and I at once made it the first story of a series. The thirtieth story of the Black Widower series is soon (as I write this) to appear.

(Isaac Asimov's Science Fiction Magazine)

Nearly half of the essays in this book are editorials taken from my magazine, and you can understand that in the last few years that magazine has meant much to me.

In the first issue, dated Spring 1977, the initial editorial described the genesis of the idea of the magazine. It was written in a jocular mood, but it is nevertheless quite truthful and here it is. (You will notice in the essay that I hoped we would "work our way up to monthly as soon as we can." We did—by the eleventh issue.)

53. ISAAC ASIMOV'S SCIENCE FICTION MAGAZINE*

I suppose I ought to start by introducing myself, even though that seems needless. The whole point about putting my name on the magazine rests on the supposition that everyone will recognize it at once, go into ecstatic raptures, and rush forward to buy the magazine.

Well, just in case that doesn't happen, I'm Isaac Asimov. I'm a little over thirty years old and I have been selling science fiction stories since 1938. (If the arithmetic seems wrong here, it's because you don't understand higher mathematics.) I have published about forty books of fiction, mostly science fiction, and about 140 books of nonfiction, mostly science.

On the other side of the fence, I have a Ph.D. in chemistry from Columbia University and I'm Associate Professor of Biochemistry at Boston University School of Medicine. —But let's not go on with the litany since I am (as is well known) very modest, and since I am the least important person involved with this magazine.

Joel Davis, the publisher, is much more important. His company, Davis Publications, Inc., puts out about twenty magazines, including the enormously successful *Ellery Queen's Mystery Magazine*. It also publishes *Alfred Hitchcock's Mystery Magazine*.

With two such magazines under his belt, visions of empire arose before Joel's eyes, and it seemed to him he ought to have a science fiction magazine as sister to these. To retain symmetry, however, he needed a name in the title and he thought of me at once. You see, I'm familiar to him because I have, in recent years, sold a score of mystery short stories to *Ellery Queen's Mystery Magazine*, and he would often catch me in suave conversation with Eleanor Sullivan and Constance Di Rienzo, the bewitching young women who occupy the *EQMM* office.

I can't say I fell all over myself with joy. The truth is I was worried. I told Joel that no science fiction magazine had ever borne a person's name on it, to my knowledge, and that the writers and readers would surely resent this as an example of overweening arrogance. He said, "Nonsense, Isaac, who could possibly accuse you of arrogance?" —Well, that's true enough.

But then I pointed out that the editors of the various other science fiction magazines were, one and all, personal friends of mine and I would not wish to compete with them. He said, "You won't be competing with them, Isaac. One more strong magazine in the field will attract additional readers, encourage additional writers. Our own success will help the other magazines in the field as well." (I consulted others and everyone agreed with Joel.)

Then I told Joel that I had a monthly science column running in one of the other science fiction magazines. It had been running without a break for eighteen years and under no circumstances could I consider giving it up. He said, "You don't have to give it up. Continue it exactly as before." (And I am doing so, with the blessing of the other magazine's editor.)

But then I had the topper. I told him that the fact was I *couldn't* edit a magazine. I didn't have the ability or the experience or the desire or the time. He said, "Find someone you can trust, with the ability, the experience, the desire, and the time, and he can be the editor."

So I did that and now let me introduce the Editor. He is George H. Scithers, an electrical engineer specializing in radio propagation, who is a lieutenant colonel (retired) in the United States Army Signal Corps and who does a bit of mountain-climbing on the side.

He has been involved with the world of science fiction for over thirty years, is an omnivorous reader in the field, and is part of fandom. He was the chairman of Discon I, the World Science Fiction Convention held in Washington in 1963 (where I got my first Hugo, so you can see what a well-run convention that was), and has been parliamentarian for several other conventions. He has a small publishing firm, Owlswyck Press, and has published several books of science fiction interest, notably the new revision of L. Sprague de Camp's *Science Fiction Handbook*. Furthermore, I know him personally, know that his tastes in science fiction are like mine and that he is industrious and reliable.

Now what about the magazine itself? Life is risky for magazines in these days of television and paperbacks so we are starting as a quarterly. What reader support we'll get is now in the lap of the gods, but if things go as we earnestly hope they do, we will work our way up to monthly as soon as we can.

We are concentrating on the shorter lengths, and there will be no serials. Novels have plenty of outlets these days, the shorter lengths relatively few. With my name on the magazine, it won't surprise you to hear that we will lean toward hard science fiction and toward the reasonably straightforward in the way of style.

However, we won't take ourselves too seriously and not every story has to be a solemn occasion. We will have humorous stories and we will have an occasional unclassifiable story as, for instance, in the case of the story by Fast in this issue.

We will have a book review column that will favor short notices of many books rather than deep essays on a few. We will have nonfiction pieces that we will try to make as science fiction related as possible. We are trying to get one that will cover a museum opening, for instance, but it's a space museum; another that compares real-life computers with those in science fiction stories.

But you can see for yourself what we're trying to do if you read this issue and, undoubtedly, we will develop in ways not easily predictable at the start.

Two last points—

For heaven's sake, *don't* send any manuscripts to me, send them to George Scithers.

And for heaven's sake, be careful where you allocate credit. If this magazine pleases you, do give the credit to George Scithers and write and tell him so. He's doing the work. —If, on the other hand, you decide it's a stinker, please send your letters to Joel Davis. The whole thing was his idea.

(Hollywood and I)

Hollywood and I don't really cross paths. For one thing, I won't travel, and if Hollywood wants me they'll have to come to Manhattan. Hollywood, in general, doesn't want me that much.

Nevertheless, there have been contacts, and I described them in the following essay.

54. HOLLYWOOD AND I*

I have hitherto firmly resisted the lure of Hollywood. I have refused to write screenplays even when invited to do so and even when my own stories were in question.

There are two basic reasons for this resistance. First, I am not visual enough to write dialogue and events that are to be interpreted primarily in the form of moving images on a screen. I'm just a word-man, and though it is a wise person who knows his powers, it is an even wiser person who knows his limitations.

Second, I am reasonably confident that in magazines and books my fiction will appear very much as I have written it. Anything I write for the visual media, however, I am certain will be tampered with by producers, directors, actors, office boys, and the relatives of any or all of these.

Yet when someone offers to pay me for an *idea*, I am likely to give in. After all, ideas aren't much.

In fact, ideas are so easy to get and are of so little consequence that, till now, I have never bothered to stipulate for a little on account before I presented one. Instead, I would just write up an idea in fair detail and, if they didn't want it, they said so, and I got nothing. In fact, my ideas have been rejected and I have been paid nothing, in consequence, on three different occasions.

* Copyright © 1979 by Davis Publications, Inc.

For instance, a gentleman approached me about a year ago and said he wanted to do a movie about little people trapped in a world of giant creatures. I said it had been done in *The Incredible Shrinking Man* and in the TV series, "Land of the Giants." He said that much better special effects had been developed and that was what counted. He just wanted a routine plot from me that emphasized various dangers the little people had to face and overcome.

I said that if he wanted excellent special effects and a run-of-the-mill idea, he should get crackerjack technicians and a hack writer and I was neither. I offered, however, to think up an unusual idea for him. He was clearly uneasy at this thought, but agreed to let me. (After all, I had neglected, as usual, to specify payment, so he had nothing to lose.)

My idea, in essence, was to introduce people landing in a spaceship on an extraterrestrial world of giant creatures and having them run into instant danger. The sympathies of the audience would be certain to be drawn to the little things trying to make it against the overwhelming strength of the enemy.

But, little by little, it was to be borne in on the audience that it was the little creatures who were the extraterrestrials and that the planet they had landed on was Earth. The little people were determined to make Earth their own, and they were both evil and dangerous. The giants were overwhelmingly the stronger on a one-to-one basis, but they were actually helpless to fight the small creatures as an organized group. Think how helpless we are against flies, considering that they are so small, evasive, and fast-breeding. Imagine what would happen if, in addition, they were as intelligent and as technologically advanced as we were.

I offered to work out the plot in full detail and to give a scientific rationale for how creatures could be as small as insects and yet be intelligent, and the methods by which we would finally defeat these intelligent insectlike creatures.

The idea wasn't taken up. The gentleman from Hollywood said it would be too expensive to do, but my own feeling was that it was too unfamiliar a notion to fit within the Hollywood cerebrum.

Oh, well, if anyone else wants to use the idea, they can. Ideas are a dime a dozen.

However, please don't write letters lecturing me on my lack of business sense. I won't do it any more.

In fact, guess what? I have suggested an idea which *was* accepted and which *will* be used (if all goes well) for a motion picture. I have signed a contract and I will be paid.

The credits will probably include "From an idea by Isaac Asimov" and I've seen the initial treatment as written by a very competent writer named Peter Beagle. I consider it great, although the producers have forced the introduction of one subplot that I don't entirely approve of and that I am trying to disinfect a bit.

I promise to keep you abreast of events in connection with this movie as best I can, considering that these editorials are written several months before they appear in print.

Then, too, I am coming to play still another role in connection with films—that of scientific consultant.

Till now, I have tended to avoid that, for some of my friends have served as scientific consultants and they have told me that, although producers pretend to listen, they don't hear a thing. However—

Surely you all know about "Star Trek," and you know that for several years now there has been talk of a Star Trek movie featuring the various actors who participated in that legendary TV series of a decade ago.

Well, the movie is coming to pass. Gene Roddenberry who has been one of the writers of the script had some trouble with the producers over a few points and he suggested they consult me. This they did. They sent me the script of the movie and I liked it very much.

Along with it were a set of questions and I answered them all, without specifying anything in the way of payment. In this case I couldn't, for Gene is a friend and I don't charge for answering the request of a friend.

There were three gratifying developments, however.

First, my answers happened to concur in almost every particular with Gene's point of view, which pleased him no end and which greatly relieved the producers.

Second, in the few places where I happened to advance small notions that hadn't quite occurred to anyone on the set, they quickly modified the script to include them.

Third, they sent me a contract that included a check, so that I got paid anyway, and, as a result, the credits may include me as scientific consultant.

What gratifies me most is neither the honor nor the money, though neither is to be despised. There is the question of the Star Trek conventions.

Over the last five years or so, about a dozen such conventions have been held in Manhattan. I have attended every single one of them and have spoken at them, signed books and, in general, participated in my usual jovial way.

Yet I have never been connected with the "Star Trek" television show in any way. I have never written any scripts; I have never suggested any ideas; I have never even been consulted over any point.

I have made this perfectly clear to the people who have organized the conventions, but they have always dismissed it impatiently. I am identified with science fiction and I have an easy rapport with the fans and that is all they care about.

Except that now I *am* connected with Star Trek and I can attend the conventions without that nagging feeling of being an impostor.

Finally, there is the matter of *I, Robot*. Harlan Ellison's script, which is wonderful, has, predictably, been met with demands for various changes by the producers. Harlan, also predictably, reacted violently to some of the demands. (I had, very early in the game, urged him to be diplomatic, but Harlan is a seething volcano who thinks "diplomatic" refers to someone who has earned a college degree.)

The producers were offended at some of what he said, and for a while the whole project hung in the balance. I wrote a letter to one of them explaining that although Harlan was a sometimes unbearable genius, the genius part was more important than the unbearable part, and that he must be allowed to say his say. It may have helped, for the last news I got was that the project had *not* been called off and that Harlan is working on the revision.

I have my fingers crossed.

AFTERWORD 54

(Hollywood and I)

I'm sorry to say that some of the hopes expressed in the previous essay did not materialize. The treatment, written by Peter Beagle from my idea, came to nothing as the movie studio decided not to invest in the motion picture. Worse yet, Harlan's movie script of I, Robot was turned down a second time, after the essay appeared. Harlan himself was relieved of his duties, rehired, refired—and I don't know what will happen next.

On the other hand, I did appear as "Science Consultant," with my name in prominent letters on the big screen, at the conclusion of Star Trek: the Motion Picture. I have also been consultant on some TV shows on both ABC and CBS, with my name in prominent letters on the small screen. Other such projects are in the offing.

My first stipulation in every case, however, is that I remain in Manhattan and that they come to me.

(*The Prolific Writer*)

And, finally, I close with an essay that deals with that characteristic of myself that is most characteristic of myself—I am a prolific writer. There are other prolific writers, of course, but I don't believe any of them matches me in my willingness to talk of the phenomenon and of myself.

When The Writer asked me to compose an essay for them on any subject I pleased that was connected with writing, I quickly produced the following, therefore. It appeared in their October 1979 issue.

55. THE PROLIFIC WRITER*

There are grave disadvantages to being a prolific writer, and if you are seriously interested in writing, it may very well be that prolificity is the last thing you want.

To be prolific means that you must be able to write quickly, facilely, and without much concern as to what improvements you might possibly introduce if you took enough time. That is precisely what you *don't* want to do if your interest is in writing well.

To write quickly and to write well are usually incompatible attributes, and if you must choose one or the other, you should choose quality over speed every time.

But suppose you do write pretty well. Isn't it possible to write quickly and easily, *too*? Surely, it is legitimate to dream of that. Any writer who has perspired his way through some bit of creation, who has worked his way through endless crossing-outs and crumplings, and who has ended uncertainly with something whose virtues seem to dim perceptibly as he gives it a final reading, must wonder what it might feel like to dash something off between yawns, so to speak, and have it read perfectly well.

Not only will a mind-wrenching job then become simple, but you will be able to turn out many more items, charge for each one, and improve your bank balance enormously.

What do you need to achieve that?

1) You have to like to write.

Without that, everything else falls to the ground and you will have to seek other daydreams. Prolificity isn't for you.

Mind you, I don't say you must have the urge to write or the deep ambition to write. That is not enough. Everyone who tries to write must obviously have the urge and the ambition to do so, and everyone would just love to have a finished manuscript on the desk.

What about the in-between, though? What about the actual mechanical process of scribbling on paper, or beating on typewriter keys, or speaking into a mouthpiece? If that is just an agonizing intermediate between the original urge and the final ecstasy, then you may be a good writer, you may even be a writer of genius—but you will never be a prolific writer. No one could stand that much agony.

No, the very act of turning it out must be actively pleasurable.

2) You must not like much of anything else *but* writing.

After all, most of us are constantly torn between desires, but for the writer who wants to be prolific, there should be no room for doubt. It's writing you must want to be doing, not anything else.

If you look out at one of those perfect days, when all nature is smiling and calling to you to get out there and enjoy life, and you say, "Oh, hell, I'll write tomorrow," then abandon all dreams of prolificity.

If you can look out at such a day and feel a sudden pang of apprehension that some loved one is going to come over and say, "What a perfect time for a pleasant walk" or "What a perfect time to go out and do thus-and-so!" then there's hope for you. (Frankly, what I do is keep the shades down at all times and pretend there's a blizzard outside.)

3) You have to have self-assurance.

If your sentences never seem perfect to you and if you are never happy unless you have revised and revised and revised until the sentence disappears altogether under the weight of erasures and interlineations, or until you have restored it full-circle to what it was originally, then how can you hope to be prolific?

You may ask, "But what if the sentence isn't good? I can't just leave it, can I?"

Of course not, but the assumption here is that you're a reasonably good writer to begin with and that it's your dream to be prolific, also. As a reasonably good writer, you have undoubtedly written a reasonably good sentence, so let it go. Once you are finished with the piece, you can go over it and change anything that really *needs* changing, and then type the whole thing over to get clean copy. But then, that's it.

Remember, change only what *needs* changing. You must cultivate an active dislike for changing and never do it without a sigh of regret.

Undoubtedly, you have read over and over again that there is no such thing as writing, only rewriting; that it's the polish that does it. Sure, but that's if you want to be a *great* writer. We're talking prolific here.

4) Never lose time.

You can replace money if you lose a wallet. You can buy a new typewriter if your apartment is ransacked. You can marry again if a divorce overtakes you. But that minute that has vanished unnecessarily will never come back, and what's more it was the best minute you will ever have, for all future minutes will come when you are older and more nearly worn out.

There are a variety of ways of saving time and every prolific writer chooses his own. Some become completely asocial, tearing the phone out of the wall and never answering mail. Some establish a family member as dragon to stand between themselves and the world. Some turn off their senses and learn to write while activity swirls all about them.

My own system is to do everything myself. I have no assistants, no secretaries, no typists, no researchers, no agents, no business managers. My theory is that all such people waste your time. In the time it takes to explain what you want, to check what they do, to point out where they did it wrong—you can do at least three times as much by yourself.

So there you are. If you want to be a prolific writer, you have to be a single-minded, driven, nonstop person. —Sounds horrible, doesn't it?

Well, then, concentrate on being a *good* writer, and leave prolific for those poor souls who can't help it.